SACRED WORDS

CONTRIBUTIONS IN
INTERCULTURAL AND COMPARATIVE STUDIES
SERIES EDITOR: ANN M. PESCATELLO

Power and Pawn: The Female in Iberian Families, Societies, and Cultures
ANN M. PESCATELLO

Tegotomono: Music for the Japanese Koto
BONNIE C. WADE

Historical Archaeology: A Structural Approach in an African Culture
PETER R. SCHMIDT

SACRED
WORDS

A STUDY OF NAVAJO RELIGION AND PRAYER

SAM D. GILL

CONTRIBUTIONS IN INTERCULTURAL AND COMPARATIVE STUDIES, NUMBER 4

GREENWOOD PRESS
WESTPORT, CONNECTICUT . LONDON, ENGLAND

Library of Congress Cataloging in Publication Data
Gill, Sam D   1943-
  Sacred words

  (Contributions in intercultural and comparative
studies; no. 4 ISSN 0147-1031)
  Bibliography: p.
  Includes index.
  1. Navaho Indians--Religion and mythology
2. Indians of North America--Southwest, New--
Religion and mythology. I. Title.

E99.N3G49   299'.78 80-659
ISBN 0-313-22165-0 (lib. bdg.)

Library of Congress Catalog Card Number: 80-659
ISBN: 0-313-22165-0
ISSN: 0147-1031

First published in 1981

Greenwood Press
A division of Congressional Information Service, Inc.
88 Post Road West, Westport, Connecticut 06881

Printed in the United States of America

10 9 8 7 6 5 4 3 2 1

COPYRIGHT ACKNOWLEDGMENTS

Grateful acknowledgment is made for permission to quote from the following
material:

Gladys A. Reichard, **Navaho Religion: A Study of Symbolism**, Bollingen Series
XVII. Copyright © 1950, 1963 by Princeton University Press. Copyright © re-

FOR JUDY

CONTENTS

FIGURES

TABLES

SERIES FOREWORD

Formed in 1974, the Council on Intercultural and Comparative Studies is a nonprofit academic organization dedicated to the dissemination of scholarship of the highest quality. The Intercultural and Comparative Studies Series presents distinguished works in four categories: history, anthropology, ethnomusicology, and linguistics. A fifth category, special series, includes works of merit not within the domains of the four more specialized categories.

The Council is especially interested in sponsoring studies of subcultures within our society and of cultures other than our own. The council also encourages interdisciplinary or multidisciplinary works that reflect the latest scholarly trends. With this series, we hope to present comparative, cross-cultural, and innovative studies that will be of value to scholars and general readers alike.

Sam Gill's *Sacred Words, A Study of Navajo Religion and Prayer* continues in the tradition of the CICS Series and meets the challenges laid out by the Council. Gill's is the first thorough discussion and study, since Reichard's work in 1944, on Navajo prayer literature. Gill's work makes a contribution in many areas: oral tradition, definition of the basic elements in Navajo philosophy, classification of Navajo ceremonies on the basis of the kinds of prayers used, and brings a highly important body of material—the prayer literature—to bear on Navajo ceremonialism, shedding much new light on the subject. In fact, one of the readers for this book, himself a Navajo specialist, classed *Sacred Words* and Witherspoon's *Language and Art in the Navajo Universe* as the two breakthrough books in Navajo studies. Gill's expertise as a historian of religions is complemented by his multifaceted talents in anthropological, folkloric, and literary analyses. We believe that Gill's book will stand as a monumental work in Navajo studies and in the larger sphere of Native American studies, and surely as a contribution to Intercultural and Comparative Studies.

Ann M. Pescatello

PREFACE

In the last quarter century the prevailing attitude in the academic study of religion has been that nonliterate peoples are not fitting subjects for the study of religion.[1] The amount of research done on the religions of nonliterate peoples by students of religion has been negligible. This is peculiar in light of two aspects of religious studies during this period. First, the field known as the history of religions has had a major influence on the many areas which comprise religious studies. This field traces a part of its origin to the nineteenth century comparative studies of religion and culture which dealt extensively with nonliterate peoples. It has remained heavily indebted to studies of nonliterate peoples for the methods and categories which have distinguished the history of religions as an academic field. This is evident in the extensive writings of Mircea Eliade who is the most eminent and influential living scholar in this field.[2] Second, during this period, and especially in the last decade, methods and definitions developed by anthropologists such as Claude Levi-Strauss, Victor Turner, Mary Douglas, and Clifford Geertz have been broadly accepted and utilized in many areas of religious studies and have greatly shaped the way many students of religion presently perceive themselves and their tasks. Yet, these anthropologists have developed and illustrated their methods and insights primarily through the study of nonliterate peoples.

Anthropology, as the study of humankind, examines religion as a human phenomenon, yet, historically, fashion has encouraged anthropologists to view religion as a medium through which to study culture and to consider the various functions which religion performs for society. While such studies provide valuable data and insight, the student of religion focuses differently. The peculiarity and nature of religion itself intrigues the student of religion, who studies culture so as to understand the nature of its religious beliefs and practices. This seems but a slight difference, but it is the difference between looking at an object through a telescope as compared to a microscope. Each view is valid and makes a contribution to knowledge. There is even a point at which these views coincide. The difference is a matter of scope and focus.[3]

While certain divisions of labor in scholarship are essential, I am not satisfied with one generally accepted between anthropology and religious studies. Dividing the study of the religions of humankind between religious studies and anthropology on the basis of culture type—high or civilized cultures to religious studies and low, simple, or nonliterate cultures to anthropology—is not useful. Certainly these very categories have been of questionable value for a long time. The distinctions between religious studies and anthropology have to do with different problems, questions, and interests, not with the subject matter or body of data. Students in religious studies should begin research in the area of the religions of nonliterate peoples. We have already seen that anthropology no longer confines its studies to nonliterate cultures, and this has been an important development.

The study of the religions of nonliterate peoples can contribute significantly to the study of religion. I entered this investigation with the expectation that I would find religious practices and systems of thought on a par with, though different from, those of the great civilizations of the East and West. My concern has been to see the religion of a nonliterate people as a whole and well-unified system of thought, expression, and action which is life-giving, meaning-giving, true, and sophisticated in the terms in which it is practiced by its believers and adherents. This work, then, is primarily a study in religion, but it is also a study in anthropology in the broadest sense of that word, for religion is one of the distinctive characteristics of humankind.

THE RELATIONSHIP OF THIS WORK TO NAVAJO STUDIES

Among Native American tribes, the Navajo people have been one of the most studied and recorded. Beginning with the midnineteenth century works of James Stevenson and Washington Matthews, ethnographic documents about Navajo culture have flowed steadily into our libraries.[4] A sizeable portion of these has included extensive documentation of ritual and mythology. In the first half of this century such eminent scholars as Clyde Kluckhohn, Leland Wyman, Gladys Reichard, Edward Sapir, Harry Hoijer, and Willard Hill recorded and described numerous facets of Navajo religious culture.

The Franciscan Fathers at St. Michaels, Arizona, and especially Father Berard Haile, added a great deal to our knowledge of Navajo religion. Father Berard's work in language and in the recording of mythology and religion amounts to the most important contribution to the study of Navajo religion. Leland Wyman spent many years editing and publishing Father Berard's manuscripts, and they still are not all published.

The field of Navajo ethnomusicology, whose subject is inseparable from Navajo religion, has benefited from the works of two outstanding scholars, David McAllester and Charlotte Frisbie. Their sensitivities to Navajo culture are unsurpassed. In addition, there are numerous records made by traders, notably those by Franc Newcomb whose reproductions of sandpaintings create an invaluable record. Travelers and visitors such as Mary C. Wheelwright also have played a significant role in collecting information about Navajo religion and culture. Government officials and the tribe itself have worked diligently to advance the knowledge of things Navajo.

Gary Witherspoon's works illuminate the areas of Navajo language and social structure in a way particularly valuable to the study of Navajo religion. Louise Lamphere maintains a steady interest in Navajo social structure and ceremonial patterns. Karl Luckert recently collected much new data about Navajo religion. Most significantly, he recorded a full nine-night performance of a ceremonial which was thought to be extinct.

The character of most of these works is descriptive, that is, ethnographic, motivated in many cases by a sense of urgency to make a record of a rapidly changing culture.

Gladys Reichard's study of Navajo religion culminated in her book *Navaho Religion,* which has been the standard work on the subject since its publication in 1950. In part, Reichard's work on Navajo religion and prayer motivated me to do the present study. Reichard's extensive knowledge of the religious elements in Navajo culture were presented in her book in several concordances. This concordancing is perhaps necessary to gain control of the data, but it is actually preparatory to an interpretive study of religion.

Reichard divided the religious data into categories such as prayers, songs, ritual, sandpaintings, and ritual symbols. Then she explained the data by giving meanings to the various religious forms in light of her interpretation of "Navajo dogma." She developed this dogma on the basis of her personal experience. Her principal interpretation is that religion is a means by which the Navajo gain control of the forces in their world, and she explained that the Navajo exercises this control by the notion of magic; a belief in a mechanical response linked to the action performed. She could dismiss the issue of the truth of the religious actions by consigning it to an erroneous belief in magic. Yet her study stopped short of the critical issues. Further, the segmentation of the religious materials into these concordance categories tends to dissolve religious vitality into so many "peculiar things," making it difficult to see the religion as a whole system in which there are many kinds of actions and symbols meaningfully integrated into any religious performance.

Reichard's work is further developed in the recent book by Gary Witherspoon, *Language and Art in the Navajo Universe* (1977). This book is especially interesting in terms of how it addresses the religious aspect of Navajo culture and how it seeks to resolve the limitations of Reichard's work. Witherspoon, whose study of Navajo culture is based in and documented by his knowledge of Navajo language, accepts Reichard's view that Navajo ritual actions are a means of gaining control. Yet he attempts to describe certain Navajo metaphysical assumptions in order to address the matter which Reichard too hastily left to magic. He sees that the Navajo base their actions on the metaphysical assumptions that language and art operate to create, control, and classify the world. The distinction between language and art is basically the distinction between formal language and nonlanguage acts. From the point of view of language studies and the studies of systems of thought, this is a very important work. But for the student who sees religion as a human phenomenon, as a dimension of the character of human existence, Witherspoon has a surprise. While he rejects the category "religion" as reflecting only "our world" and as having no possible application to anything in the Navajo universe, he accepts the terms "ritual" and "art" without comment on any possible limitations to purely Western meanings. Witherspoon seems to associate things spiritual and mythological with the term religion for he tends to avoid these in his discussion of Navajo metaphysical assumptions about language and art. From the perspective of the study of religion this is disappointing, because it is obvious that Navajo views of language and thought have a religious character even to the extent of the personification of "speech" and "thought" as mythological persons, that is, as deities. The results of Witherspoon's study of Navajo culture remain important to the study of Navajo religion, but he has translated anything which we would commonly associate with religion into language categories which results in an awkwardness and lifelessness which surely is not necessary.

I have aspired to approach Navajo religion in such a way that the gap explained away by Reichard's notion of magical control can be filled and yet to do so in a way that would enhance our appreciation of the validity and creativity of Navajo religion as it is performed and lived.

While much material has been collected related to Navajo religion, its beliefs and practices, and while there has been much organizing and classifying of this material, there has actually been little interpretive study of Navajo religious processes. We have either a description of the religion, that is, a set of facts, or the bracketing of what appear to be nonpragmatic aspects of the religion as peculiarly interesting though untrue, or the awkward translations of religious data to serve social scientific theories.

Facts about Navajo religion do not interpret themselves to us; only the questions with which we approach the facts do that. There are no studies that approach the facts of Navajo religion with questions like: What can Navajo religion reveal to us about the nature of religion and hence the nature of humankind? What is the basis for the truth in Navajo religion? How does Navajo religion truly accomplish for Navajos what they say it does and what does that tell us about religion? These questions frame the more specific aims of this study.

THE AIMS OF THIS WORK

An important question to ask is, Why prayer? What is there about Navajo prayer which makes it an appropriate vehicle to understand the processes of Navajo religion? First of all, in his study of prayer Frederick Heiler said, "in prayer do we grasp the peculiar quality of the religious life."[5] By that he meant that as a speech act between a human being and a deity, as a divine-human intercourse, prayer embodies in its distinctive nature that which is peculiar to religion itself. Even a cursory view of Navajo religion gives an appreciation of the central position of prayer. Prayer begins and ends all things and often reaches grand poetic proportions when performed as a central and essential part of most ritual acts.

These factors are complemented by the existence of an extensive record exceeding three hundred prayer texts totaling more than fifteen thousand lines, although lines are a somewhat ambiguous measure. Then, too, there is the structural study of Navajo prayer by Gladys Reichard, published in 1944, which also suggests the importance of prayer. Certainly prayer is not the only focus for the study of Navajo religion, but it offers great potential.

My hypothesis has been that a structural study of Navajo prayer can contribute much to our understanding of Navajo religion. This is particularly true when prayers are considered to be complex ritual acts whose performances engage and are informed by elements of mythology and the cultural contexts in which they are performed. My hypothesis is that a description of the structuring principles which operate in the performance of Navajo prayer acts will reveal the premises and categories upon which Navajo religious processes are based. The method by which I have approached this study is described in Chapter One.

While I have focused this study on Navajo prayer, this has been primarily a means to "see" and to appreciate the complex symbolic system of Navajo religion. As it will become clear in Chapters Five through Twelve, I was led by the study of Navajo prayer to probe nearly all areas of Navajo mythology, ritual, and religious iconography. For nearly every rite, every symbol complex, and every category of mythology, I have examined the existing descriptive data and expository studies in order to interpret the particular in the light of an understanding of Navajo religious thought. In many cases my interpretation differs from what other scholars have stated. My central concern was two-pronged—the study of Navajo prayer and the study of Navajo religion—which, while separate at the outset, became identical by the conclusion. I found that to understand the one is to understand the other.

Recently much attention has been given to the element of performance by scholars in the fields of folklore and oral traditions.[6] They have begun to show us that the elements of context and style in specific performances of any oral act are essential to our fuller understanding of it. The bulk of this work demonstrates precisely this point. For example, Chapter Five, shows that the same prayer can be said in one context to request and effect a smooth and healthy birth and in another to request and effect rainfall in a period of drought. In studies of performance it has rarely been possible to incorporate the formal structure of a many-layered context with the formal structure of the text, yet that has often been possible in this study.

This work also investigates the issue of the interrelationship between formality and freedom in cultural forms, especially in ritual. We tend to think that formality and freedom are opposed to one another, the more of the one, the less of the other. Since ritual by its very nature requires formality we tend to think it stifles freedom of expression and creativity. Particularly when the form has high repetition and long memorized speeches, we assume that freedom is the price paid. In this study I have found that formality is the very key to the Navajo idea of freedom and creativity. This should encourage us to rethink our ideas about freedom and creativity.

This study has helped us to understand how prayer acts are effective in the terms described by Navajo people, that is, how prayer is an instrument of creation and change in the Navajo world. We can appreciate the powers engendered in the performance of prayer acts. We can see the truth of Navajo religious acts more in the terms stated by Navajo people.

Finally, I have been concerned with the nature of prayer as a nearly universal religious phenomenon. Remarkably little study has been devoted to the general nature of prayer, particularly odd when we recall its central role in religion. Our understanding of the nature of prayer and its efficacy in the world needs to be carefully reexamined, and this study of Navajo prayer has afforded me the perspective from which to do this.

My family and I lived with a family on the Navajo Reservation near Cow Springs, Arizona, during the summer of 1973 at which time I initiated research on this project. I have made occasional visits to the Navajo Reservation since then as well as making inquiries of Navajos in Phoenix, but the majority of my research has been confined to published and manuscript sources. I learned sufficient Navajo language to do limited analysis of prayer texts in Navajo.

Finally, it should be noted here that the Navajo language has a non-gender specific pronoun. This creates a problem when translating into

English. The repetitive use of both male and female English pronouns is awkward. This text reluctantly uses the masculine pronoun although it does not denote exclusively masculine actions, and the reader should be aware of this.

NOTES

1. This position was stated for example by W. C. Smith in "Comparative Religion: Whither—and Why?" in *The History of Religions: Essays in Methodology* edited by Mircea Eliade and Joseph M. Kitagawa (Chicago: University of Chicago Press, 1959), pp. 31-58. This position has not gone without criticism, but nonetheless, even the history of religions has become a field primarily concerned with the historical study of the religions of the great civilizations.

2. While Eliade's works are too numerous to cite, his many contributions are considered in *Myths and Symbols: Studies in Honor of Mircea Eliade* edited by Joseph M. Kitagawa and Charles H. Long with the collaboration of Jerald C. Brauer and Marshall G. S. Hodgson (Chicago: University of Chicago Press, 1969). It contains a bibliography of his works as well.

3. See E. E. Evans-Pritchard, *Theories of Primitive Religion* for a critical review of the major social scientific perspectives on the study of religion. See also Gill's "Native American Religions," *Bulletin, The Council on the Study of Religion* 9:2 (1978): 125-28, for a research agenda for a religious studies approach to the study of Native American religions.

4. Consult the bibliography for the publications of these scholars and those to be named in the following paragraphs.

5. Frederick Heiler, *Prayer: A Study in the History and Psychology of Religion* (New York: Oxford University Press, 1932), p. xv.

6. See for example the collection of essays *Folklore: Performance and Communication* edited by Dan Ben-Amos and Kenneth S. Goldstein (The Hague: Mouton, 1975) and especially the article by Dell Hymes, "Breakthrough into Performance" which is in that volume. See also Gill's "Native American Religions: A Review Essay," *Religious Studies Review* 5, no. 4 (1979): 251-58, which comments on how this perspective is particularly important to the study of Native American religions.

ACKNOWLEDGMENTS

There are many to whom I am deeply grateful for help and support in my study of Navajo religion and culture. I would never have had the courage to begin or the capacity to see the vitality of this subject were it not for Professors Jonathan Z. Smith and Michael Silverstein who were my teachers at the University of Chicago. I have learned much from them. The works of Professor Smith continue to shape my approach to the academic study of religion in ways for which I am grateful. Among students of Navajo culture Professor David P. McAllester has been my most careful and helpful critic. His many years of sensitive study of the culture contributed much to the accuracy and completeness of my work.

In my contact with Navajo people, I especially want to thank Mrs. Bonnie Betoney and her extended family who hosted my family and me and served as skilled ambassadors, interpreters, and good friends. Many Navajos took time to patiently respond to my questions, but I would especially like to thank Clark Etsitty and Carl Gorman for their continuing friendship and help.

Since the mid-1970s, I have come to believe that my initial basic research findings needed to directly address certain vital issues in the study of religion and culture. I also felt the work needed to be stated in terms more appropriate to the Navajo. At that point, Professor Dell H. Hymes

evaluated my project and offered extensive critical comment and sugges-
tions. With this help and support I was able to move towards my aspira-
tions for the study. I want to thank Professor Hymes and acknowledge
the contribution he has made to this study.

I want to thank my wife, Judy, who listened and responded, who read
and challenged, and who sympathized and encouraged. I also wish to
express my appreciation to Ann Pescatello and to those at Greenwood
Press who have been so helpful throughout the publication process.

During my Navajo studies I have received much needed financial support from several grants. The American Philosophical Society supported
my research for the first two summers which enabled me to do much of
the basic field and library research. The Museum of Northern Arizona
provided excellent library and research facilities as well as a summer research fellowship. Much of the writing was made possible by an Arizona
State University faculty grant-in-aid. Other support came from the Lilly
Endowment Grant awarded to Richard E. Wentz which provided me with
time to concentrate on teaching and research in the area of Native American religions. To all these people and institutions I express my sincere
appreciation.

SACRED WORDS

CHAPTER ONE

THE SACRED WORDS OF PRAYER: AN INTRODUCTION

It must have been my background in mathematics and computer science that riveted my attention to the curious foldout pages of prayer diagrams in the back of Gladys Reichard's little monograph *Prayer: The Compulsive Word* (1944). I had read the beautiful Nightway prayers recorded and freely translated from the Navajo by Washington Matthews in the nineteenth century, and I was moved by the poetic imagery and the kinetic force of the words. Navajo prayers are not unfamiliar to the English-speaking world. They are sprinkled throughout the popular literature of the American Southwest. They are common in numerous anthologies of Native American literature. They have even been the inspiration for the title of N. Scott Momaday's Pulitzer Prize winning novel, *House Made of Dawn*. Navajo prayer passages such as "to walk in beauty" are identified with the very core of Native American religion.

Reichard's book shows that Navajo prayers are far richer and more complex than the few commonly quoted lines would suggest. In her inquiry into the nature of Navajo prayer, Reichard set the stage for a more extensive study of Navajo prayer. This is such a study. It is not so much an extension of Reichard, nor even a correction of her work, as it is an activity whose inspiration was sparked by a few hints dropped by Reichard, not only in her book on Navajo prayer, but throughout her publications on Navajo religion. This study is in many ways very different from Reichard's work. Part of that is no doubt due to the change in academic climate during the more than a quarter of a century which has benefited from major developments in the study of religion, especially in the area of ritual utterances. Still, this work is in the spirit and at one with the interests of Gladys Reichard.

The diagrams which first attracted me to the study of Navajo prayer were the result of Reichard's formal analysis of Navajo prayer texts. She is the first and only person to have attempted such an analysis. Her principal interest was in the analysis of rhythm and repetition of words in prayer texts. This interest in patterns of repetition dates back to her analysis of the rhythmic repetition in the beadwork and embroidery designs of the Thompson River tribes which she did in the early 1920s. She wanted to discern the principles underlying the color patterning in the designs. Her method was to assign letters to the colors represented so that she could chart these for purposes of analysis.[1]

Her approach to Navajo prayer was similar. She began with a sample of twenty-five prayer texts from a variety of Navajo ceremonials. In each she assigned letters to what she recognized as lines and advanced to the next letter only with a change in rhythmic pattern within the line. Thus, she was able to diagram the prayers for purposes of analyzing the form of the rhythmic repetition of the phrases within them.[2]

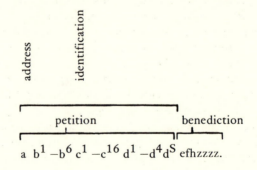

At the initial level of her analysis, Reichard did nothing more than describe the rhythmic repetition within prayers as though it was nonfunctional and without significance. This is reflected in the base line of her diagram. But Reichard placed labels on certain segments which suggests that the rhythmic structure of prayer has significance. She made these divisions on the interpretation of the content of prayers. At one level she divided the prayers into invocation, petition, and benediction. She did not say how she distinguished the invocation, but she indicated that she placed "under 'petition' the lines which show what the patient [the one praying] wants and under 'benediction' what he gets."[3] At another level she divided the prayers into another set of components. These are "an address to deity, . . . the reason for his coming to the patient's aid, . . . the symbol which he carried, . . . the behavior of the deity, . . . the concern the deity feels for the patient, . . . [and] . . . monotonous repetitions of ritualistic acts taken up motion by motion and advancing step by step."[4] It is notable that the boundaries of the components derived by interpretation roughly correspond with points of change in the rhythmic structure.

Reichard also suggested a way to classify the prayers into two groups on a structural basis. She noted that some prayers were composed of grouped repetitions of entire prayers while others were but a single prayer. Further she suggested that these two types of prayers correlate with distinctions in the contexts in which they are uttered. While she offered this "merely as a suggestion," she stated rather clearly her belief that "the form of the prayer may be considered subordinate to its purpose."[5]

Since my first intrigue with Reichard's study of Navajo prayer, I have examined the prayer texts not included in Reichard's publication for which she prepared the diagrams, and I have discovered that there are innumerable errors. (A detailed critique of Reichard's work is given in Appendix A.) Her approach is not clearly stated, and the criteria for her analysis of form and content are usually indeterminate. Still, the vision Reichard undoubtedly saw and followed in her study of Navajo prayer is clear, and her work suggests the great potential for the structural analysis of Navajo prayer.[6] This volume is such a study.

Since Navajos hold prayer central to their ceremonial practices, reciting prayers at the climactic moment of most Navajo ritual acts, the structural analysis of prayer as a religious act promises to be a particularly fruitful way to understand the extremely complex and diverse system of action and thought that is Navajo religion. This study seeks this understanding.

The implications of Reichard's study of prayer, as I see them, can be simply stated. The first is that Navajo prayers can be described in terms of their structure at levels both internal and external to the prayer texts. The second is that the structure of prayers is significant.

By recognizing that prayers are key components in the entire Navajo ritual system, the analysis of their structure and its significance can be extended well beyond the prayer texts to include the related elements of ritual, the mythology upon which Navajo ritual is based, and the cultural milieu in which the performance of ritual takes place.

A collection of some three hundred prayer texts, amounting to more than fifteen thousand lines, served as the base for the analysis of the constituents or building blocks on which Navajo prayers are constructed. This analysis was done with little regard to context, but with a concern to define the constituents in terms of the content as well as the rhythmic and stylistic form. This analysis produced twenty distinct constituents of prayer out of which all Navajo prayer texts can be formed and is discussed in chapter 2.

The description of the constituent structure of the three hundred prayers served, in turn, as the base for the classification of prayer texts. Eight distinct classes have been identified. When the prayers that comprised each class are considered in the ceremonial contexts in which they are performed, there is a high degree of correlation between the structural classification of prayers and an indigenous classification of ceremonials. This strongly confirmed the premise that the structure of Navajo prayers is significant and it established the basis for a much broader analysis of Navajo prayer and religion. This classification is explained in chapter 3.

The eight classes of prayers were next considered as complex ritual acts that included not only the prayer texts, but contiguous ritual elements, the corresponding bodies of mythology, and the relevant elements from the cultural situation in which the prayer acts were performed. The analysis of these eight classes of prayer acts is the concern of chapters 5 through 12.

Heretofore, the principal approach to the study of Navajo religion through its rituals has been to isolate the various ritual components from their performance contexts and to organize them in concordances or to make them the subjects of separate studies. The emphasis has been primarily descriptive based largely on surface features. But one cannot understand the full significance of individual elements of the ritual process unless they are seen in light of their place in entire religious events. It has been clearly shown that the depth of understanding, the fullness of description, increases in proportion to the breadth of context that can be accounted for in a coherent system.[7] While this study of Navajo prayer acts is based on a description of the structure of prayer texts apart from their context, it strives to achieve an understanding of the interrelationships between elements of Navajo religion at all levels. It seeks to describe the structuring principles that operate in the composition and performance of religious acts. It seeks an understanding of the basic premises, categories, and principles of Navajo religion and the sacred words of prayer.

NOTES

1. Gladys A. Reichard, "The Complexity of Rhythm in Decorative Art," *American Anthropologist* 24 (1922): 183-208.

2. Gladys A. Reichard, *Prayer: The Compulsive Word* (New York: J. J. Augustin, 1944), Figure 1.

3. Ibid., p. 41.

4. Ibid., pp. 22-25.

5. Ibid., p. 36.

6. The approach that Reichard was moving toward in her book on prayer was unique among Navajo studies in her era and remains so to the present. Marian W. Smith may have had this approach in mind when she suggested in *Prayer: The Compulsive Word* that Reichard "opened up a whole new field in religion which as yet has failed to be explored." See her, "Gladys Armanda Reichard," *American Anthropologist* 58 (1956): 914.

7. For two important articles on this matter see Jonathan Z. Smith, "I Am a Parrot (Red)," *History of Religions* 10 (1972): 391-413 and Clifford Geertz, "Thick Description: Toward an Interpretive Theory of Culture," in, *The Interpretation of Cultures* (New York: Basic Books, 1973), pp. 3-30.

CHAPTER TWO

THE STRUCTURE OF NAVAJO PRAYER TEXTS

A search through the published and manuscript materials on Navajo religion resulted in a collection of some three hundred prayer texts. In length they range from as short as a few words to thousands of words requiring perhaps as much as two hours for their recitation. While a considerable number of these texts were available in both Navajo and English, many of them were recorded only in their English translation, and many of these are subject to criticism.[1]

Recorded prayer texts are usually found in either of two types of material. The most common source is in mythological literature. Much of Navajo mythology relates the origin of the various ceremonials and incorporates a description of the first performance of the ceremonial. When presented in its fullest form, this description includes all of the songs and prayers. It is, in effect, a prototype for the performance of the ceremonial by Navajos. The other common source for Navajo prayer texts is in the literature which describes observed performances of ceremonials.

Both of these sources present problems in the analysis of prayer acts. While the prayer texts recorded in mythology are generally more complete and often have accompanying comments about the significance of the prayer in the context of the events of the myth, they are usually not part of a ritual performance within Navajo culture. Therefore, the situational context and the variability within the ritual context is indeterminate. Then, most prayer texts which were recorded and incorporated in a description of an actual ceremonial performance were not recorded during the ceremonial, but in a special session after the ceremonial. Consequently, these texts are often appended to the description and not clearly referenced to their position in the specific ritual context. Beyond this the recording of the extensive nonverbal aspects of the prayer recitation are almost wholly missing.

It is difficult to judge the collected prayer texts in terms of all possible prayer texts. Certainly there are some prayer texts which for various reasons have been more easily and frequently recorded than others. Perhaps some texts of important types and contents have never been recorded. For some contexts our understanding would be increased with more extensive and more accurate recordings of prayer texts. Although we never can have enough information, the body of existing recorded texts offers an excellent base upon which to conduct this study.

THE CONSTITUENT ANALYSIS OF THE PRAYER TEXTS

The initial problem in dividing prayer texts into constituents is how to recognize and define the various constituents and how to distinguish where one terminates and another begins. Yet familiarity with the character of Navajo prayer texts shows there are relatively obvious changes in the style and rhythm of the phrasing within prayer texts. Further, certain passages which appear in one prayer may appear in other prayers in nearly the same words, yet surrounded by different passages. A short prayer text may help to illustrate how such a constituent analysis can begin.

1. Who travels with his body, young man,
2. For you I have made a sacrifice,
3. For you I have prepared a smoke,
4. My feet for me you shall restore,
5. My legs for me you shall restore,
6. My body for me you shall restore,
7. My mind for me you shall restore,

8. My voice for me you shall restore,
9. Your magic power with which you were bothering
   me you shall take out of me,
10. Your magic power with which you were bothering me
    you have taken out of me.
11. For a point far away from me you have left,
12. To a distant place you have taken it,
13. This very day I shall become well again,
14. This very day my body will be cooled,
15. Just as long ago my condition was, so I shall go
    about,
16. With my body light in weight I shall go about,
17. With my body cooled I shall go about,
18. Long life happiness I am, therefore I shall go
    about,
19. At my front it is pleasant, therefore I shall
    go about,
20. At my rear it is pleasant, therefore I shall go
    about,
21. Below me it is pleasant, therefore I shall go about,
22. Above me it is pleasant, therefore I shall go about,
23. My surroundings are pleasant, therefore I shall
    go about,
24. My speech will be pleasant as I go about
25. Pleasant again it has come to be
26. Pleasant again it has come to be.

Without any knowledge of the context in which such a prayer might
be uttered or the various nuances of these words in Navajo culture, there
are certain rather obvious candidates for distinct constituents in this
prayer text. Line 1 refers to a "young man" and a description of his
attribute, "who travels with his body" (context reveals that this is rattlesnake). We may assume that the pronominal "you" in line 2 is this same
person. Line 1 may then be tentatively considered a definable constituent
with its distinguishing feature the designation of the one to whom the
prayer is directed. Lines 2 and 3 are stylistically similar (this is correct
in the Navajo language as well). They both refer to the preparation of

something for the one to whom the prayer is directed by the one speaking the prayer. These lines are a constituent distinguished as an announcement of preparations made by the one praying for the one to whom the prayer is addressed. Again there is a stylistic change between lines 3 and 4 while a parallel construction exists in lines 4 through 8. These five lines are repetitions with the change of but a single word from line to line. The word changes, which constitute a catalog—feet, legs, body, mind, voice—give coherence to the passage through systematic reference to parts of the human being. This passage is another likely constituent. Other prayer constituents are found in the same manner in lines 9 through 12, 13 through 17 or 18, 19 through 24, and 25 and 26.

The three hundred prayer texts were analyzed in this fashion. I wanted to describe each prayer text by a set of prayer constituents without lines or passages left over. Furthermore, it was necessary to be able to describe each constituent in terms based on an interpretation of the content and not simply in formal terms. This was desirable, although perhaps not essential, to prepare for the later analysis of the larger prayer act. The elements of coherence were investigated in every prayer constituent. Elements considered were theme, motif, style, phrasings, actions, and catalogs (lists appearing within a constituent) in the attempt to designate distinctive features.

Obviously numerous sets of constituents might be designated, but in this part of the analysis an attempt was made to define as constituents those passages in which form and content most clearly distinguished coherent units. The constituent analysis was done on the basis of an evaluation of the texts, that is, from my own sense of what features were distinctive. Yet these constituents reflect Navajo categories, for they can be stated in Navajo language. I worked primarily with English translations, using the available Navajo texts to be sure that the features designated as distinctive existed in Navajo language and were not introduced through translations. Still, this analytical exercise claims little in terms of increasing understanding of Navajo prayer or religion. It is done to provide a formal description upon which to base studies leading to a fuller understanding of the Navajo perspective on prayer and religion.

The examination of the three hundred prayer texts resulted in the designation of twenty prayer constituents and satisfied the purpose for which the analysis was conducted. The size of the various constituents ranges from as small as a word or short phrase to as long as a passage of fifty phrases or groups of phrases, but none are so long as to make comparison between various examples of the constituent overly complex and burdensome. As an analytical aid and in order to maintain control over the more than fifteen thousand lines of prayer text, all incidents of every constituent were compiled.

A discussion of each of the constituents follows. The set of constituents is given in Table 1. Several terms are used in these presentations which require clarification. The individual constituents of a prayer text are often referred to as constituent "units," in order to indicate elements of the set of constituents defined. The word "constituent" by itself may imply anything found in a prayer and has a freer than desired connotation. The term "catalog" has been adopted to designate a feature which occurs in a great number of Navajo prayer passages.

> My feet for me you shall restore,
> My legs for me you shall restore,
> My body for me you shall restore,
> My mind for me you shall restore,
> My voice for me you shall restore.

These five lines are exact repetitions except for a single word in each line. The term "catalog" is used to indicate the list of parallel changes in a group of repetitious contiguous phrases. In the example given, the catalog would be the list: feet, legs, body, mind, voice.

CONSTITUENT UNITS OF NAVAJO PRAYER TEXTS

Place Designation (Unit A)

In a large number of the prayers there is a designation of place, either by proper name, for example, "at Whirling Mountain," or by description, for example, "in the house made of dawn."

Proper name place designations are mostly mythological locations, many being names of mountains, such as Whirling Mountain and Dark Mountain. The "sacred mountains" are the place names most commonly identified in physical geography.

TABLE 1

Navajo Prayer Constituents

Constituent Designation	*Distinguishing Feature*
A	Place designation
B	Name mention
C	Offering/smoke
E	Plea for assistance
F	Statement of relationship with a Holy Person
G	Association/identification with a Holy Person
H	Injunction to affect
I	Assertion to affect
J	Homeward journey of a Holy Person from the home of an Earth Surface Person
K	Removal and dispersion of foreign malevolence
L	Procurement of protection
M	Removal and dispersion of native malevolence
N	Consequence of protection—attack avoided
P	Journey of a Holy Person from his home to the home of an Earth Surface Person
Q	Journey of a Holy Person to the house of an evil one in search of a lost Earth Surface Person
R	Recovery/restoration of the lost Earth Surface Person
S	Journey of a Holy Person returning the lost Earth Surface Person to his home
T	Restoration of the Earth Surface Person upon his return home
U	Restoration/recovery
V	State of blessing

The other major form of place designation is the description of a place, often a home.

In the darkness home,
In the sky blue home,
In the home of evening twilight,
In the dawn home. (MMH # 1)[2]

Natural phenomena are common descriptive features such as dawn and darkness, clouds and lightning, or flint and agate. The association of these descriptions with color and cardinal direction is extensive. A house may be designated by naming its mythological residents: "In the home of First Man" (RMGW # 3).

Other kinds of place designations are common: "In the center of wide cornfield on a floor of fabrics" (BW # 10), and a combination of proper place name and place description, "At Sky-reaching-rock,/At the house of darkness" (SMHR # 4).

The distinctive feature is simply the designation of place. Place designation normally occurs separately, but it may be incorporated in other constituent units. Here it is usually not designated as a separate constituent although it certainly could be.

Place designations normally refer to mythological geography and are associated with mythological characters and events. The place designation in prayer is clearly a special, and perhaps sacred, place.

Name Mention (Unit B)

In all prayers, with the exception of a few short prayer formulas, the name of a Holy Person *(diyin dine'é)* is mentioned. This "name mention," is the distinctive feature of a separate constituent of prayer texts. Although it most commonly appears by itself, it nevertheless occurs within other constituents on occasion.

In the common form of name mention there are three possible components—a descriptive name, a proper name, and a title. The descriptive name tells the attributes or features, usually physical, which identify the Holy Person. Navajos use the same principles in giving names to each other.[3] A common feature in Navajo naming practices gives rise to problems in English translations. The English word "sun" is the translation for either of two Navajo words. *Jóhonaa'éi* is "day carrier in space" or "who carries a round object here and there in daytime" and clearly refers to the Holy Person who is the sun. *Shá* simply refers to the physical orb of the sun. In a prayer "sun" as a name mention would clearly be a reference to *jóhonaa'éi*. Still the translation of name often introduces an ambiguity not present in the Navajo.

The title, "Chief," is frequently a part of the name mention and is usually modified by the designation of sex—"Youth" or "Young Man" and "Maiden" or "Young Woman."

All forms of name mention may be combined, as in the example "White Coyote who howls in the dawn below the east, Young Man Chief" (SMGH # 6). Note that the phrase "who howls in the dawn below the east" is a descriptive name designating a Holy Person in human-like form as "Young Man Chief." This form of name mention associates the Holy Person with the coyote by proper name and by attribute, that is, howling, but at the same time it clearly distinguishes the Holy Person in human-like form from the coyote animal.

An infrequently used form of name mention establishes the Holy Person as speaker. "I am Talking God, as I say this" (BW # 7). Thus as one speaks the prayer, he is identifying himself with the Holy Person whose name is mentioned.

Offering/Smoke (Unit C)

In many prayer texts there is an announcement that an offering and/or smoke have been prepared. This is the distinctive feature of another constituent unit. These phrases appear together most frequently in the highly standard formula "I have made an offering for you, I have prepared a smoke for you," but on rare occasions they appear separately. The Navajo stem, *gheel*, translated above as "offering," is occasionally translated as "sacrifice." When the offering phrase occurs alone, it is sometimes followed by a specific description of the offering: "This day I have made you an offering,/A nice jet, of this I have made you an offering," (RMGW # 2), repeating this phrase through a catalog of jewels and types of pollen. Tobacco is never mentioned. In the very few examples where "smoke" is mentioned by itself it is referred to as tobacco: "Today I have given you my tobacco" (BFHW # 5).

A few prayers state the purpose of the offering. This statement of purpose may incorporate the description of the offering. Two kinds of purposes are stated for making an offering. One is in order to get rid of something undesirable which was brought about by the person to whom the offering is made.

> Because you have thought of me in the
> past by ugly means, and have bothered
> me with ugly intent as proven,
> I have made this sacrifice to you. (SMGH # 3)

In this case it appears that an offering is a persuasive means to remove ill intentions.

The other reason is in order to obtain something desired, such as holy medicine,

> To obtain your holy medicine
> So that your medicine be a cooling one,
> I have made your sacrifice. (FH # 5)

or desired weather and the resulting bounty,

> Although there are many hardships
> These are not for what I am making offering
> The finest of dark clouds for that I have
> made an offering to you
> That is what I came after. (RCH # 7)

This form suggests that the offering of a gift may result in a reciprocal gift, that there is a reciprocal relationship between the one praying and the one addressed.

Since the offering and smoke phrases are never combined and since tobacco is not included in these specifically named as *gheel*, it appears that the offering of jewels and pollens are distinguished from the preparation of smoke or the offering of tobacco.

Plea for Assistance (Unit E)

The words *nánooshkąhgo 'ánidishni*, rendered as "I plead with you, therefore I say this to you," are not very common in Navajo prayer vocabulary.[4] Still, in a few prayer passages an urgent request for assistance seems to be the distinctive feature, as in, "Today I desire your assistance" (SMGH # 4). This may be stated in a phrasing common to Navajo prayer as a fact accomplished.

> This day I have secured your help,
> This day I have looked up to you for assistance,
> Pleading with you, therefore I say this to you. (RMGW # 4)

The plea may include the "name mention" (Unit B), "Earth I beg of you/ Changing Woman I beg of you" (BW # 5). One form of this constituent incorporates an elaborate catalog of the attributes of the Holy Person (see NM # 6). This gives highly specific traits to the Holy Person and to the desired results for which the plea is being made. The theme of this constituent unit is the existence of a problem whose solution is beyond the resources of Earth Surface People.

Statement of Relationship with a Holy Person (Unit F)

Occasionally in a prayer the distinctive feature of a passage is the statement of the establishment, or desired establishment, of a relationship with a Holy Person. Commonly it is the use of kinship terms combined with a description of reciprocity.

> This day I have become your child,
> This day I have become your grandchild,
> Just as I say to you, you shall act,
> Just as you say to me, I shall act. (SMHH # 1)

It may name the Holy Person. The kinship terms are always those of "child" and "grandchild" and usually include both generations in the relationship. On some occasions the statement of reciprocity precedes the statement of kinship which then indicates that the motivation for starting the relationship is for the well-being gained through such a relationship.[5] A similar idea of relationship is expressed in a hunting prayer but without the use of kinship terms. "In the future that we may continue to hold each other with the turquoise hand" (SWH # 2).

Association/Identification with a Holy Person (Unit G)

In a large number of prayers, a section, sometimes reaching elaborate proportions, draws an association or identification with a Holy Person. A variety of styles and phrases are used.

1. When you came upon me by means of your feet of dark medicine you have thereby perfectly restored my feet. (FH # 7)
2. May the power that enables you to inhale also enable me to inhale. (FH # 7)
3. May the means that keep your feet in health also keep my feet in health. (FH # 7)
4. By means of your feet may I go through life. (BW # 5)
5. His feet have become my feet, thereby I shall go through life. (EH # 1)
6. By which it is pleasant at your front, by that it is pleasant at my front. (EH # 2)
7. Let the dark flint which arises to protect you, always arise to protect me. (BSGW # 3)
8. Give me the light of your mind, that my mind may be strong. (RSC # 1)
9. [as a holy person speaking] "Whatever makes it blessed before me, that shall make it blessed before you. (BSGW # 1)

The association/identification is extended by the repetition of the words of association with catalogs of objects. The most common catalog is the ordered sequence of body parts and functions: feet, legs, body, mind, voice. This catalog may be elaborated, but the sequence normally corresponds with an upward movement from the feet. Other catalogs base the association/identification on attributes of clothing, propensity for health, ability to approach game, capacity for protection against dangers, or the conditions of blessing.

From a consideration of the phrasing of this constituent and the catalog items, it appears that the association/identification is made with the Holy Person for the purpose of obtaining the power or means that provides a state of health or blessing, that is, with the holiness that distinguishes Holy People.[6]

Injunction to Affect (Unit H)

A large number of prayers center on a constituent which directs the Holy Person to make, remake, or restore the vital parts of the sufferer, an injunction to affect the one praying. The catalog—feet, legs, body, mind, voice—is almost always used in this constituent unit, for example, "This very day you shall remake my feet for me, . . ." (BFHW # 1). A few instances of this constituent omit the catalog and utilize a summary form: "This very day you shall make him whole again. This very day you shall put him in perfect condition again" (FH # 5). This unit is stated as an injunction, never as a plea.

Assertion to Affect (Unit I)

This unit, which asserts that "I" will affect "you" by making, dressing, or restoring, is not to be misunderstood as a quoted statement of a Holy Person. The "I" is clearly the one praying or his representative, the "singer," and the "you" is clearly the Holy Person named in the prayer.

Almost all instances of this constituent utilize a very complex form. For example the passage may begin: "Properly I have restored your former condition. Your feet I remade for you," continuing the repetition through the standard catalog. Then the catalog phrase is continued in numerous versions indicating redressing and remaking with various pollens and jewels. This example concludes: "By this means I have made you alive again, By this means you have moved again, By this means you took leave" (SFH # 1). Once again, the catalogs of body parts and garments are strongly associated with life, movement, and health—a state which indicates holiness.

Homeward Journey of a Holy Person from the Home of an Earth Surface Person (Unit J)

A considerable number of prayers describe the journey of a Holy Person departing from the home of the one praying and moving along trails returning home and entering. This prayer constituent unit seems to "talk" the Holy Person home.

> From the rear center of my home you took
> leave,
> From the center of my home you took leave,

At the fireside of my home you took leave,
At the side corners of my home you took
    leave,
At the entrance of my home you took leave,
At the trail that starts away from my home
    you took leave,
At trails leading away from my home you
    took leave,
Along the trail on rainbow, along the trail
    on pollen you took leave,
Where your home first came into view you
    have arrived,
At the entrance of your home you have
    returned.
You left for the place called the white
    house,
You left for square rooms of the white house.
Into the trail white pollen lies here and
    there you have reentered,
Yonder in the rear of the room upon the floor
    of pollen you have returned. (SFH #1)

The enumeration of the distinctive points along the journey is not
unique to this constituent (see Units P, Q, and S), but is relatively standard
for every description of a journey between the earth surface and the
realms beyond. Since these journey passages are so extensive and since
the destination seems critical to the meaning, this has been used as part
of the distinctive feature.

This constituent is very stable from one instance to another with
changes only in the description of the house to correspond with the
various Holy People named.

Removal and Dispersion of Foreign Malevolence (Unit K)

The general theme of the removal and dispersion of malevolence is not
uncommon in prayer texts. The source of malevolence is always identified
as foreign. The distinctive features of this constituent must include both
the theme of the removal and dispersion of the malevolence and the
identification of the malevolence as issuing from a foreign source. The

latter feature distinguishes this constituent from its counterpart which
focuses on native malevolence (Unit M).

> From the terminal of this flash on the white man's enemy
>   ghost, its weapon, its witchery, its magic spell, the filth
>   of its pores, with which it had bothered my interior.
> Which moved in a mass in my interior,
> Which moved as a heavy mass in my interior,
> Shall be headed from there farther on,
> It has gone farther on without it.
> With its ugly witchery its moving power is moving farther
>   away from me,
> The sound of its moving power is farther away from me,
> It has gone farther to his dwelling place and has vanished
>   there.
> It has changed into water,
> It has changed into dew. (EH # 3)

Here the foreign malevolence is described as influencing the sufferer by
traveling about in his interior as a heavy mass. The object which carries
or represents the malevolence is *be'iinzįįd*, translated as "its witchery."
This passage utilizes the common Navajo style of presenting a sequence
of time and space slices to describe the act of removal and dispersion.

Procurement of Protection (Unit L)

Many prayer texts have a distinct passage which focuses upon the procurement of protection from a Holy Person. The passage is usually worded
as an injunction rather than a plea, and it usually is developed upon a
catalog describing the weapons or protective garments of the Holy Person
whose protection is sought. "With your dark pollen shoes you will rise
to protect me/With your dark pollen leggings you will rise to protect me,"
continuing through a catalog which mentions garments, hat, mind, and
voice (SMGH # 5). Another type begins, "The zigzag lightning and dark
flint that flutters from the tip of your shoulders with these you will rise
in my defense," moving through the catalog: hands, mouth, and eyes
(SMGH # 2). The type of danger is rarely made specific, and the source
of danger is rarely mentioned.

There are many variations in this constituent unit. The catalogs may vary in length while the protective garments may vary in material and color. The weapons and articles of protection, such as hoops, also differ widely and are associated with varied colors and materials. Several passages may be strung together to present this elaborate description of the garments and weapons of the Holy Person from whom protection is sought. The common feature is the injunctive phrase, "rise to protect me."

Removal and Dispersion of Native Malevolence (Unit M)

This constituent, paired closely in style and purpose with Unit K, is focused on the removal of malevolence from a native, that is a Navajo, source. More examples of this constituent have been found than of Unit K, but that is probably not a wholly accurate reflection of their incidence in Navajo culture. The constituent which describes the removal and dispersion of native malevolence has a distinctive composition.

> This very day you shall take out of me your magic [spell]
>> by which you are bothering me,
> Away from me you shall carry it,
> Far away from me you shall take it,
> Far away from me you have taken it. (BFHW # 1)

From this passage it appears that the suffering borne by the one praying is thought to be the result of a "magic spell" *(álííl)* inflicted by the one to whom the prayer is directed. This suggests that the special powers of Holy People may be used by them for malevolent, as well as benevolent, effects on Earth Surface People.

This passage is stylistically consistent with many others in Navajo prayer. It directs rather than requests. It juxtaposes a sequence of still moments, like photographs, in such a way as to accomplish a movement through time and space. In some instances this is carried to grand proportions. (See particularly RMGW # 2f.) The term "witchery" *(be'iinzįįd)* is sometimes used here rather than "magic spell" *(álííl)*, suggesting that native witches, and perhaps native ghosts, are the sources of the malevolence.

The recognition of this constituent as a whole is not as difficult as identifying its distinctive features since one aspect of it is absent. The dispersion of malevolence is primary. The removal may be described in detail or it may simply be an understood aspect of the dispersion. The difficulty lies in the recognition of the source of the malevolence as "native" rather than "foreign." From the known examples the foreign source is always explicitly stated, for example, "the Ute enemy's," or "the white man's," but the native source is not explicitly stated. Thus in this constituent it is necessary to identify the source of the malevolence by the recognition that it is attributed through possessive pronoun to the one addressed in prayer. This is distinctive since Navajos do not address foreigners in their prayers.

Consequence of Protection—Attack Avoided (Unit N)

This passage, describing the consequence of obtaining protection is related to the constituent describing the procurement of protection (Unit L). Yet in their appearance in prayer texts these two constituents are distinct and occur independently of each other. This constituent describes the failure of the "witchery" *(be'iinziid)* attack, indicating that it was stopped, and that it was turned upon its source. The effect the "witchery" has when it is turned upon its source may be added. The ugly one that is the source of this malevolent power is *naayé'ii,* which may be translated as "monster."

> The two dark pollens that you hold, you will cross to protect
>   my path.
> Then the witchery of the ugly one will reach just so far,
> Then its witchery has reached only so far.
> Its witchery will give up in despair without reaching me.
> Its witchery will stumble without reaching me, so I say this.
> The witchery of the ugly thing has gone from me,
> Its witchery has returned upon it,
> Its witchery has returned down into its interior,
> With its witchery its mind could not function,
> It was simply lockjawed,
> It closed its eyes,
> It became immovable,
> It did not move. (SMGH # 5)

A passage may be added which describes the state of safety which succeeds the rebuffed *naayé'ii* attack.

Monster missed, monster missed me,
I am safe, safe at last,
May my winters be many,
May my winters be many. (SMGH # 5)

Journey of a Holy Person From His Home to the Home of an Earth Surface Person (Unit P)

This journey sequence is distinctive for its point of departure—the home of the Holy Person—and the destination point—the home of an Earth Surface Person. The journey style is consistent with similar passages, but the length of the journey may vary. A brief description of the home of the Holy Person is usually followed by a sequence of places, such as the trails and fields where the Holy Person travels. The passage may end with the journey in progress or with an account of the entry into the home of the Earth Surface Person where the Holy Person sits down with the sufferer.

Coming from the home of dark medicine,
Coming from the floor of dark medicine,
Coming from the square rooms of dark medicine,
Along the out trail controlled by dark medicine,
Along the trail at the tip of dark medicine,
You who travel with the aid of white cloud. (FH # 1)

Journey of a Holy Person to the House of an Evil One in Search of a Lost Earth Surface Person (Unit Q)

There are few recorded incidences of this constituent, but its length and elaboration make it outstanding among prayer constituents. The journey is made in at least two segments. Generally, it begins with a description of the departure of the Holy Person from his home, then jumps to the point where the search is to begin. It describes the Holy Person searching through mountains, clouds, mists, mosses, and waters; several of each identified by a standard sequence of colors. The search continues toward the home where the Earth Surface Person's means of life are held captive. This requires crossing over several pairs of dangerous door guards, always red in color. Finally, the journey ends when the Holy Person enters the hogan and overtakes the one who has been lost. This entire journey is described by a sequence of from twenty to fifty moments referenced to place. In each of these moments there is usually a description of the Holy Person in his garments with his weapons and instruments undertaking a particular type of action.

> From the center of the earth,
> Enemy Slayer, using his dark staff,
>   comes in to search for me,
> With lightnings flashing before him,
> With lightnings flashing behind him,
> He comes in to search for me,
> Using a rock crystal and a talking prayerstick,
> He comes in to search for me.
> Below the east, he comes in to search for me,
> Farther on, he comes in to search for me,
> Beyond that place, through a dark mountain,
> Enemy Slayer, using . . . [as above] with lightnings. . . .
> Farther on. . . .
> [Continuing in this manner through three yellow
>   mountains, and four white mountains. Then the
>   journey of search is conducted through one dark,
>   two blue, three yellow and four white clouds, mists,
>   mosses, and waters for each color.]
> Farther on, he comes in to search for me.
> Beyond that place, at the door of the Darkness Hogan,
> Where a pair of red coyotes lie with heads reversed,
> Enemy Slayer tosses these apart with his dark staff
>   and thus he comes in to search for me,
> With lightnings . . . [as above]
> [Continuing in this manner Enemy Slayer moves past
>   a pair of red bluejays, red hoot-owls, and red screech
>   owls.]
> Farther on, he comes in to search for me,
> At that place, in the west corner of the Darkness Hogan,
>   behind the Traveler in Darkness,
> Where my feet lie,
> Where my legs . . . [body, mind, voice, speech, power
>   of movement] lie.

I came in, searching for all these.
Farther on, . . .
At that place, . . . Whirling Darkness,
  [as above]
At that place, . . . Spreading Darkness,
  [as above] . (BSGW # 1)

A shift in pronoun to "I" indicates that the one praying has, in prayer, accompanied the journey of the Holy Person. Health and life are associated with a form in human shape with feet, legs, body, mind, and voice.

Recovery/Restoration of the Lost Earth Surface Person (Unit R)

Associated with the successful search (Unit Q) is an act of recovery or restoration which may be distinguished as a separate constituent of prayer. Its distinctive feature is the act of recovery which includes the restoration necessary to prepare the lost Earth Surface Person for the return.

The most common form of this constituent begins with a statement by the Holy Person that he has recovered the lost one and that they are preparing for the return. This is followed by a description of an act of recovery. The Holy Person uses one of the implements he carries to encircle the head of the lost one. With this gesture the person is turned around in preparation for the return journey. The recovery acts are in the form of a reorientation.

"I came searching for you; you and I will begin our return,
  my grandchild.
We two are now leaving, my grandchild,"
  Enemy Slayer says to me;
With talking prayerstick in his right hand, he encircles me
  with it, in a sunwise direction, and places it in my right
  hand;
Encircling me, sunwise, with a rainbow, he turns me, sunwise,
  toward himself;
"We two will now start back, my grandchild."
  he says to me;
"We two are now leaving, my grandchild," he says to me as I
  return to stand upon the rainbow. (BSGW # 1)

Journey of a Holy Person Returning the Lost Earth Surface Person to His Home (Unit S)

The complexity and detail of the journey of a Holy Person from his home in search of a lost Earth Surface Person (Unit Q) is surpassed only by the complexity of the journey returning the lost one to his home. This constituent usually begins with an account of that journey of search in reverse sequence. A difference between the journey of search and the journey of return is that one is more elaborate than the other. Once the return is made to the point where the search began, a further journey sequence describes the return from that point to the home of the Earth Surface Person. This journey may be greatly elaborated to include a journey to the tops of the sacred mountains, through the fields of the Earth Surface Person, and into his hogan to a point in the back corner, mentioning all of the significant points of his house. The end of the journey is usually when the Earth Surface Person is placed in the back corner of his hogan, the safest and innermost place, sitting with one or more Holy People. Again, the fact of a journey is not in itself the distinctive feature although it is essential. The distinctive features are the points of departure—the place where the Earth Surface Person had been recovered—and destination—the home of the Earth Surface Person.

Restoration of the Earth Surface Person Upon His Return Home (Unit T)

Upon the return of the lost Earth Surface Person to his home, a passage describes the reuniting of the person with all of the things which are in and around his home with which he was formerly associated. This constituent may be elaborately developed. Generally, the first reassociation is made with the home and the physical body of the Earth Surface Person.

> "This is your home, my Grandchild!" he says to me as he sits
> down beside me;
> "I have returned with you to your home, my grandchild!"
> he says to me as he sits down beside me;
> "Upon the pollen figure I have returned to sit with you, my
> grandchild!" he says to me as he sits down beside me.
> (BSGW #1)

The association is continued through fire, food, resting place, feet, legs, body, mind, voice, speech, and power of movement. To this may be added the reestablishment of relationships with all of one's relatives, the repossession of all of one's physical belongings, the reassociation with one's environment extending outward to include the whole world, and the reestablishment of relationships with the Holy People, especially in their association with long life, health, and blessing.

Restoration/Recovery (Unit U)

A passage in many prayers describes the restoration and recovery and the state which shall succeed when this is accomplished.

This passage usually focuses on the condition of one's body and its capacity to act when restoration and recovery are won.

> Nicely I shall rise again.
> Nicely I shall heal up,
> Nicely my body shall be cooled.
> Nicely pains shall move out of me,
> Nicely moving away from me shall take place.
> Nicely I shall go about as my condition was formerly,
> In the same condition I shall go about.
> Nicely I shall walk out,
> Perfectly immune to sickness I shall go about.
> With my body perfectly cooled I shall go about,
> Filled with energy I shall go about,
> Nicely you shall walk me about. (BFHW # 1)

On some occasions this passage focuses on restoration of internal body parts and indicates the defeat of monsters whose attacks cause internal harm.

> Nicely you shall put my foodpipe in its former condition
>   again!
> Nicely you shall put my windpipe in condition again!
> Nicely you shall put my heart in condition again!
> Nicely you shall put my nerves in condition again!
> Nicely I shall walk about, without ailment I shall go about,

Unafflicted by sickness I shall go about!
Without monsters seeing me I shall be going about,
Without beings which are evil seeing me I shall go about,
With monsters dreading me I shall go about,
With monsters respecting me I shall go about,
Governed by this I shall be going about,
After conquering monsters I shall be going about,
After accomplishing this with monsters I shall be going
    about. (EH # 1)

Restoration may certainly be described in terms other than physical
well-being. It may be cast in literally global proportions.

That with which I speak, today blessing is restored,
That with which I speak, today, on earth blessing is restored.
From everywhere blessing is restored to me,
From within the home up above blessing is restored to me.
From the coming rains blessing is restored to me,
From where zigzag lightning flashed blessing is restored to me,
From the highest points where light first hits blessing is
    restored to me,
From where the dawn rises in the east blessing is restored to
    to me,
From where horizontal blue rises blessing is restored to me,
From where twilight rises in the west blessing is restored
    to me,
From where the darkness rises in the north blessing is re-
    stored to me,
From everywhere blessing is restored to me,
According to that, long life-happiness, that which I am,
    no harm will come, so I am saying. (BW # 21)

This passage suggests that Navajos believe that suffering results when one
does not have a proper relationship with the surrounding world and consequently that relief is acquired by reestablishing relationships with
everything in the environment. The consequence, as described in this
constituent, is that a person becomes the center of an entire world of
blessing. Restoration is described in terms of physical health and a fertile
environment.

State of Blessing (Unit V)

Almost all Navajo prayers conclude with a passage indicating the imminence or presence of a state of blessing. This highly formulaic passage may be uttered as a prayer by itself. In it there is considerable possibility for variation.

A summary of the forms will provide a general outline of the vocabulary and ideology of the important Navajo notions of "blessing." "May an environment of blessing surround me," states the theme for a large number of these constituents. It may be stated in the very general phrase, "In beauty may I walk" (NM # 1), or it may be more highly specified as in the standard formula

> May it be blessed before me,
> May it be blessed behind me,
> May it be blessed above me,
> May it be blessed below me,
> May it be blessed all around,
> May speech from me be blessed,
> May all my surroundings be blessed. (BW # 8)

Greater specificity may be added by indicating things in one's surrounding environment for which blessing is desired, such as possessions, crops, animals, and relatives.

"May I become a blessed one," is the theme of another large group of these constituents. The terms "long life" and "happiness" are strongly associated with this theme. "As one who is long life, happiness I shall go about" (BFHW # 1). "May I be long life, happiness" (BW # 5). An alternate translation renders long life and happiness as proper names.

The conclusion of this constituent, and sometimes the composition of the entire constituent, is the repetition of a short formula rendered variously as: "In beauty it is finished" (NM # 7), "Pleasant again it has come to be" (FH # 9), and "It has become beautiful again" (SMGR # 2). Generally, the English words beauty, happiness, blessing, and pleasant are all renderings of the Navajo word hózhǫ́.

Dew, pollen, rain, mist, long life, happiness, vegetation, old age, cornbeetle (ripener), the possession of fabrics and jewels, and the abundance of relatives are all terms which are strongly associated with blessing (hózhǫ́). Wherever they are found, the idea of blessing is suggested.

THE STRUCTURE OF NAVAJO PRAYER TEXTS

The prayer text near the beginning of this chapter may be divided into six of the twenty constituent prayer units instead of twenty-six lines. In sequence it is: name mention (A), offering/smoke (C), injunction to affect (H), removal and dispersion of native malevolence (M), restoration/recovery (U), and state of blessing (V). The surface level of the structure may be represented in symbolic form simply as A C H M U V.

At this point these constituents may be linked together for a general interpretation of the prayer. A Holy Person is named (A), he is offered a gift, and a smoke is exchanged with him establishing rapport and a relationship of reciprocity (C). On the basis of this relationship, the one named is directed to restore or remake the one praying (H), who appears to be suffering. The source of this suffering is described in the next passage which assigns to the Holy Person the responsibility, by asking him to remove and disperse the "magic power with which you were bothering me" (M). This act is described as it progresses and is followed by a description of the succeeding state, first in terms of the conditions of restoration and recovery (U) and then in terms of the acquisition of a general state of blessing in the whole environment (V).

Navajo prayers are often repeated either at one sitting or on succeeding days. Significant changes are made from one recitation to another, yet the items changed have a relationship to one another. Consider, for example, the first prayer in the set of four Red Antway Thunder prayers. Each of the prayers has the structure A B C E N L N. Several of the corresponding units do not have identical compositions in all four prayers, yet the variations from one prayer to another complement one another. Consider the following examples from the text of the first prayer in the set with the corresponding changes for the other three prayers in the set given in brackets.

> In the skies, at one [two, three, four]
> A   opening[s] of the sky,
> In the inside rear of the home of dark
>   [white, blue, yellow] cloud,

> B Dark [White, Blue, Yellow] Thunder, Young Man
>   [Woman, Man, Woman].

This day I have made you an offering,
C A nice jet [turquoise, jet, turquoise], of this I have made
    you an offering,
    A nice white bead [jet, white bead, jet], of this I have made
    you an offering,
    A nice turquoise [white bead, turquoise, white bead], of this
    I have made you an offering,
    A nice abalone [abalone, abalone, abalone], of this I have
    made you an offering.
    A nice dark sparkling rock [same in all four], of this I have
    made you an offering,
    A nice blue pollen [same], of this I have made you an offering,
    Nice pollen [same], of this I have made you an offering.

. . . .

    With your dark [white, blue, yellow] flint shoes you will
L   rise to protect him!
    With your dark [white, blue, yellow] flint leggings. . . .
    With your dark [white, blue, yellow] flint garment. . . .
    With your dark [white, blue, yellow] flint hat. . . .
    With your dark [white, blue, yellow] flints and the zigzag
    [straight, zigzag, straight] lightnings which you hold in
    your hand, you will rise to protect him! (RMGW # 2a)

This example includes place designation (A), name mention (B), offering/ smoke (C), and procurement of protection (L). Note that in place designation the alterations occur as a sequence of numbers and colors. In name mention the sequence of colors is repeated, but there is an alternation between sex designation of the Holy Persons. This same alternation pattern is again indicated in the jewel offering. Here three jewels—jet, white bead, and turquoise—are presented in alternations two at a time so that every combination of ordered pairs which can be composed from the three jewels is presented. This example indicates that these alterations are not only a stylistic consideration, they have religious significance as well.

    In order to indicate these complementary relationships in the structure diagrams, subscripts have been added to show that such a relationship exists.

1. $A_1 B_1 C_1 E \ N \ L_1 N$
2. $A_2 B_2 C_2 E \ N \ L_2 N$
3. $A_3 B_3 C_3 E \ N \ L_3 N$
4. $A_4 B_4 C_4 E \ N \ L_4 N$

In Appendix C these relationships are indicated in this manner for each prayer.

NOTES

1. Perhaps some comment on the knowledge and use of Navajo language required for the study of Navajo prayer is relevant here. The language used in Navajo prayer has a relatively limited vocabulary. No more than two or three hundred words would probably provide a vocabulary that would cover most prayer texts. This limited vocabulary allows one to work with Navajo language and with translations of prayer texts by studying the grammar. Fortunately, a number of language scholars have provided extensive discussions of many of the critical terms in the vacabulary of prayer. But a further point needs to be emphasized. With the methods of analysis used here, the concern has been to identify constituents of prayer at a level above that dependent upon the accurate translation of every word. Since it is the character of much of Navajo prayer to be highly repetitious and formulaic, a distinctive passage in a prayer is usually recognizable even if it is inaccurately rendered in English. In other words, while knowledge of Navajo grammar and the vocabulary of Navajo prayer are obviously essential, it is not essential to be fluent in the language to do this study of Navajo prayer.

2. Alphanumeric designations are used to identify prayer and to make reference to the prayer text. See the introduction to Appendix C for reference details.

3. See the Franciscan Fathers, *An Ethnologic Dictionary of the Navaho Language* (St. Michaels, Arizona: St. Michaels Press, 1910), pp. 118-78, and Gladys A. Reichard, *Social Life of the Navaho Indians with Some Attention to Minor Ceremonies* (New York: Columbia University Press, 1928), pp. 96-107.

4. For a discussion of these words see Father Berard Haile, *Legend of the Ghostway Ritual in the Male Branch of Shooting Way* (St. Michaels, Arizona: St. Michaels Press, 1950), p. 262, n. 392.

5. So far as I have been able to discover, the establishment of a relationship of reciprocity with a Holy Person has gone without comment in the literature except for David Aberle, who, in his article "The Navaho Singer's 'Fee': Payment or Presentment," in *Studies in Southwestern Ethnolinguistics,* ed. Dell Hymes (The Hague: Mouton, 1967), pp. 15-32 includes this relationship by extension but without utilizing this prayer passage which makes explicit and descriptive reference to it.

6. The term "holiness" is used here to indicate the special powers and special attributes of the Holy People. Robert Young and others have objected to the use

of the common translation "Holy People," and I am certain there will be objection to my use of the term "holiness." While it may carry moralistic connotations in certain usages, the word "holy" when used to indicate a deity has reference to no more than the designation of an entity with special power. According to Young, the core concept of Holy People *(diyin dine'e)* is the possession of special power. Clyde Kluckhohn and Dorothea Leighton made a similar argument supporting the use of the word "holy" in *The Navaho* (Cambridge: Harvard University Press, 1946), p. 180.

CHAPTER THREE

CLASSIFICATION AND HIERARCHY: PRAYER TEXTS AND CEREMONIALS

Some of the constituents of Navajo prayers clearly state the purpose of the prayer while others are of a preliminary or secondary character. For example, place designation (A), and name mention (B), tend to help establish the proper context for the intention of the prayer, and as would be expected, these appear very commonly in prayer texts. Other constituents, such as the removal and dispersion of foreign and native malevolence (K and M), describe an action which is apparently central to the purpose of the prayer utterance. The proposition that the structure of prayer correlates with its purpose suggests that the set of prayer constituents which appears to bear the purpose of the prayer may possibly be used to meaningfully classify prayer texts. The prayer constituents which seem most likely to state the central purpose of the prayer are:

1. Association/identification with a Holy Person (G),
2. Injunction to affect (H),
3. Assertion to affect (I),
4. Removal and dispersion of foreign malevolence (K),
5. Procurement of protection (L),

6. Removal and dispersion of native malevolence (M), and

7. Recovery/restoration of the lost Earth Surface Person (R).

Using the structure diagrams for the full corpus of collected texts (see Appendix C), an attempt can be made to classify the prayer texts by dividing them according to the presence of one or more of these core constituents. Each class of prayer texts would then reflect a prayer purpose. An examination of how the constituent units in the classification group relate to each other and which prayers remain unclassified by this effort will indicate the adjustments necessary to establish a complete classification of Navajo prayers.

Other than association/identification (G), which occurs with most constituents, the other core constituents rarely occur together in the same prayer texts. This makes immediately possible several distinctive classifications. Assertion to affect (I), removal of foreign malevolence (K), and procurement of protection (L) never occur in texts with any other constituents in the classification group except association/identification (G). Recovery/restoration (R) which is always associated with the set of journey and restoration constituents (Q, R, S, T) never occurs with any other units in the classification group. Injunction to affect (H) never appears without removal of native malevolence (M), but there are some occurrences of the removal of native malevolence (M) without any other units in the classification group. The examples of removal of native malevolence (M) constituents in this group have prayer purposes which correspond to the source of the native malevolence. Those which occur with an injunction to affect constituent (H) are concerned with the removal of ill intentions caused by Holy People. Those which occur without this constituent (H) are concerned with the removal of malevolence caused by native ghosts and witches.

After classifying all compatible prayer texts in this manner, the remainder of the corpus constitutes texts with a structure which contains association/identification (G) without any other of the constituents in the classification group and those that do not contain any of the classification group of constituents. The first of these two remaining groups reveals a large number of texts which consist primarily of association/identification by itself, association/identification and state of blessing (V), and these two constituents preceded by the Holy Person's journey to the home of an Earth Surface Person (P) and various combinations of constituents A through F. When association/identification (G) and state of blessing (V) occur together, there is strong concern for the acquisition of a state of blessing by association with the inherent means and powers of life associated with the Holy People. However, when the association/identification constituent occurs with the Holy Person's journey to the home of an Earth Surface Person (P), the focus is on the association of Holy People with medicine, restoration, and health. This suggests two classifications with different prayer purposes—one directed toward the acquisition of life and blessing by association with the Holy People; the second directed more specifically toward the recovery of health by establishing an association with the source of health, the Holy Person.

After removing all of the prayers that are classified by these means, there remain unclassified only those which are composed of the state of blessing constituent (V) without specification of any means for obtaining it. This small group of prayers may be associated in their purposes with the group in which association/identification (G) occurs without other members of the classification group and without the preceding journey of the Holy Person to the home of an Earth Surface Person (P).

The result of this classification is eight classes of prayer texts based on their formal structure. Each class can be described by a distinctive prayer purpose, by a specific and unique structure, and by a number of characteristic, if not distinctive, themes, catalogs, and other features. This schema can accommodate all of the Navajo prayer texts considered for this study.[1] The constituent structures of the prayer classes may also be designated symbolically.

The classification in terms of distinctive purpose is as follows:

1. Prayers of Blessing

The prayer purpose which distinguishes this class is the identification/association with the means of life, blessing, and holiness of the Holy People. It appears to be uttered for the purpose of acquiring blessing, in a situation where no specific suffering or malady is apparent. This class includes three structural types which may be diagrammed:

$$(A) \ldots (F) \ G \ (U) \ (V),$$
$$(A) \ldots (F) \ V,$$
$$(A) \ldots (F) \ G^n \ V^n \ (U) \ (V)$$

where n is some repetition of these units for n combinations of Holy People named.[2] A very common catalog in this classification is: feet, legs, body, mind, voice.

2. Prayers of Restoration/Recovery by Reidentification/ Reassociation with the Means of Health

This class of texts reflects the notion that restoration and recovery may be gained by reidentification and association with Holy People who are the means of health and life. The structure is $(A) \ldots (F) \ P \ G \ (U) \ (V)$. The constituent describing the journey of the Holy People to the Earth Surface Person (P) occurs only in this class of prayers, but it is not cited as the distinctive constituent unit because it does not appear to carry the purpose of the prayer utterance. The "feet, legs, body, mind, voice" catalog is common to this class.

3. Prayers of Restoration by Expulsion of Foreign Malevolence

This class is important, although only a few recorded texts are known, because it and the next class represent types of prayer purposes quite different from the others. The structure is $(A) \ldots (G) \ K \ (V)$. Here a catalog of internal organs tends to replace the feet, legs, body, mind, voice catalog.

4. Prayers of Restoration by Expulsion of the Malevolent Influence of Native Ghosts or Witches

This class, somewhat related to the previous class, is also small in representative texts. This class is distinguished from the preceding one by identification of the source of the bothersome malevolent powers. The malevolence referred to here is thought to have its source in native ghosts and witches. The constituent units are also distinct from class 3. The constituent structure is $(A) \ldots (F) \ M \ (N)$. Emphasis is on internal organs of the body rather than the catalog mentioning feet, legs, body, mind, voice.

5. Prayers of Restoration by the Removal of the Malevolent Influence of Holy People

The purpose of this kind of prayer is to remove a magic spell or power attributed to the Holy People which is causing suffering. This power is not represented as an object within the body of the sufferer as it is in classes 3 and 4. It is not apparent from the constituents alone why a Holy Person has turned against the person praying. The structure is (A) . . . (G) H M (U) (V). Again, the catalog—feet, legs, body, mind, voice—is important.

6. Prayers of Restoration by the Recovery, Return, and Reassociation with the Means of Health *(Ha'áyátééh sodizin and ch'ééhoyátééh sodizin)*

The Navajo terms which name these prayers are very important, but discussion of them will be reserved for later. The prayers of this class are perhaps the most distinctive in style of all prayers. They are built upon long journey sequences for the search, recovery, and return of the lost means of life and health of the one praying. The constituent structure is (A) (B) Q R S (T) (G) (V).

The important idea of the representation of the means of life and health in human-like form is strongly apparent in the recovery constituent (R) in which the catalog—feet, legs, body, mind, voice—is almost always present and also at the point of the reassociation of the lost means of life with the one who lost them (T).

7. Prayers of Procurement of Protection Against Potential Attack *(ach'ah sodizin)*

This group of texts is distinctive for its concern with prevention of potential attacks by the malintentioned rather than with the relief of some existing malady. The catalogs focus on the garments and weapons of protection rather than the body parts themselves. The structure is (A) . . . (G) L (N) (V). The constituent describing the consequence of gaining protection does not occur outside of this class of prayers although it is not present in all examples.

8. Prayers of Restoration by Remaking/Redressing the Holy Person's Means of Health and Life

This class of prayer is notable since it is the Earth Surface Person who is restoring the means of holiness to the Holy Person. This suggests that Navajos feel that potential illness may be suffered by the Earth Surface Person who has disturbed a Holy Person. Restoration results in undoing the injury to the Holy Person by remaking/redressing his means of holiness and returning it to him. This is the purpose of this class of texts which has the constituent structure (A) (B) I (J) (T) (V). The catalog—feet, legs, body, mind, voice—is standard in the passage of the prayer having to do with the remaking and redressing (I).

This classification of Navajo prayer texts reveals a number of notable factors. It shows that prayers can be distinctly classified in terms of both their constituency and the syntactic arrangement of the constituents. It shows that the entire corpus may be considered in relationship to the purpose for the prayer utterance. The purposes of many prayers are to attain health on the one hand and holiness on the other. It shows that most classes of prayer utilize the catalog—feet, legs, body, mind, voice—which suggests that health and life are represented in human-like form. Those classes of prayers which do not utilize this basic catalog are concerned with the internal organs of the body, and they are characterized by distinctive features concerned with the removal of malintentioned foreign objects from inside the body.

THE GENERAL STRUCTURE OF NAVAJO PRAYER

A study of the structures of the individual prayer texts and the several classes of prayer texts shows that all prayers share, to a degree, a common pattern or structure both in terms of purposes and the syntactic arrangement of constituent units. Generally, all prayers have the following four part structure.

$$\left(\begin{array}{c} \text{Establishment} \\ \text{of a} \\ \text{Relationship} \end{array} \right) \left(\begin{array}{c} \text{The Motivating} \\ \text{Problem or} \\ \text{Situation} \end{array} \right) \left(\begin{array}{c} \text{The Solution} \end{array} \right) \left(\begin{array}{c} \text{State Upon} \\ \text{Solution} \end{array} \right)$$

Of course, many prayers do not have a specific constituent unit or units representing each of these parts. The problem or motivating situation and the means to gain a solution are commonly combined. The problem statement is often an implication of the required solution. A number of constituent units can serve in a number of distinctive capacities, making the rigid assignment of each constituent to any functional role impossible.

These factors do not upset the descriptions of the structure of the prayers and classes. These descriptions indicate that it is not only the utilization of one or two specific constituents, but rather the specific selection and syntactic organization of all of the constituents that is essential to the composition of any prayer. The structuring principles by which prayer constituents are selected and organized are at the heart of the way in which a prayer communicates a specific message to the Holy People and to other Earth Surface People as well as the way in which it evokes a whole system of religious symbols. These structuring principles have not been fully revealed on the basis of the descriptive analysis and classification of the prayer texts. The prayer constituents constantly refer to the mythological, ritual, and situational contexts in which they occur. To achieve an understanding of the deeper meaning of prayer demands a fuller study of the structuring principles that operate at the prayer act level, that is, when prayer is performed in a particular situation in the ambience of the Navajo tradition of mythology and ritual.

To this point Navajo prayer has been revealed as having a communicative function between people as well as between Earth Surface People and Holy People. The style of the language used in prayer suggests that it has a performative function as well as a petitionary function that is, that it evokes and affects as well as informs.

PRAYER AND CEREMONIAL CLASSIFICATIONS

The major basis for the descriptive analysis and classification of Navajo prayer texts is that the structures of prayer texts correlate with their purposes. The prayers are uttered at the climactic moment in ritual performances, and the prayer utterance constitutes a prayer act which incorporates relevant mythological and situational factors. From this it is expected that the classification of prayer texts according to their purposes should correlate with a classification of prayer acts. This means that there should be a high degree of correlation between the classification of prayer texts and the classification of ceremonials.

The principal approach used to determine and show the whole system of Navajo religion has been the classification of Navajo ceremonials. A list of ceremonials was begun before the turn of the century by the Franciscan Fathers at St. Michaels which they published in *An Ethnologic Dictionary of the Navajo Language* in 1910. The first major effort at classification is recorded in the journal articles by Father Berard Haile and, collaboratively, by Clyde Kluckhohn and Leland C. Wyman in 1938. Other classifications have appeared regularly since then, notably that of Gladys Reichard in 1950, a further effort by Kluckhohn in 1960, and an expansion and restatement of Kluckhohn by Lamphere in 1973.[4] The history and comparison of these classifications is an important story in the history of the study of Navajo culture and religion. It is critically presented in detail in Appendix B.

While Father Berard's approach was focused more on the thought and ideology reflected in the schema of Navajo ceremonial classification, as was Kluckhohn's 1960 work, the simple descriptive categorization done by Wyman and Kluckhohn has provided the basic classification which has been most useful. Even so, Father Berard's schema shows a deeper sensitivity to the principles of Navajo religion which make the entire gamut of ceremonials cohere as a religious system. Wyman and Kluckhohn distinguished six classes of ceremonials.

1. Blessing Way

2. Holy Way (7 subgroups)

3. Life Way

4. Evil Way (2 subgroups) [herein referred to as Uglyway]

5. War Ceremonials

6. Game Way

The occurrence of the prayer texts in their ceremonial context (where known), reveals a very close correlation between this ceremonial classification and my classification of prayer texts. These factors are summarized in Table 2.

TABLE 2

Correlation of Classifications of
Prayer Texts and Ceremonials

Structure Diagrams for Classifications of Prayer Texts	Ceremonial Classification of Most Common Incidence
1. (A) . . . (F) G (U) (V)	Blessingway
(A) . . . (F) V	
(A) . . . (F) G^n V^n (U) (V), $n = 1, 2, . . .$	
2. (A) . . . (F) P G (U) (V)	Lifeway
3. (A) . . . (G) K (V)	Enemyway
4. (A) . . . (F) M (N)	Uglyway
5. (A) . . . (G) H M (U) (V)	Holyway
6. (A) (B) QRS (T) (G) (V)	Prayer ceremonies and most other classifications
7. (A) . . . (G) L (N) (V)	Prayer ceremonies and most other classifications
8. (A) (B) I (J) (T) (U) (V)	Remaking rites (not classified by Wyman and Kluckhohn)

This provides a basis for a classification of Navajo prayer acts, that is, a classification of the prayer texts including the ceremonial and cultural contexts in which they are uttered. The classification of prayer acts may be presented in a schema which designates the problem or motivating situation, the statement of the means to respond to this situation, and the state of resolution. There is general correlation between the concern to which the prayer is directed and that of the ceremonial with which it is closely associated. That correlation will be considered in depth. Diagrammatically it is presented in Table 3.

To this point a classification of Navajo prayer texts has been described and it has been shown that the motivations and concerns of these classes of prayers, as revealed in their constituent structures, generally correlates

TABLE 3

Motivating Purpose of Prayer Acts by Class

Class of Prayer Acts	Motivating Purpose
1. Blessingway	Identification/association with the means of life, blessing, and holiness
2. Lifeway	Restoration/recovery by reidentification, reassociation with the means of health
3. Enemyway	Restoration by expelling foreign malevolence
4. Uglyway	Restoration by expelling the influence of native ghost or witch
5. Holyway	Restoration by removal of bothersome influence of Holy People
6. Liberation	Restoration by recovery and reidentification/reassociation of life forces
7. Protection	Obtain protection against various kinds of potential harmful influences
8. Remaking	Restoration by remaking/redressing the life force of a Holy Person

with that of the ceremonials in which they are uttered. This indicates that there are relationships between the structure of prayer texts and the structure of the complex religious acts in which they occur. This hierarchy of structure has not been fully described, yet it is integral to understanding the capabilities of prayer acts to both communicate specific messages and to be effective and meaningful religious acts. The description and classification of prayer acts provide the base for a fuller analysis of Navajo prayers; they describe the hierarchy of structuring principles that operate and give significance and force to these complex religious acts. It is like beginning with a single melodic line in music and then considering it in the midst of a complex musical score. In this way we begin to appreciate how prayers have the capacity to be infinitely creative and responsive to very specific needs in the culture.

Since the prayer acts correspond closely with the major classifications of Navajo ceremonials and their corresponding myths and since the prayer acts engage a wide range of elements within Navajo religion, this study of Navajo prayer acts is also a study of much of Navajo religion. By necessity this study must consider the majority of Navajo myths, rituals, and religious situations.

Before the individual classes of prayer acts are considered, it is essential to present a discussion of Navajo mythology and ritual processes in order to provide a general overview from which to deal specifically with the interrelationships among the details.

NOTES

1. A few prayer texts have not been classified because they are incomplete.
2. Parentheses indicate optional constituents.
3. Father Berard Haile, "Navaho Chantways and Ceremonials," *American Anthropologist* 40 (1938): 639-52, and Leland C. Wyman and Clyde Kluckhohn, *Navajo Classification of their Song Ceremonials* (Menasha, Wisconsin: Memoirs, American Anthropological Association, no. 50, 1938).
4. Gladys A. Reichard, *Navaho Religion: A Study of Symbolism* (New York: Pantheon Books, 1950), pp. 314-37, Clyde Kluckhohn, "Navajo Categories," in *Culture in History: Essays in Honor of Paul Radin* ed. Stanley Diamond (New York: Columbia University Press, 1960), pp. 65-98, and Louise Lamphere and Evon Z. Vogt, "Clyde Kluckhohn as Ethnographer and Student of Navaho Ceremonialism," in *Culture and Life, Essays in Memory of Clyde Kluckhohn,* eds. Walter W. Taylor *et. al.,* (Carbondale: Southern Illinois University Press, 1973), pp. 94-135.

CHAPTER FOUR

NAVAJO MYTHOLOGY AND RITUAL PROCESSES

Navajos believe that the life and power of their mythology depends upon its being retained in the memory of the people and that to record the mythology is to risk its possible misuse, or worse, to take away its vitality. Still, with the help of Navajos, thousands of pages of mythology have been recorded which afford an almost limitless opportunity to read and examine this mythology for the purpose of gaining further appreciation and understanding of the Navajo people and their religion.

The oral traditions of the Navajo remain alive due, in part, to their intimate relationship with Navajo ritual processes. For the Navajo, ritual and myth are so interdependent that neither could exist without the other. Huge portions of mythology center on the incidents and procedures of the first occurrence of a particular ceremonial. The ritual process is described so carefully that it amounts to a prototype for all subsequent performances of the ceremonial.

THE ERAS OF SACRED HISTORY[1]

Navajo mythology is complex and tells many tales. It is difficult to obtain an overall picture of how these many stories are related to one another and how the whole body somehow coheres. One way that remains consistent with Navajo thought is based on the recognition that all of the stories find a place within one of several major eras of sacred history, a history which took place "in the beginning." The Navajo story of the creation begins far below the surface of the present Navajo world. The first era unfolds with the journey by the predecessors to the Navajos through a number of lower worlds and concludes with their emergence onto the present earth surface. The second era begins with the emergence at the center of the surface destined to become Navajoland. The second era is an era of creation during which the earth surface was formed into what is now known to the Navajo people. Covered with water and nearly landless at the emergence, the events of the era of creation transform this world into a place of incomparable beauty. This beautifully ordered world is the setting for the third era in which mythic heroes, in establishing Navajo culture, also introduced disorder and ugliness into the world thus threatening its destruction. The heroes suffered as a consequence of their actions and were restored by ceremonials performed by Holy People which resulted not only in the restoration of the heroes, but also in the restoration of order to the world. The heroes learned the ritual processes and how they are to be used while the ceremonials were being performed for them. With this knowledge they became the progenitors of the ceremonial ways which have been performed throughout Navajo history. Origins for many Navajo ceremonials are told in the stories of the era of the heroic adventurers.

The Era of Emergence

The sacred geography encountered in the journey of emergence reveals the Navajo conception that in the beginning there already existed a number of world structures stacked one on top of another. These worlds, numbering from two to fourteen, are depicted as platters, one suspended above another or as hemispheres stacked one on top of another. The journey of emergence begins in the center of the lowest level moving upward through world after world with a series of episodes recounted for each. The journey concludes with the emergence onto the present earth surface.

Insect, animal, and bird peoples inhabit these lower worlds. While they have some nonhuman characteristics, they have the power of speech, and they live and act according to customs and practices that would be familiar to Navajo people.

The upward journey is a forced movement due to the misconduct of these peoples. Each world offers the promise of happiness and a good life to its inhabitants, but they are unable to maintain the proper relationships with one another. They quarrel constantly and though they try, they are unable to avoid committing acts of adultery and incest. After repeated warnings by the chiefs of the oceans which border the four sides of these lower worlds, floods are unleashed which threaten to engulf them. They flee upward to the next world.

This pattern of events is repeated for each of the lower worlds. The geography and physical character of the lower worlds is usually carefully described. The imagery generally points out the barrenness of the landscape and the watery threat that constantly surrounds these worlds. They are not dark but are each cast in a different hue. Most versions note that the sun and moon did not yet exist. One could discern the passing of time by the shifting of the dominance of color from one quadrant to another through each of the four cardinal directions.

Disorder, if not chaos, is the mood associated with the lower worlds. Much of the action can be characterized as disruptive or illegal. There is an unmistakable association between the pending forces of destruction and the acts of misconduct.

A theme which emerges with increasing urgency as the emergence journey proceeds is the need to establish dependable relationships to bring about an orderly world. The sequence of acts which lead only to watery chaos begins by negative means to determine the necessary character of the desired world. The people who are to direct the creation of a new world upon emergence, First Man and First Woman, are born and are given the sacred objects from which will arise the form of the new world. Yet along with their acquisition of certain powers of creation, First Man and First Woman also learned the ways of witchcraft.

Navajo people consider the lower worlds to be dangerous places inhabited by the ghosts of the dead and witches. In the emergence journey there is no gradual evolution of forms culminating with the entrance onto the earth surface. There is little suggestion of womb imagery. There is no gradual increase of light, and only the slightest suggestion of an increase of knowledge. No metamorphosis accompanies the emergence process. As will be elaborated upon later, even First Man and First

Woman, the directors of the creation process, are destined to return to the lower worlds to serve as the chiefs of witchcraft. In mythology the lower worlds are identified with the condition referred to by the Navajo word *hóchǫ* which designates an ugly and unhappy environment.

The Era of Cosmic Creation

At the rim of the emergence place, a new era of sacred history begins. The earth surface is found covered with water and under the control of water birds. After the waters are drained and dried by the wind people, First Man and First Woman begin to whisper to each other, planning what will be created on the earth surface. They build a sweathouse and enter it to continue making plans. When the plans are made others that had emerged with them enter the sweathouse. First Man performs two ceremonial acts using his medicine bundle, his collection of sacred objects, to reveal its creative power. With the first ritual act, two groups of "human forms" arise from the bundle and are designated as the materials out of which the life forms of all things are to be created. The second ceremonial act, which is performed over these human forms, gives rise to a beautiful young man and woman who represent the means of life for all things as they proceed through time. The medicine bundle is shown to be the source of life containing both the substance of life and the means by which life is maintained through time. The Navajo concept of life is tied closely to the power of the sacred medicine bundle.

After these preparations are made in the sweathouse, the party constructs and consecrates a ceremonial house, or hogan, in which to create life on the earth surface. The creation hogan is a microcosmic structure which stands at the center of the world, at the emergence place. Its four support pillars are identified with the cardinal directions, and in the creation ceremony its floor represents the earth surface. The party enters the creation hogan, and on the floor First Man constructs, in a manner resembling a painting in sand, representations, in human form, of the life forms of things to be created on the earth surface. He uses the materials (sacred jewels) from his sacred bundle. These human-shaped life forms will reside within the physical forms of the mountains, plants, animals, and other physical features which are to live upon the earth surface. After making the inner forms, they are "dressed" in representations of their physical outer forms by the application of sand designs.

The creation of this microcosmic world lasts all night. It is accompanied by the singing of the creation songs. At dawn, a smoke is prepared as a vehicle to transport the representational forms to their corresponding places on the earth surface. In effect, they are transformed from the symbolic ritual world to the nonsymbolic world of the earth surface.

First Man and First Woman send the human-shaped life forms of dawn and evening twilight on a tour of the earth surface to inspect the creation. Ascending each of the mountains "the two sat down side by side. As they viewed the scene below they found it extremely beautiful."[2]

During the process of creation, it becomes clear that the Navajo concept of life is expressed through the image of a nonphysical form in human shape which stands within the physical form, giving it life. The Navajo refer to this inner form as *bii'gistíín,* "one who lies within it," or as *bii'siziinii,* "in-standing one."[3] These life forms are often perceived as named people with distinct attributes. They may be addressed and engaged in relationships. A review of the various Navajo perceptions of the inner life form shows that they associate it with things they regard as living. This may occur in complex and nested arrangements. For example, the Navajo perceive separate identities and personalities for the inner life forms of the sacred mountains. Some of the Holy People, who may be represented as masked figures *(ye'ii)* in ceremonials, are identified as the in-dwellers of these mountains. From another perspective the life form associated with mountains collectively in the songs of creation is identified as Mountain Woman. Earth Woman is also named as one of the inner life forms of the earth and is often paired with the Sun as a male figure in the celestial region. Thus, it appears that the Navajo notion of the inner life form is a generalized expression of their concept of life at whatever level they perceive it. The life forms generally have names and forms of representation that are distinct from the outer or physical form, yet it must be stressed that Navajos perceive the inner and outer forms as inseparable in that they are wholly interdependent.

The creation story reveals that while the inner life forms for the many living entities differ from one another, they are at base all the same. They all arose from the medicine bundle which is the latent reservoir out of which life becomes manifest. One life form differs from another not in the substances which compose it or the source from which it arises, but rather in the shape it takes and the place and character it is given as ordained by the acts of creation. All life forms are also accompanied by, or identified with, the means by which life is maintained through time. This kinetic power is represented by a beautiful young man and woman in the sweathouse and they are identified as long life and happiness.

A concept which occupies a central position in Navajo religious thought is communicated by the words *są'ah naaghái̇ bik'eh hózhǫ* which is normally translated by the phrase "long life and happiness." According to Gary Witherspoon's analysis of the Navajo term, "*są'ah* refers to the completion of the life cycle through death in old age, and *naaghái̇* refers to the continual reoccurrence of the completion of the life cycle." *Bik'eh* means " 'according to it' or 'by its decree'." "*Hózhǫ* refers to the positive or ideal environment. It is beauty, harmony, good, happiness, and everything that is positive, and it refers to an environment which is all-inclusive."[4] In other words, the term signifies that the continual reoccurrence of the completion of the life cycle through a death in old age is a state that is part of an all-inclusive environment of beauty. Hence, the animating or kinetic aspect of life produces a world which is beautiful. This is precisely the state observed at the conclusion of the sacred era of creation.

After the world is given life, a figure known most commonly by the name Changing Woman is born, and her activities are central to the concluding story cycles in the era of creation. Her parents are the beautiful young man and woman who represent long life and happiness. Twins born to Changing Woman rid the earth surface of monsters, produced through adulterous or unnatural sexual acts, thus preparing it for habitation by Navajo people. Changing Woman is given First Man's sacred bundle and with it the power of creativity. Before First Man reluctantly yields the bundle to her, he makes a copy of it to use as the source of his witch power upon his return to the lower worlds. With the sacred powers Changing Woman creates corn. Then from balls of epidermal waste which she rubbed from her body, mingled with cornmeal, she creates the first Navajo people.

The era of creation concludes with the departure from the earth surface of the Holy People, who had been instrumental in the creation processes. After their departure they are not to be seen or heard again on the earth surface through ordinary senses, yet they remain present and active in all things.

The birth of Changing Woman made it possible for the process of creation to be disassociated from the people who emerged from the lower worlds. Changing Woman takes her name from her distinguishing ability to grow older through time, and upon reaching old age, to repeat the cycle of life again and again. She is like the passing seasons. She is the personification of *sǫ'ah naagháii* and is identified with the environment of extreme beauty *(hózhǫ́)*. Changing Woman is the Holy Person who represents and controls time—the medium and process of life. She is fittingly the child of Long Life and Happiness. Identified with the kinetic life process, holding in her possession the sacred bundle that contains the sacred objects from which all life is made, Changing Woman is a singular embodiment of the powers of creation and the sustenance of all earth surface life.

The creation process, which began in the barren dungeons of the lower worlds, struggling against a background of infidelity, adultery, witchcraft, incest and the constantly rising waters of chaos (a world characterized as *hóchǫ́*), somehow retained the seeds of life to eventually emerge upon the earth surface. Once gained, the earth surface became the scene where these seeds, sown even by those who knew evil ways, sprouted in the drained mud to grow into a world which could only be described as extremely beautiful *(hózhǫ́)*. The powers of creation were passed on to Changing Woman who became identified with beauty and fertility. Her twin sons made the world safe from the terrifying monsters and, thus, won a victory over the threat of disorder not conquered in the lower worlds. In this way the earth was made a place suitable for the existence of the Navajo people who were created by Changing Woman.

The view from the rim of the emergence place makes it clear that Navajos perceive their world as an interdependent and interacting duality. At the conclusion of the creation era, the balance of the world rests upon the rim of the emergence place. It is here that the interdependent parts of the duality meet and interact. All things meet at the center of the world and give definition and meaning to their counterparts: the era of emergence and the era of creation, the lower worlds and the earth surface, *hóchǫ́* and *hózhǫ́*, disorder and order, chaos and creation, the outer physical form and the inner life form, the Earth Surface People and the Holy People, "our side" and "their side," death and life.

The Era of the Heroes and the Origin of Ceremonials

In the sacred era which follows the cosmic creation there is a shift from the rim of the emergence place to the outer boundaries of the created

world, from the center where creation unfolded and on which it is balanced,
to the periphery, where the significance of order and the consequences of
trespassing are tested. The mythology that describes the origin of Navajo
ceremonials also investigates the significance of creation through the action
of its characters who violate the order established in creation. Furthermore, it confirms and extends the aspect of Navajo religious thought which
portends that the impending threat to creation is an essential element in
the maintenance of a significant life. As the creation of the Navajo world
as an environment of beauty *(hózhǫ́)* was set against a background of disorder *(hóchǫ́)* which characterized the lower worlds, the maintenance of
order *(hózhǫ́)* through time is set in the context of the continual presence
of the potential collapse of that order.

The era of the origin of the ceremonials is an era of heroic adventures.
The heroes, invariably in the process of a journey, enter forbidden terri-
tories or violate some regulations. As a consequence, they suffer in any
number of ways. When the heroes are unable to get out of their predica-
ments, Holy People come to aid and relieve their suffering by performing
ceremonials which restore them. The enactment of the ceremonials not
only brings restoration, but it initiates the heroes into the knowledge of
the ceremonial ways. The heroes are allowed to go home to teach the
ceremonial to a successor, but they must return to live permanently in the
domain of the Holy People. The myths which describe in detail the ceremonial performances are the archetypes for the Navajo ceremonials.

At the surface level the stories of this sacred era reveal the ceremonials
by describing the occasion of their first performances. But as several
studies have shown,[5] these stories also serve as a guide to the Navajo way
of life. Where in the era of creation the concern is with the establishment
of proper places and relationships for things in the world, the era of the
origin of the ceremonials is concerned with how one lives in that world.
It deals with the boundaries of both places and relationships. It deals with
the relationships which are necessary for life, such as the relationships
between hunter and game, between a man and wife and women who are
not his wife, between in-laws, between the living and the dead, between
a Navajo and a non-Navajo, between a person and the plants and animals
in his environment, between Earth Surface People and Holy People. The
stories which tell of this era define the Navajo way of life. They deal with
life in progress through time and across space. They test limits and thus
reinforce those limits.

In speaking of the organization within their oral tradition, Navajos use the metaphor of a tree. Ordinarily they refer to the cosmic creation mythology as the trunk of the tree with the various adventure stories of the heroes as branches extending out from the trunk. This metaphor is particularly appropriate since many of the hero stories, and the ceremonials whose origins they recount, share extensive story cycles before they branch off into separate stories and separate ceremonial ways. Navajos tell many versions of the specific branching relationships within certain groups of ceremonials. Although there is no evidence that Navajos regard the emergence mythology as the root portion of this tree, it seems a consistent extension of this metaphor.

The recitation of myths may occur on numerous occasions. While it might be expected that a formal recitation of the myth would accompany the performance of the ritual, this is not always the case. Indeed, there are even singers who may learn the ritual processes of a ceremonial without learning the myth that accounts for the origin of these processes to the point of being capable of reciting the story in an oral performance. Short portions of myths are often told informally to illustrate a point or to teach a lesson. There are seasonal restrictions which may be observed in the recitation of some myths. While some may be told at any time, others are restricted to winter, which is defined as the time after the first frost and before the first spring thunder. The rationale Navajos give for this practice is that during this period certain forces and beings, such as snakes, lightnings, and thunders, are sleeping or not present, so that to talk about them and to tell their stories would consequently be safe.

The style of myth recitation is an area which has received far too little consideration. Most myth texts have not been recorded on the occasion of a formal telling. Still it is clear that singers have considerable latitude in how they tell the story in terms of both style and content. Humor plays a significant role in the recitation of many myths and stories. This extends far beyond the telling of the often humorous tales of Coyote, the Navajo trickster.[6] The myth recitation is accompanied by liberal gesturing which is used most commonly to clarify points in the myth such as how far or high something was or how a certain act was performed. Points of humor are eagerly anticipated and told with relish. Pauses for laughter are frequent, and sometimes the point of humor is repeated for a second round of laughter. When the myth recitation is being interpreted into English at the same time, this allows a fourfold opportunity to enjoy the humor. Singers also commonly withhold a portion of a myth so that they do not reveal all of their knowledge, a situation they would consider as endangering them.

THE NAVAJO RITUAL PROCESS

Almost all Navajo ceremonials are motivated by a certain need, most commonly that felt by a single individual. The need may arise out of the accession to a particular stage in the life cycle or out of the events peculiar to an individual's life. For example, when a girl experiences her first menses, it is time for her first *kinaaldá* ceremony which is a puberty rite. In it she is made into a woman and her preparation for marriage is initiated. On other occasions, particularly the suffering of ill health, the appropriate ceremonial is not always obvious. On this occasion, the person and his family begin to review the past in an attempt to discover some transgression or error of the sufferer that might have given rise to ill health. The etiology of the disease is the focus in this effort, rather than the symptoms as such. If this is unsuccessful they procure the assistance of a "seer" *(eé'deetjhii)* who, through methods of divination, "sees" the causal factor and recommends the ceremonial which will most appropriately rectify the situation.

With the knowledge of what ceremonial is needed, someone approaches one knowledgeable in the ceremonial procedures, its songs and prayers, on behalf of the sufferer. The approached person is known as a "singer" *(hataałii)* and is distinct from a curer *('azá'oonitigi)* who has a much narrower range of ceremonial activity. The "singer," if available, will set a date and place for the ceremonial performance and consider the versions and ritual acts which would be appropriate for the situation. Except for members of his own family, the singer never performs a ceremonial without compensation, but David Aberle (1967) has suggested this is more for maintaining the proper relationships of reciprocity than it is a professional fee.

In the intervening period before the ceremonial begins, preparations are made. These normally include the cleaning of the ceremonial hogan, the collection of medicines and materials to be used in the ceremonial, and the preparation of food for the guests and participants. The ceremonial begins with the ritual blessing of the ceremonial hogan on the evening of the day the singer arrives. The majority of ceremonial activity will take place within this sacred structure. The person (sometimes persons) for whom the ceremonial is performed is known as the "one-sung-over" *(bik'i nahagha)*. The common rendering of this term as "patient" is too confining and in many cases actually misleading.

The common duration for Navajo ceremonials is either two, five, or nine nights. The Navajo reckoning of time in the ceremonial context places the nights before the days, so a two-night ceremonial begins at sundown on one day, includes the next day and its night (the second night) ending at the dawn which concludes the second night. A nine-night ceremonial lasts for nine nights and the intervening eight days.

Navajo ceremonials are composed of a relatively small number of constituent rites or ceremonies, and each of these ceremonies is composed of ritual acts involving sacred objects and manual and vocal actions.[7] Each performance of a ceremonial involves a complex process of selecting components and ordering them at several levels. This process is controlled by a hierarchy of structuring principles. We have already seen the first levels of these principles in the description and classification of prayer acts. Yet there are other levels of structuring principles that function when the prayer acts are in the various contexts of performance. In describing these principles we will achieve a deeper understanding of how prayer acts, and even the ritual process in general, may be used to respond creatively and meaningfully to almost any conceivable circumstances.

NOTES

1. A fuller development of some of the material in this chapter can be found in Gill's, *Songs of Life: An Introduction to Navajo Religious Culture* (Leiden: E. J. Brill, 1979).

2. Leland C. Wyman, *Blessingway: With Three Versions of the Myth Recorded and Translated from the Navaho by Father Berard Haile, O.F.M.* (Tucson: University of Arizona Press, 1970), p. 137. See Gill, *Songs of Life,* Plates I-III for creation iconography.

3. Father Berard Haile, "Soul Concepts of the Navaho," *Annali Lateranensi* 7 (1943): 68.

4. Gary Witherspoon, "The Central Concepts of Navajo World View (I)," *Linguistics* 119 (1974): 46-58 and *Language and Art in the Navajo Universe* (Ann Arbor: University of Michigan Press, 1977), pp. 15-32.

5. See especially Katherine Spencer, *Reflections of Social Life in the Navaho*

Origin Myth (Albuquerque: University of New Mexico Publications in Anthropology, no. 3, 1947) and *Mythology and Values: An Analysis of Navaho Chantway Myths* (Boston: American Folklore Society, Memoirs, vol. 48, 1957).

6. Barre Toelken's article "The 'Pretty Language' of Yellowman: Genre, Mode, and Texture in Navaho Coyote Narratives," *Genre* 2 (1969): 211-35 is an example of a study giving some attention to the style of presentation.

7. For more detailed information see Clyde Kluckhohn and Leland C. Wyman, *An Introduction to Navajo Chant Practice* (Menasha, Wisconsin: Memoirs, American Anthropology Association, no. 53, 1940).

CHAPTER FIVE

BLESSING PRAYER ACTS

Frank Mitchell, who was a well-known singer of Blessingway, began his recitation of the story of Blessingway to Father Berard with an important statement about its relationship to other Navajo ceremonials. He said,

You see, as for the beginning of this particular line, it, like all lines, originated at the Place of Emergence and much could be told of them. You see, of the many different chant lines that were to be, it is the first to start from there. Blessingway was first used to place Earth and Sky in a position facing each other. The condition of [life on] the surface of this earth and likewise on the sky below which we were to live, was established first of all they say.[1]

It is well known that Navajos consider Blessingway central to Navajo ceremonials in a position cogently described by Long Moustache as the "spinal column of songs."[2]

It seems essential to begin the analysis of Navajo prayer acts with those which occur most frequently in Blessingway ceremonials.

BLESSINGWAY RITUAL PROCESS

An examination of a prayer text in more than one prayer act will show the principles in the ritual process which make the prayer act meaningful to a specific situation. Also, a brief account of the basic elements in Blessingway *(hózhǫ́ǫ́ji)* is necessary because the term is used to designate a wide variety of ceremonial acts. It may designate ceremonies for the blessing of a new house, a girl's puberty rite *(kinaaldá)*, and the creation ceremonials which took place at the beginning of time. Blessingway prayer acts may occur in other ceremonials which can be considered a part of the Blessingway complex, such as rain ceremonies, seed blessings, weddings, and numerous forms of prayer ceremonies. The variety and flexibility of the ceremonial way is distinctive. Gladys Reichard once remarked that she had seen a number of ceremonials which were called *hózhǫ́ǫ́ji* but no two of them were alike.[3]

Even with the flexibility of the Blessingway ritual process enabling it to respond to diverse needs, it has a fairly standard ritual constituency. Normally it includes four ceremonies: the consecration or blessing of the ceremonial hogan, the intoning of a litany prayer, the administration of a bath, and an all-night singing ceremony. It is usually a two-night ceremonial, but there are situations when it may be reduced to but one night or less.

Consecrating the Ceremonial Hogan

The consecration, or blessing, of the ceremonial hogan is performed at sunset on the first night as the initiating act in the ceremonial. Within the hogan, which has already been cleaned and prepared, a new fire is lighted and the singer enters through the door, which always faces east, and moves clockwise (sunwise to the Navajo) around the interior marking with corn pollen or corn meal the four support poles (or lowest roof beams in cribbed-roof style hogans), one corresponding with each of the cardinal directions. The singer does not complete the full circuit by moving from the fourth pole to the entrance, but retraces his steps to the entrance. On the return circuit the singer strews corn meal upon the floor of the hogan. The singing of a set of Chief Hogan or Talking God Hogan songs, whose texts identify this structure with the creation hogan constructed at the emergence place, accompanies the ceremony. The songs identify the four support poles with the inner life forms of that first ceremonial structure. They are four of earth's inner life forms, all female. Since that first hogan was a microcosm, this rite serves to identify the commonplace Navajo home with the structure of the entire Navajo world.

In this first ceremony a ritual or sacred space is set aside. It is identified with the center of the earth and with the structure in which earth surface life was created. It is thus consecrated as a space in which the Holy People who created the earth in the beginning may once again communicate with earth people and perform acts of creation.

Intoning a Litany

A litany prayer ceremony may follow the consecration of the hogan. The one-sung-over, the singer, and guests enter the hogan to take their places on the floor. The singer applies pollen to the tongue and top of the head of the one-sung-over while saying a brief pollen prayer. The one-sung-over holds the principal Blessingway ritual object, the mountain soil bundle, while reciting the prayer with the singer in litany fashion. At the conclusion of the prayer the singer presses the mountain soil bundle to the body of the one-sung-over in a ritually prescribed manner and a communal pollen prayer concludes the prayer ceremony.

The genesis of the mountain soil bundle is described in Navajo mythology in the events when Changing Woman revealed the knowledge of Blessingway to the Navajo people. It is a representation of her medicine bundle which was the same medicine bundle brought to the earth surface by First Man and out of which came all of earth surface life. The structure of the mountain soil bundle maintains the complementary dual pattern which is basic to Navajo religious thought. Soil must be collected from the four sacred mountains which stand at the perimeter of the Navajo world in each of the cardinal directions. The soil from each mountain is given an application of pollen and wrapped in an unwounded (ritually killed) animal skin. A jewel (semiprecious stone) corresponding to the jewels in First Man's medicine bundle is attached to each of these sacks, retaining the directional associations. Two cylinder stones decorated with faces representing Long Life and Happiness *(sq'ah naaghaii bik'eh hózhǫ́)* are placed at the center of the four bags and all are tied together, covered with pollen, and wrapped in a buckskin. A white shell is tied to the buckskin outer wrapping at a point corresponding with the bag of soil from the east mountain to serve as a means of orienting the whole bundle.

The mountain soil bundle is identified with the medicine bundle of First Man and with the creative powers of Changing Woman. Its structure represents in its jewels and soils, the substance from which life is given form, and in its stone cylinders the animating forces of life, long life and happiness. Its shape and design are that of a world created in beauty *(hózhǫ́)*, and correspond with other manifestations of that shape in the ceremonial hogan and the surface of the earth itself.[4]

The mountain soil bundle is pressed to the various parts of the body of the one-sung-over from the feet to the head. This ritual gesture associates and identifies the one-sung-over with the attributes of the bundle, and is a principal element in the acts of creation in the mythic archetypes. It is used to place the representations of the inner life forms within their outer forms. This ritual gesture of associating corresponding body parts is used to confirm the complementation between paired entities, such as the earth and sky or White Corn Boy and Yellow Corn Girl (the inner life forms of corn).

Administration of Bath

The one-sung-over sleeps in the ceremonial hogan and arises the next morning to ritually greet the dawn with a pollen offering and a pollen prayer. The essential ceremony to be performed during the morning is the bath ceremony. A platform for the bath is made of sand or clean soil usually collected from a cornfield. A yucca root is ritually collected to make the suds which are prepared in a Navajo woven basket (whose woven design echoes the shape of the hogan). A circle and cross are inscribed in pollen by the singer on the sand platform and upon the suds in the basket. The one-sung-over takes his place on the platform. His jewelry, or hard goods, may be washed first. Then the hair is washed. The whole body may then be bathed and dried by a ritual application of corn meal. The mountain soil bundle may be applied again to his body, and the one-sung-over leaves the ceremonial hogan upon a trail of pollen

and corn meal drawn on the floor. The archetypes in Blessingway mythology suggest that the bath ceremony serves a dual purpose: to purify
the one-sung-over and to prepare him for the singing of the Blessingway
songs during the all night singing which will follow.[5]

All-night Singing Ceremony

The all-night singing (called the "no-sleep" ceremony) may include the
preparation of a small drypainting during the afternoon upon the floor
of the hogan. It is constructed of cornmeal and various plant pollens,
ground flower petals, and charcoal. It is quite different from the other
drypaintings or sandpaintings which are made of different materials and
which are used in a different way.

The night, from sundown until dawn, is spent singing Blessingway
songs, repeating those songs which have been sung in the ceremonial up
to that point and including still others. Prayers may be said at intervals
throughout the night. Brief intermissions may be observed. As dawn is
anticipated, the dawn songs are begun, and with first light, the one-sung-
over arises and exits from the ceremonial hogan. Moving toward the east,
he "breathes in the dawn" which is a gesture that Navajos say is "to become one with it."[6] The "no-sleep" corresponds in the mythological
archetype of creation to the final preparation of the inner life forms,
their association with the representations of their outer physical forms,
and the transformation of these from symbolic to nonsymbolic forms.

The Blessingway ritual process is the Navajo way of creation. It is
modeled upon the events of creating life on the earth. As a way of creation it produces a ritual identification with the era at the beginning of
time and with the emergence place at the center of the world. The first
ceremony consecrates an enclosure and space, bestows life upon it, and
establishes it as a sacred or holy place because of its design and its location at the center of the world.

The words of the litany prayer and the application of the mountain
soil bundle follow the pattern of the archetype of the creation of the
earth in that they associate and identify those praying with the life principles of the world.

The bath ceremony purifies and prepares the one-sung-over for the
singing of the Blessingway songs which conclude the "no-sleep" cere-

mony. The symbols and songs of the bath associate him with the events of the creation of the earth surface and place him in a ritual environment characterized as *hózhǫ́*.

Perhaps the climactic moment of the "no-sleep" ceremony is when the one-sung-over, surrounded by his family and friends, sings the Blessingway songs and intones the Blessingway prayers. When Changing Woman taught these songs and prayers to the Navajos she said, "These will direct you as you live on in the future, and they will direct your mode of living. And should there be any mishap in things on which life depends, which enable you to live, all will be put in proper shape again by means of them, the body will be restored again by means of them."[7]

At dawn, the one-sung-over is directed outside of the sacred enclosure and away from the center to the east to greet the dawn. He is directed away from the ceremonial identification with the timeless sacred era of creation in order to reenter the ordinary world of Navajo life.

THE EARTH'S PRAYER

In the mythological archetype of Blessingway, the prayer that is perhaps most central to the creation process is the prayer known as the Earth's Prayer or the Prayer to the Inner Forms of the Earth. It is recited at the moment when the inner life forms of the earth are transported to their proper places within the physical forms in the world. It is synonymous with the moment of creation. The late Frank Goldtooth of Tuba City, Arizona said of the function and origin of the Earth's Prayer that

when this earth was being made the prayer was said. Then this blanket was placed over the object which was to become the earth and repeatedly taken off like making smoke signals. Then they [those who were performing the ceremony] uttered some kind of word, then they threw the blanket upward like making smoke signals. Four times that happened. Each time the earth got larger. They made the earth and the prayer together.

Echoing this statement, Andrew Woody of Tuba City, Arizona, said that "the words of the prayer were made when the world was being made.

The words followed the process of the world creation." Asked about the relationship of the prayer to the world, he responded, "They are the same thing."

The text of the prayer is extensive and the structure is complex, although only two distinct constituents are used, the association/identification with a Holy Person (G) and desired state of blessing (V). The text begins with an extended passage which identifies the one praying with Earth and Sky at the sacred body points. Even this catalog is very elaborate. The association/identification is made not only by body part correspondences but with a set of attributes attached to each body part.

> Earth's soles where dark cloud, male rain, dark water,
>   rainbow lie across them with pollen, that same dark cloud,
>   male rain, dark water, rainbow lies across my soles with
>   pollen as I say this.
> Sky's soles where dark mist, female rain, blue water,
>   sunray lie across them with pollen, that same dark mist,
>   female rain, blue water, sunray lies across my soles with
>   pollen as I say this.

The statement of blessing (V) uses the usual form of declaring a state of blessing before, behind, above, below and all around, but it too is more elaborate.

> Before Earth with small blue birds it is blessed,
>   with small blue birds before me it is blessed as I say this.
>   (BW #1)

These two constituents of the prayer are repeated, for Earth and Sky, but in the reverse order with Sky being named first. Then the entire prayer in these two parts is repeated for eight other pairs of the inner forms of the earth: Mountain Woman and Water Woman, Darkness and Dawn, Evening Twilight and Sun, Talking God and Calling God, White Corn and Yellow Corn, Pollen and Corn Beetle (Ripener), Changing Woman and White Shell Woman, Long Life and Happiness. The diagram of the constituent structure of the prayer text is

$$(G_{(a,b)} \ V_{(a,b)} \ G_{(b,a)} \ V_{(b,a)})^9$$

where a and b are the members of a pair of Holy People and the super-script indicates the repetition of the double prayer set for nine pairs of Holy People.

In the context of the Blessingway ritual process which focuses exten-sively on the events of creation, the Earth's Prayer corresponds with the ritual process and with the intent of the mythological archetype. It asso-ciates and identifies the person praying with the inner life forms of the earth, thus establishing for that person the conditions upon which life depends (G). It then describes the condition of blessing *(hózhǫ́)* (V) which is the consequence of these relationships. The statement of the prayer is reiterated or enacted in the applications of pollen and the mountain soil bundle, the primary symbols of life, to body parts which correspond to those named in the prayer.

The Earth's Prayer can be found in several Blessingway ritual contexts. By examining a couple of these prayer acts it can be shown how blessing prayer acts accommodate the very specific needs for which they are per-formed.

THE EARTH'S PRAYER IN A CEREMONIAL FOR
AN EXPECTANT MOTHER

Father Berard obtained a description from a singer of this ceremonial known as Little Big Water. He described the ceremonial as follows:

Well, if I am told to hold a no-sleep for a pregnant woman I'll at once conduct the "its day" [closing day] without spending a night.

Soil from a straight current is raked together ahead with the current, without raking it backwards, and is brought in a blanket. On this the bath is administered with songs of How Changing Woman Was Picked Up or with Cornbeetle songs.

And drying with cornmeal differs. At her soles it is applied forward, and all other applications are made downward to the back of her neck. The pollen again is mixed with unraveling medicine and in this shape the pollen is applied. That is applied to her in exactly the same way as the cornmeal was applied. After that a prayer is offered for her employing Earth's prayer. [Little Big Water gives the additions to the prayer which apply to this particular situation.]

After that one merely observes closing day until sunset. And after dusk one merely begins songs. Any time during the night, if one decides upon another prayer, a mate to the same one is available, one may again say the very long one for her. At the conclusion they are alike, whereas the songs that I enumerated for you all are used in the no-sleep.

All pollen applications are made downward only. And at dawn he employs the songs of How Dawn Gave Birth as dawn songs.[8]

Comparing this description to others of Blessingway ritual process there appear to be several significant differences which are attributable to the situation. The Blessingway ceremonial performed for an expectant mother is shortened in length from two nights to a single night. The soil for the bath platform is taken from a flowing stream, and it is collected by a motion which goes with the current. Normally the soil is collected from a cornfield. The application of pollen and the drying with cornmeal after the bath is done in a downward direction, opposite the normal foot to head direction. The songs selected to accompany the bath and the concluding dawn rites appear to be different from the songs normally used for these parts of Blessingway ritual. A special addition to the Earth's Prayer is made, yet the major portion of the prayer remains unchanged.

The intonement of the Earth's Prayer appears essential to this Blessingway ceremonial. Although not specified explicitly, the prayer is probably said by the singer and the expectant mother in litany fashion with the mother holding the mountain soil bundle.

The passage which Little Big Water added to the Earth's Prayer to fit it to the situation continues the statement of the condition of blessing (V) and is added after each of the pairs of the inner forms of the earth have been addressed. This special passage deals quite directly with the situation at hand.

> From the heart of Earth, by means of yellow pollen blessing
> is extended.

From the heart of Sky, by means of blue pollen blessing is
   extended.
On top of pollen floor may I there in blessing give birth!
On top of a floor of fabrics may I there in blessing give birth!
As collected water flows ahead of it [the child] , whereby
   blessing moves along ahead of it, may I there in blessing
   give birth!
Thereby without hesitating, thereby with its mind straightened,
   thereby with its travel means straightened, thereby without its
   sting, may I there in blessing give birth!
As water's child flows behind it whereby blessing moves along
   behind it may I there in blessing give birth!
Thereby without hesitating, thereby with its mind straightened,
   thereby with its travel means straightened, thereby without
   its sting, may I there in blessing give birth!
With pollen moving around it, with blessing extending from
   it by means of pollen, may I in blessing give birth!
May I give birth to Pollen Boy, may I give birth to Cornbeetle
   Boy, may I give birth to Long Life Boy, may I give birth
   to Happiness Boy!
With long life happiness surrounding me may I in blessing
   give birth! May I quickly give birth!
In blessing may I arise again, in blessing may I recover, as one
   who is long life happiness may I live on!
Before me may it be blessed, behind me . . . , below me . . . ,
   above me . . . , in all my surroundings may it be blessed,
   may my speech be blessed! It has become blessed again,
   it has become blessed again, it has become blessed again,
   it has become blessed again! (BW # 15)

The prayer text speaks directly to the situation. This added passage
expresses the desire for an easy delivery of a healthy baby. The most
common phrase in this passage is "may I there in blessing give birth!"
Father Berard noted that certain alterations could be made to the prayer
based on whether the expectant parents desire a boy or a girl. The phrases
"may I give birth to Pollen Boy," ". . . to Cornbeetle Boy," " . . . to Long

Life Boy," " . . . to Happiness Boy," may be changed so as to refer to each of these as "girl," in order to express the desires of the parents in the prayer.[9]

Father Berard's notes also show that the phrase "As collected water flows ahead of it," refers to the soil collected for the bath platform from the bottom of the flowing stream, and this should signify that "the babe should not hesitate, its mind should be straight on this point, it should arrive quickly without leaving a 'sting' which would injure the mother."[10] The imagery of the fluidity of water is utilized as a metaphor in the passage to indicate the way in which the birth is desired. It also appears to be an allusion to the physiology of childbirth, when, in easy birth, the amniotic fluid washes the infant out with it.

The phrase "With pollen moving around it," carries the imagery of the application of pollen made immediately prior to the recitation of the prayer. The downward pollen application, contrasting with the usual direction from the feet up, also expresses the desire for the birth of the child.

Given that the prayer text speaks directly to the situation at hand, especially through the special passage added, there is much more to be appreciated about how the structure of the prayer act serves the motivating situation. There are overt indications of the correlations and interdependence between the text and the context which already have been shown in the preparation of the platform for the bath ritual. Since the bath rite is the major ritual act conjoined to the prayer recitation in this performance of Blessingway, it is important to consider its interrelationship with the prayer recitation as part of the blessing prayer act. In doing this, the ritual of the bath will be considered, including the songs of the bath rite and the mythology which describes the archetypical performances of this rite.

The bath rite is a distinctive and essential act in Blessingway ceremonials. It is certainly not unique to Blessingway, but in no other ceremonial is it so central and important to the ritual process. In Blessingway mythology there are several descriptions of the ritual bath which must be considered in order to establish a frame for interpreting the levels of meaning which may be associated with the bath ceremony. Three descriptions of bath rituals occur in the story of the puberty rites (kinaaldá) for Changing Woman and two others appear in the story of the abduction and return of the children to whom Changing Woman teaches Blessingway in order that it may be given to the Earth Surface People.

All of the descriptions of the bath ceremony in Blessingway mythology are closely associated with Changing Woman and, therefore, with the powers of fertility, fruition, and creation. The bath ceremonies which are a part of *kinaaldá* must be of particular significance for an expectant mother who probably was once the subject in this puberty rite version of Blessingway. In this rite the pubescent girl is identified with Changing Woman, and her acquisition of maturity and the accompanying powers of creation are recognized and honored. The mythological archetypes for *kinaaldá* are the puberty rites of Changing Woman and the bath rites in these stories merit review here.

Talking God performed *kinaaldá* for Changing Woman. At dawn on the last day of Changing Woman's first *kinaaldá,* Talking God entered the ceremonial hogan and into a white shell basket he poured white shell dew, turquoise dew, abalone dew, jet dew, and dew of dark cloud. As he sang the dawn songs, he bathed Changing Woman's hair in this collection of dew. Then she ran toward the dawn, encircled a white shell standard, and returned. That done, white clay and red ocher were mixed with water and applied to her. "That white clay was applied first from her legs upward and represented her growth to be. Downward application again represented future giving birth. At her arms the same was repeated, on her upper body and on both her cheeks."[11] As soon as the sun arose, Talking God laid down spreads of white buckskin, crystal doeskin, white cotton, a crocheted fabric, and a white robe. He placed Changing Woman upon these spreads and by rubbing her, he shaped her into the form of a woman. Changing Woman was then prepared to receive the instructions and the powers with which she would create all of the living phenomena on the earth. This process is begun with songs and prayers of the Twelve Person Group.[12] The specific motivation for bathing Changing Woman is not indicated, but it appears to prepare her for receiving the powers of creation. The bath is associated with the application of clay and ocher which are said to represent "growth" and "future giving birth" which are to be the primary attributes of Changing Woman. The downward application of pollen in this rite confirms and amplifies the interpretation Father Berard reported for the direction of application in the ceremonial for the expectant mother.[13]

Changing Woman's second *kinaaldá* is given to prepare her for marriage to Sun.[14] Again, at dawn on the last morning of the ceremonial Talking God enters with the same basket of white shell in which he has gathered the same collection of dews. The bath occurs in two parts. In the first part, Talking God removes the red ocher and white clay from Changing Woman with the various dews. Then, as Changing Woman bathes herself, the songs of "How Dawn Gave Birth" are sung and the four dawn children—Dawn Boy, Sunray Girl, Yellow Afterglow Boy, and North Girl—are born and placed in the four directions. The simultaneity of the bath with the birth of the dawn children constructs an association between the act of creation and the materials of the bath—the various dews and the white shell basket. And Changing Woman is associated with these materials of creation as she bathes in the foam which arises from the basket.

The third Blessingway story of relevance to the bath rite is also concerned with the procreativity of Changing Woman. It is in the act of bathing that Changing Woman becomes pregnant with twin sons.

Now it seems that at sunset there was a place down the hillside called dripping water. Thinking, "I will bathe," she went over there; perhaps she was thinking, "The man may visit me again." It seems that over there she undressed completely and bathed herself. So it seems, she lay down below the water which dripped down [and she let] it drip into her crotch.[15]

First Man and First Woman, with whom Changing Woman lived and who were in charge of the first acts of creation upon the Emergence, told her to "go ahead to the water, go again, let him do it again." And she did so.

After she undressed, as she was busy with herself [bathing S.G.] as on the first occasion, in that [same] manner the man [Sun's inner form S.G.] came upon her again. Then it seems [he said to her S.G.], "Now in this manner, First Man has ordered that all giving birth [reproduction] will be yours [i.e., you will be in charge of it], vegetation and everything which exists on the surface of the earth shall give birth, and you shall be in charge of fabrics of all kinds, jewels of all kinds. . . ."[16]

All of the incidents of Changing Woman's bathing are directly associated with the powers and means of creation. It seems that through the bath the powers of creativity are obtained and acts of creativity are effected.

The other descriptions of the bath ceremony in Blessingway mythology occur in the story of how Blessingway is given to the Navajos by Changing Woman. She abducts two children and takes them to her home so that she can teach them Blessingway ritual and its prayers and songs. Before they are allowed to enter her home she insists that they be bathed.

They should have entered the home of Changing Woman, but when people discovered that they stink they were left this side somewhere at the Tree-grove-slope. So there will be a bath with herbs exactly four times and when the bad odor has absolutely left them then they may enter. When the two have entered there, Blessingway prayers and songs, as they should be, will be placed in their interiors.[17]

Here bathing seems to be concerned with the purification of the bad-smelling children in preparation for entering the home of Changing Woman to learn the sacred details of Blessingway.

After learning Blessingway from Changing Woman the children are sent home. They reappear in the cornfield at the point where they had disappeared. Before telling the others what they learned from Changing Woman they take a ritual bath. The preparation for the bath includes the offering of a jewel basket with jewel eggs left at the summit of the four sacred mountains and the collection of a pinch of soil from each of these mountains, referring to the preparation of the mountain soil bundle, the primary ritual object of Blessingway.

Brought here the soils were placed upon an unwounded buckskin, mirage [stone] and pollen were applied to them. White Corn Boy then prepared soapsuds in water for the boy, whereas Yellow Corn Girl prepared the soapsuds in water for the girl. That is called the bath at the cornfield, because the two children had returned at the cornfield.[18]

Each of the children was dried in cornmeal and pollen was applied to them. The details of this bath ritual are similar to the children's other bath ceremony, but the context precludes purification as the central motivation for this bath performance since they are returning from a very pure and sacred place. It appears rather to celebrate the return of the children,[19] and to sanctify them in preparation for the recitation to their own people of the sacred knowledge learned from Changing Woman. The reference to the basket and jewel offerings and the mountain soil bundle associates this bath with the bath ceremonies of Changing Woman.

The mythological archetypes for the bath rite consistently suggest that in Navajo thought the bath rite is a medium through which one acquires the means and powers of creativity. The strong association and identification with Changing Woman and all that she represents has great affinity with the specific situation of the expectant mother.

The songs of the bath rite constitute another element in the prayer act for the expectant mother. According to Father Berard, the bath may be performed using either the songs "How Changing Woman was Picked Up" or the "Songs of the Cornbeetle." According to Kluckhohn and Wyman the "Songs of the Cornbeetle" are the standard songs used for the bath ritual.[20] Either set of songs has relevance in establishing a context for the meaningful recitation of the Earth's Prayer.

The "Songs of the Cornbeetle" occur in Blessingway mythology in the story of the mating of corn. Changing Woman has control of the events of creation by this time, and she performs a number of acts of creation in order to establish vegetation and animal life on the earth.

She spread down one of these white shell unwounded skins, one of turquoise, one of abalone, and one of jet, four unwounded skins she laid down. Then by running her hand over the white shell corn, she made a drawing of its roots, she drew its tassel and its face, she made markings for its mouth and eyes, its ears and nose, and by moving mirage over it four times she formed its genitalia. And by moving her hand over the blue corn she reproduced its parts in the very same manner, but for this one she made its genitalia of rising haze. After that she applied mirage to the male side, rising haze to the female side. She then moved her hands over them four times, then began to sing to them.[21]

The song which she sang is a corn placing song which, according to Father Berard, is similar to the cornbeetle (ripener) songs and may be used for the same purpose.[22]

> '*e ne ya,* one has placed it, *ni yo o.*
> Now Earth one has placed, long life one has placed,
>   happiness one has placed, *ni yo o.*
> Now Sky one has placed, long life one has placed,
>   happiness one has placed, *ni yo o.*

[The song continues in the same way naming Mountain Woman, Water Woman, Darkness, Dawn, Evening Twilight, Sun, Talking God, Calling God, White Corn, Yellow Corn, Pollen, Cornbeetle (Ripener), White Shell Woman, Changing Woman, Long Life, Happiness.] [23]

This song describes the placement of the inner forms which are to give life to the corn. Those Holy People named correspond with the ones mentioned in the Earth's Prayer. As the inner life forms of the earth, they are essential to the creation of life. Upon preparing the forms to become the corn, Changing Woman gives these forms life by placing within them these nine pairs of Holy People. Each of the Holy People is placed along with the pair, long life and happiness, the personification of the force of life. The placement does not complete the act of creation. The story continues.

Immediately after that the inner forms of Blanca Peak and other mountains began to arrive here. "Arise!" the two [personifications of corn] were told. The two arose there, a young man and a young woman unequaled in beauty arose side by side. At once she [Changing Woman] applied pollen to the young man's feet along the skin coils, then upward as she went along she applied it to his legs, his genitalia, his chest, palms, ending at the tip of his tongue. Then she put some into the mouth of that young woman wiping her tongue at the same time. Then she repeated the same on the woman's side and also put some into the young man's mouth. [24]

The creation of corn is concluded with the dressing in pollen of each of the corn figures Changing Woman has drawn, White Corn Boy and Yellow Corn Girl, by a process of application which is concluded with the transfer of pollen from each figure to the mouth of the other, thus attaching them to one another in a gesture of their interdependence. The use of the cornbeetle (ripener) songs in mythology places them in an ambiance of creativity and suggests that they are vital.

Another cornbeetle (ripener) song tells of the creation of Pollen Boy and Cornbeetle (Ripener) Girl by Talking God and Calling God in the home of Changing Woman.[25] Pollen Boy and Cornbeetle (Ripener) Girl are inseparable from White Corn Boy and Yellow Corn Girl who were created by Changing Woman. They are associated in the manner of corn with its pollen.[26]

In these songs the creation of Pollen Boy and Cornbeetle (Ripener) Girl is accomplished by making clothing, moccasins, leggings, and garments of pollen; by making the mind, voice, and head-plume of pollen; and by making wings of jewels. The process of creation takes place upon the floor of the home of Changing Woman. The pollen is used to draw the figures of Pollen Boy and Cornbeetle (Ripener) Girl in the same manner as Changing Woman drew the figures of White Corn Boy and Yellow Corn Girl in her act of creating them. The songs describe the construction of a pollen painting on the floor of a hogan and the subsequent acts by which Talking God and Calling God give life to the pair.

The use of either of these cornbeetle (ripener) songs to accompany the bath ceremony for an expectant mother would direct her attention to either of two primal creation events. Not only do they describe the process of creation, they account for the origin of fertility and fruition itself in the birth of the figures White Corn Boy and Yellow Corn Girl, Pollen Boy and Cornbeetle (Ripener) Girl. The extensive reference to the creative powers represented in the application of pollen and cornmeal inform the expectant mother of the significance of these applications made to her body during the ritual bath.

The alternative set of songs to accompany the bath, "How Changing Woman Was Picked Up," begins

> Now on the summit of Gobernador Knob he found her,
>   he found her, *ni yo o.*
> Talking God found her, he found Changing Woman,
>   *ni yo o.*
> Now dark cloud, male rain, rainbow and collected waters
>   lay there when he found her.

Cornbeetle's frequent call with its pretty voice lay there
when he found her.
As long life-happiness he found her.
Before her it was blessed, behind her it was blessed when
he found her, he found her *ni yo o*.[27]

The theme of the songs changes with each new song while maintaining
the same pattern to form a ten song set telling the story of the birth of
Changing Woman. The story begins with First Man and First Woman
making a plan. Then, in the direction of Gobernador Knob, First Man
holds up a representation of the inner life forms of the earth which he
takes from his medicine bundle. As a consequence of this act, a number
of events take place atop Gobernador Knob. Dark clouds form and it
rains upon the mountaintop. Rainbows and sunrays are seen around the
mountain while cornbeetles and small dark birds are heard giving their
calls. First Man approaches the mountain summit on each of four consecutive days from four different directions, but he is unable to reach
the summit until the fourth day. There he finds a babe who is Changing
Woman. She is described as in the form of a sandpainting. "The babe
lay over there on a layer of crystal sand, smoothed out as nicely as possible by hand as it were."[28] Talking God appears and they argue over who
is to raise her, but First Man wins. The songs with which First Man picked
her up and started home with her became Changing Woman's songs, "How
Changing Woman Was Picked Up." The songs associate Changing Woman
with complementary sets of weather-related phenomena which were
apparently instrumental in creating her: dark cloud, male rain, rainbow,
collected waters, and the call of the cornbeetle (ripener); and the complementary set: dark mist, female rain, sunray, water's child and dark
small bird's call. These instruments of creation were found lying with the
babe whom they helped to create when First Man directed the powers
of the inner forms of the earth toward the mountaintop. The drypainting
which gave form to Changing Woman corresponds to the way in which
Changing Woman proceeded in her creation of White Corn Boy and
Yellow Corn Girl. The two events of the birth of Changing Woman are
clarified in an explanatory note which the myth narrator appended to the
story.

You can see now that this is the child of the young woman and man of exceeding beauty [long life and happiness S.G.] who, as I mentioned earlier, had arisen from that medicine bundle which he never laid aside to become the inner forms of Earth. It is clear too that she originated here at Gobernador Knob where he held that same medicine bundle up in that direction, as they say.[29]

The expectant mother, when she recites the Earth's Prayer in the ritual context of the Blessingway ceremonial given for her, is not only expressing but also satisfying her desire for an association/identification with the representation of all life, the inner forms of the earth, so that her child, upon its birth, may have life and so that her own life may remain unharmed. "Thereby without its sting, may I there in blessing give birth." The expectant mother expresses her desire in the prayer to have the birth of her child take place in the "way" ordained in the beginning that all things should be created and given life. The prayer act, including the ritual of the bath, serves to give the expectant mother the powers of creation. The prayer act also focuses these powers upon the specific creative act of childbirth by such things as the manner of selecting the bath soil and the downward applications which occur at the conclusion of the rite. By taking the bath and intoning the prayer the expectant mother is prepared to use her powers of creation in the act of giving birth to her child.

THE EARTH'S PRAYER IN A RAIN CEREMONY

A study of the Earth's Prayer performed in a very different ceremonial context will demonstrate the principles of transformation that adapt Blessing prayer acts to specific situations.

In 1938 Willard W. Hill published an account of a rain ceremonial which he had witnessed. According to his investigation, it was not frequently performed and few knew how to perform it. Hill did not identify the rain ceremonial as a form of Blessingway, but its ritual process and prayers clearly identify it with Blessingway. He indicated that one of its prayers could be used in Blessingway. The rain ceremonial begins with the blessing of the ceremonial hogan. In this rite the first modification to the situation is noted. The cornmeal is strewn about the floor of the hogan to the recitation of the prayer formula, "May it rain for us today."[30] The songs which are sung the first evening also express the desire for rain. They begin

> I usually walk where the rains fall
> Below the east I walk
> I being the Talking God
> I usually walk where the rains fall.[31]

A person is chosen to participate in the litany recitation of prayers since this ceremonial is not motivated especially by the needs of an individual. The first extensive prayer is said on the first evening after the completion of the song. It is the same prayer which Changing Woman gave to the children when she told them about the mountain soil bundle and its powers of creativity.[32] It was the last thing she gave to them before their return.[33] The structure of the prayer text is

$$1) \ A_1GV_1, \ 2) \ A_2GV_2.$$

The passage associating and identifying the one praying with Holy People (G) goes

> Blanca Peak and San Francisco Peak regularly look at each
>   other,
> San Francisco Peak and Blanca Peak regularly look at each
>   other.
> With their feet I shall walk about,
> With their legs I shall walk about,
> With their means of traveling I shall walk about,
> With their torso I shall walk about,
> With their mind I shall walk about,
> With their voice I shall walk about,
> With their head plumes I shall walk about,
> That which extends out of their head tops,
> By means of it I shall go about pleasantly,
> That which surrounds them [the mind] it shall also
>   surround me

By means of it I shall go about pleasantly,
Surrounding me the mountain ranges and the beauty which
    extends up their slope,
By means of it I shall go about pleasantly.[34]

Hill calls this one of the most important of Navajo prayers and says that
it can be used in Blessingway ceremonials. The significance of this passage
in the context of Blessingway mythology is clear. To the boys who were
being made progenitors of Blessingway, Changing Woman had given instruc-
tion on the significance and use of the medicine bundle. She had shown
them how to replicate it from soils of the sacred mountains. With the
bundle they would hold the source of creative power modeled upon her
bundle and the sacred pattern of the world. This prayer is concerned with
the creation of an environment of beauty, *hózhǫ́*.

In the rain ceremonial, following the prayer recitation, pollen is passed
sunwise around the hogan and all present put some in their mouths,
some on their heads, and sprinkle some away from themselves while they
say a pollen prayer, such as

May it be pleasant
May it rain for me today
So that I may raise a big crop of corn of all colors, white,
    yellow, blue, grey
May I enjoy the beautiful flowers that may be brought
    by the rain
May my stock get fat. (RCH # 3)

On the morning of the next day, the songs which were sung the night
before are sung again, but the often repeated line "I usually walk where
the rains fall," is replaced with the line, "I walk where there are an
abundance of crops." Upon completion of the song another prayer is
said. Hill does not identify the prayer by name, but it is a simplified form
of the Earth's Prayer. It addresses only the first fourteen of the eighteen
Holy People, omitting Changing Woman, White Shell Woman, Long Life
Boy, and Happiness Girl.

During the day prayersticks are prepared. They are made of either
"drifted stalk" or "water scum." Either one or two may be made. If two
are made there is

a blue one representing "green earth," and a black one symbolizing "dark sky." If only one is used it was always black. This stick was first painted black. Then with more black paint, two clouds representing rain, and two chains of zigzag lightning were drawn on it. If a blue prayerstick was also used, the clouds and lightning were painted in yellow. . . . After the painting was finished, the butt end of the prayerstick was plugged with the downy feather of either the nighthawk, swallow, or hummingbird. The nighthawk was the thunder bird, the swallow the rain bird, and the hummingbird was thought to be associated with water.[35]

Upon completion of the preparation of the prayersticks, they are placed on a piece of unwounded buckskin in a basket. Then all who wish to participate take yucca baths. The singer stands and, holding the basket with the prayersticks, intones a prayer. The message of this prayer is not specifically for rain, but for the abundance of vegetation and animal life on the earth. This correlates with the progression reflected in the change in the theme of the song on the second day from "I usually walk where rains fall," to "I walk where there are an abundance of crops." Further, the prayer acknowledges that the source of this abundance lies not with rain, but with the perfect union of "green earth" and "dark sky" represented by the prayersticks over which the prayer is said. This is consistent with the pattern of the acts of creation throughout Blessingway mythology. Here again the rain, as water, is not the source of life, but the essential medium through which it is transmitted.

In this prayer act the recitation of the Earth's Prayer is placed in the ritual context carefully adapted to the expressed need for rain. The pollen prayer formulas, the songs, the preparation of prayersticks all express this urgent need. The mythological context with which these ritual acts are identified reveals something of the ideology behind the rain ceremony. It is not rain which is actually sought, rather it is the reinstatement of the order of the world, characterized as an environment of beauty, hózhǫ́. This state assures good crops, beautiful flowers, and fat livestock. The preparation of the prayersticks illustrates that this comes about as a result of the proper relationship between the earth and the sky, which in mythology is personified in various ways. Rain is the mediator and the tangible evidence of the proper relationship.

SUMMARY OF BLESSING PRAYER ACTS

The consideration of these prayer acts which incorporate the recitation of the Earth's Prayer, perhaps the most representative and important of Blessing prayers, has revealed a distinctive and essential characteristic. All Blessing prayer acts are in one way or another basically acts of creation or re-creation. The entire class of Blessing prayers is heavily dependent upon the theology, ideology, and ritual process exemplified in the creation stories of Blessingway mythology.

The most basic prayer constituent associates the one praying with a Holy Person (G). The analysis of the Blessing prayer acts has shown that the meaning and power of this act of association and identification with Holy People rests upon the Navajo understanding of the nature of life and creation. In the Navajo view, the life force can be represented as a human-shaped form which all living things must have within them.

The essential composition of the association/identification prayer constituent (G) is basic and formulaic. The body parts—feet, legs, body, mind, voice—are listed as the basis for association/identification. This passage in Blessing prayers corresponds to the placement of the inner life form within the various things created in primal times. In the recitation of this passage the original acts of creation are repeated. In a sense the world is re-created, and the person praying is made an integral part of that creation by being associated and identified with the holy ones upon whom all life depends. At the most generalized level the recitation of the passage responds to a need to acquire access to the source of life. But as has been shown, other elements in the prayer act serve to tailor the message and to direct the power of the prayer to meet very specific needs.

The description of the desired state of blessing (V) is a basic constituent of Blessing prayers. Blessingway mythology shows that blessing succeeds from things being in their proper places, as assigned in the acts of creation. Blessing (hózhǫ́) is synonymous with proper order. There is a "way" for everything and that "way" is blessed because it was so decreed in sacred history. The passage may either petition directly that this "way" be reinstated, or state that it has once again come to be. The desired state of blessing is dependent upon the establishment of proper order, consequently the passage describing the state of blessing normally follows upon the passage which accomplishes an association/identification with the Holy People. When the state of blessing (V) appears by itself it usually takes the petitionary form.[36]

All of this begins to suggest why Blessingway is "the spinal column of songs," but that will become clearer with the consideration of other prayer act classifications.

NOTES

1. Wyman, *Blessingway*, pp. 343-44. Frank Mitchell's recent autobiography contains much valuable information on Blessingway. See *Navajo Blessingway Singer* (Tucson: University of Arizona Press, 1978).

2. Quoted in Wyman, *Blessingway*, p. 5.

3. Reichard, *Navaho Religion*, p. 734.

4. See Gill, *Songs of Life*, Plate V for iconography of mountain soil bundle. See David P. McAllester and Susan W. McAllester, *Hogans: Navajo Houses & House Songs* (Middletown, Connecticut: Wesleyan University Press, 1980), for texts and photographs related to hogans.

5. See Gill, *Songs of Life*, Plates XIV-XVI for ritual bath iconography.

6. Kluckhohn and Wyman, *Navaho Chant Practice*, p. 104.

7. Wyman, *Blessingway*, p. 465.

8. Ibid., pp. 335-37.

9. Ibid., p. 337 n.235.

10. Ibid., p. 336 n.234.

11. Ibid., p. 163.

12. Ibid., pp. 164-67.

13. It is notable here that the usual Navajo connotations of ritual reversal are exorcism, evil, or ghosts. The only discussion of Navajo ritual reversal I know is in Reichard's *Navaho Religion*, pp. 181-84. In the example of the reversal of the direction of application for the expectant mother, not even opposition of the usual associations is intended, and the stated representation is a very positive concern, "future giving birth." See Gill, *Songs of Life*, Plates XLV-XLVI for *kinaaldá* iconography.

14. Frisbie and others have confirmed that the second *kinaaldá* should be done on the occasion of the second menstruation.

15. Wyman, *Blessingway*, pp. 196-97.

16. Ibid., p. 187.

17. Ibid., p. 226.

18. Ibid., pp. 294-95.

19. Reichard's informant, RM, confirmed this when he indicated that the "bath represents the restoration of the children kidnapped from the garden" (*Navaho Religion*, p. 623).

20. Kluckhohn and Wyman, *Navaho Chant Practice*, p. 92. The Navajo term *'anił'tánii* rendered as "cornbeetle" is a mistranslation as are the common alternatives "grasshopper" and "corn bug." The Navajo term means "ripener" and this was used by Reichard, *Navaho Religion*, p. 422 and Wyman, *Red Antway*, p. 20.

21. Wyman, *Blessingway*, pp. 200-1.

22. Ibid., p. 210, n.161.

23. Ibid., p. 201.

24. Ibid., pp. 201-2.

25. Ibid., pp. 210-11.

26. Ibid., p. 204 n.159.

27. Ibid., pp. 141-42.

28. Ibid., p. 140.

29. Ibid., p. 143.

30. Willard W. Hill, *The Agricultural and Hunting Methods of the Navaho Indians*, Yale University Publications in Anthropology, no. 18 (New Haven, 1938), p. 75.

31. Ibid.

32. Wyman, *Blessingway*, pp. 283-90 (BW #9).

33. This prayer is again found in the version of Blessingway recorded by Father Berard Haile from River Junction Curly. In this instance it is in the context of the remaking of the mountains (BW #21).

34. Hill, *Agricultural and Hunting Methods*, p. 78.

35. Ibid., pp. 81-82.

36. The class of Blessing prayers appeared to be of three structural types. On the basis of the analysis of the Blessing prayer acts, the distinction between these types was found to have little significance. It appears that stylistic considerations may be the major distinction. There are no major prayers which have the structure (A) . . . (F) V. These prayers are usually brief and accompanied by a ritual act such as pollen application or strewing. They are not uttered in the formal manner common to major prayers. Still these short prayer formulas appear to be very important to the ritual process and may be an important way in which a ritual process is channeled toward a specific situation. The importance of these prayers has often been overlooked and they remain unrecorded throughout most of the ceremonial descriptive literature.

CHAPTER SIX

LIFEWAY PRAYER ACTS

Lifeway prayers are very similar in constituent structure to Blessing prayers in that they focus upon the association/identification of the one praying with the Holy People (G). Still, they are distinguishable by the inclusion of the unique passage describing the journey of a Holy Person from his home toward the home of the one praying (P). The structural diagram is (A) . . . (F) P G (U) (V).

The constituent analysis suggested that the prayers acknowledge that there has been some severance with or impairment to the means of life and health, but the etiology of this disorder is not apparent from the constituent analysis of the prayer text. The apparent purpose of these prayers is similar to that of the Blessing prayers, the association/identification with a Holy Person (G), but the wording suggests that the association is more directly for the purpose of the restoration of health.

The known examples of Lifeway prayers all come from the same ceremonial, and all are found in Father Berard's recording of Flintway (1943). The ethnographic record is not adequate for other ceremonials where it is likely that similar prayers occur.[1] Flintway is a ceremonial performed for the purpose of healing internal injuries and the restoration of consciousness and vitality.[2] Accidental injury seems to be the predominant source of these ills. Wyman and Kluckhohn have further enumerated the uses of Flintway and associated ceremonials.[3]

On the basis of the available descriptive material, it appears that Flintway has a highly flexible ritual process accommodating a great many situations. Quite a number of special rituals which are optional to Flintway have been described. A "preliminary" form of Flintway may be used to ascertain its effectiveness in given situations.[4] Some Flintway prayers are said to accommodate special situations. They may be said at almost any time during the ceremonial including trial or preliminary performances.

THE CONTEXTS AND COMPOSITION OF LIFEWAY PRAYER ACTS

Although Father Berard recorded the Flintway prayer texts apart from the ceremonial description, he provided a basic description of the general ritual environment of the recitation of a prayer so that some general outline of Lifeway prayer acts can be developed.

All of the Lifeway prayers in Flintway are very similar. They differ from one another primarily in terms of the name mention and the phenomena associated with those named (B). Father Berard provides a description of the prayer act which seems to be standard for the recitation of any Lifeway prayer in Flintway.

The singer administers the bath first, after which he directs the patient [one-sung-over] to tie the offering to the cranebill. This is a flint arrowhead or a jewel for a man, a bead or shell for a woman patient, which they tie on the male and female [cranebill] pouch, respectively. . . . These gifts are not removed from the pouch so that, in time, they become heavily decorated with flints, jewels and the beads. During the prayer the patient [one-sung-over] holds the two pouches in his hands with their heads turned toward himself. The singer usually sits facing the patient [one-sung-over] while reciting the prayer, which the patient [one-sung-over] repeats verbatim.[5]

B Dark Male Crane,

C   I have made a sacrifice to you!

P   Coming from the home of dark cloud, from the floor of dark cloud, from the square rooms of dark cloud, along the out-trail controlled by dark cloud, along the trail at the tip of dark cloud, you who travel along with the aid of dark cloud!

G   When you have come upon me by means of your feet of dark cloud you have thereby wholly restored my feet [legs, body, mind, and voice] !

May the power that enables you to inhale also enable me to inhale, may the power that enables you to exhale also enable me to exhale, may the power that enables you to utter a word also enable me to utter a word, may the power that enables you to speak also enable me to speak!

May the means that keep your feet in health also keep my feet [legs, body, mind, and voice] in health!

U   With its aid you have nicely made me whole again, you have perfectly restored me! You have put me back into my former condition!

May you nicely raise me on my feet, do walk out nicely! May you cause me to walk about nicely! May it be pleasant wherever I go!

V   May it always be pleasant at my front wherever I go! May it always be pleasant in my rear wherever I go! Pleasant again it has come to be, pleasant again it has come to be![6]

This "Prayer to the Crane" is repeated naming several others: White Female Crane, Blue Male Crane, Sparkling Female Crane, Wind, Big Fly, Changing Woman, Sun Carrier, Pollen Boy, and Cornbeetle (Ripener) Girl. Appropriate changes are made for the corresponding house descriptions and related phenomena. The other prayers in Flintway differ only in the name mentions and the corresponding phenomena.

The principal constituents to be considered in Lifeway prayer acts are the bath ceremony, the cranebill pouch to which the offering is made, and the prayer recitation proper.

Flintway Bath Ceremonies

Father Berard described several bath ceremonies in Flintway, although none appear to be explicitly connected with the recitation of prayer.[7] All follow the general pattern as previously described for Blessingway, but the songs accompanying the bath emphasize its medicinal qualities. For example, the song sung during the bath preparation begins,

> Holily he placed it in water. . . . Exactly at the rim of whirl-
> ing earth he puts it in water. . . .
> Gila Monster dark male put it in water. . . . In a jet basket
> he placed it in water. . . .
> Soaproot, dark-colored, he placed in water. . . . Its dew, dark-
> colored, he placed in water. . . .
> Dark medicine, living medicine he placed in water, its dew,
> with a cooling effect, he placed in water. . . .
> Which makes one whole again, which makes one perfect again
> he placed in water. . . .
> Long life, happiness he placed in water, in a holy way he
> placed it in water. . . .[8]

And the song sung while the bath is being given begins,

> In a holy way he flushed it from you. . . . Exactly at the rim
> of whirling earth, dark male Gila Monster flushed it from
> you. . . .[9]

Careful attention is given to the strewing of medicines and pollens upon the basket of bath water, and the significance of each strewn line is indicated. Following the bath the "Songs of the Earth's Inner Forms" are sung to accompany drying the one-sung-over. These are Blessingway songs associated with the "Earth's Prayer."

Like similar bath ceremonies in Blessingway, the Flintway bath ceremonies can be considered acts of purification and acts of sanctification closely associated with creation and with Changing Woman so as to provide access to the source and means of life. Blessingway ideology is also borne in the elements of the bath ritual—the pollen and cornmeal, the yucca and water, and the "Songs of the Earth's Inner Forms." In Flintway the bath focuses slightly more upon the medicinal qualities of the bath, for the bath water contains the medicine "which makes one whole again."

The Cranebill Pouch

The one-sung-over makes an offering to the cranebill pouch and holds it as he recites the prayer. In Flintway mythology the cranebill pouch represents the medicine pouch of Gila Monster which he used in the original performances of the Flintway ceremonial. It is a highly meaning-ful object as the following review of Flintway mythology reveals.

The protagonist, a young man traveling with his family, departs to hunt for food. During his expedition he finds a handsome young woman with whom he converses. He spends the night with her and they have sexual relations. She neglects to tell him until later that she is the wife of White Thunder. Continuing on his hunt, the young man pursues some mountain sheep until he is able to kill one of them. The animal's "left horn had been struck by lightning, the mark of zigzag lightning could be seen on that horn. He also observed that its eye was missing on that same left side."[10] An omen. Upon skinning the animal he laid the meat in several heaps. But as he did so the sky began to cloud over and it began to rain, forcing the hunter to take shelter under a spruce tree. He held his arrows under his garments in order to protect them. The lightning struck the ground near him three times. After each time a voice from the sky was heard saying, "He has not yet been struck. He does not lay his arrows aside!" Hearing this the hunter wondered what would happen if he leaned his arrows against the spruce tree, so he tried it.

"There now! He has removed his arrows!" the voice up above said, and at that instant lightning again struck the earth. This time thunder had evidently shattered him beyond recognition, he was gone. Nothing but a streak of blood flowing away could be seen.[11]

Upon his failure to return, the hunter's family went in search of him. They discovered what had happened to him, and they sought the help of Gila Monster. Gila Monster demonstrated his powers of restoration by cutting himself up and scattering his various parts broadly about which were, according t ˙ his powers, gathered together, reassembled, and he was restored. In order to do this, first, he made offerings to the thunder, the earth, the sky, the sun, the moon, and every other being. Then he instructed his servants, "After I have now cut myself up ye shall go to the east, to the south, west and north. There you shall scatter my parts, and even my blood, which there may be, ye shall cast with the soil in every direction."[12] Having done this the wind people and the sunlight people began to search for and gather together the parts of Gila Monster which they reassembled upon a fabric. Then life was restored to the re-assembled body.

The two winds then ran out through his interior in opposite directions, which made him able to breathe again and gave life to his nerves. The sun threw his light upon him, he was enabled to wink. Then it seems his two agate pouches stepped over him from the east side and back again. Then from the south side the two stepped over him and back again. That done he sat up again, he arose, he was restored they say.[13]

Having shown his powers of restoration, Gila Monster indicated that in this same manner he would restore the hunter, and he immediately set about doing it.

This part of the Flintway myth illustrates the character and function of Gila Monster's pouch. The pouch of Gila Monster is composed of two human-shaped agates which function to return life to the reassembled body of Gila Monster by stepping over him and which may also be used by Gila Monster to restore life to others. The human-shaped form of the pouch is confirmed in a number of explicit references in Flintway mythology. In the ceremonial performances in Flintway mythology, a number of associations with the pouch are drawn. It is associated with the medicine administered to the hunter. It is used to stir the medicine when mixed with water, so that upon drinking the medicine water, his body "changed into sky, and . . . into earth" so that he became long life and happiness.[14] The pouch is identified with weather-related phenomena. As Gila Monster explained, "The medicine of the rainbow stepped across him, while the medicines of straight lightning went about in his interior. Now through these he has become holy."[15]

The medicine pouch is a power capable of restoring life, and it is activated by its association with and utilization of water and weather-related phenomena. It is a means for a person to regain his inner life form, as indicated by his identification with the earth and sky, long life and happiness.

The human-shaped agate pouches are closely associated with flint. Father Berard noted that the agate pouches are identified with flints which are jingled during the songs,[16] and that these flints and the arrow head-shaped flints which are tied to the cranebill pouches should be agate flint "in imitation of the live agate pouch of Gila Monster."[17]

After giving the ceremonial for the young hunter, which serves also to transmit the knowledge of the ceremonial to him for the later use of Earth Surface People, Gila Monster made representations of his own pouches in the form of cranebill pouches. He said, "This earth surface people shall possess in days to come."[18]

The cranebill pouches are complex ritual objects carefully prepared from the bodies of cranes in a ceremony just for that purpose.

The brains and all particles of flesh are removed from the bills, after which the bone is thoroughly dried in the sun. Particles of the crane's heart, lungs and stomach are evaporated, chips of jewels are stuck into them, and these parts are then replaced within the bill in their natural order. The skin of the crane's breast and back is left on the bill and is now slipped over the reed joints, which are perhaps a good span in length. [Reeds are placed within the crane skins as containers, S.G.] The reeds obtained from Oraibi and Taos are containers for medicines of Flintway, of which samples are inserted with the fingers. Pueblo foods are added to the medicines. And the whole is stoppered with red ocher and with pitch taken from a lightning-struck tree. The reed is then wrapped with unwounded buckskin thongs. The male pouch is decorated with flints in the shape of arrowheads, the female bill with olivella, aba-lone, white bead and other available shells.[19]

The very construction of the cranebills embodies many of the features noted in the pouches of Gila Monster. It is a crane's body cut into pieces and reassembled in its proper order. It is a container of medicine. It is associated with lightning and water through the flints, the pitch from the lightning-struck tree, and the various shells from water animals. And it is associated with the earth through the presence of the red ocher. The cranebills are prepared in pairs, one male and one female, and recall the many paired representations of the inner life forms of the earth.

Now, why is the crane chosen for this central religious object? The crane as a bird is introduced into Flintway through songs which focus on the bird's characteristic migratory habits.

> *woya . . . wo . . . ya ni . . . yo* . . . In the path of male crane,
>   at the ends of the sky, his feathers lie strewn in his rear. . . .
> In the path of long life, in the path of happiness his feathers
>   lie strewn in his rear, *wo . . . ye . . . e . . .*[20]

The cranes here are depicted on their migratory "path" leaving only feathers behind. But later in the song the cranes make their return.

> Upon the return of the male crane speech is shouted. . . .
> Now upon the return of long life speech is shouted. . . .
> Now upon the return of happiness speech is shouted. . . .[21]

In other words, people shout when the cranes return. Gila Monster says of the cranes, "Those beings continue to give birth and take very good care of their young which they pack back and forth."[22] By migrating the crane best cares for its young, a wise and admirable act. As the song indicates, the return of the crane is an omen of the return of conditions which are good for life. That is why the crane returns with its children. It knows where conditions for life are good and always goes there. Since the crane is always on the path of long life and happiness, its return signals the return of long life and happiness, the life-sustaining forces. The crane is chosen for the re-creation of the medicine pouches of Gila Monster because it represents the power of restoration or return of life. Through their structure and composition the cranebills, as ritual objects, are homologous with the pouches of Gila Monster.

While the cranebills can be considered a distinctive feature of Flintway, substitutions can be made if they are unavailable. Father Berard learned that

if there be absolutely no pouch in the neighborhood, and unexpectedly a critical case comes up, no mention is made of the absence of the pouch,

[but] four fresh herbs are plucked [for medicine] . These are carried in addition to flint points [arrowheads] , and one sings with these for a pouch.[23]

The herbs have at least part of the capacity for representing the medicine pouch of Gila Monster because of their medicinal association and their annual life cycle of dying and returning to life. Since there is no mention that they are not the pouch, the herbs are thought of as the cranebills and would, therefore, carry all of the associations of the cranebills. The substitution in this case appears to have little, if any, negative effect on the significance of the pouches.

The structure and function of the cranebills is homologous in many respects to the mountain soil bundle of Blessingway. Both are representations of the primary religious objects and the sources of power in the events of sacred history which account for the origin of the ceremonial practices. Both are given by Holy People for the future use of Earth Surface People and the Holy People make clear that these are representations modeled upon the original objects rather than being imitations of them. Both are held by the one-sung-over during the litany recitation of prayers. Both embody in their structure and composition the whole range of meanings developed in the mythological events and communicated in the prayer acts. Throughout the interpretive literature these objects are referred to as having "magical" power. It is clear from this analysis that the source of this "magic" is in their truly remarkable power to represent and to communicate.

THE SIGNIFICANCE OF LIFEWAY PRAYER ACTS

The constituency of the prayer texts can now be considered in light of the network of associations which has been described as emanating from the several known elements which compose the prayer act.

All examples of this class of prayers begin with a very simple name mention (B). The names mentioned are in either of two general groups. In one group are those Holy People who are associated primarily with the events in Flintway mythology. The others are associated with the cause of the injury. These appear in specific prayers keyed to the cause of the accident or injury incurred. For example, "Prayer to the Stone" is said on the occasion of injuries which "may be caused by a stone, or a tree, which falls upon or rolls over a person,"[24] and "Prayer to the Horse" for an injury by a horse. These prayers all mention the name of the source of injury in one part and conclude with what is called the blessing part which consists of two repetitions of the prayer, one naming Pollen Boy and the other Cornbeetle (Ripener) Girl. In the specification of the name mention the message of the prayer is made responsive to the particular situation.

Upon the first recitation of the phrase "I have made a sacrifice to you," (C) the one-sung-over attaches either a flint or shell (depending upon his or her sex) to the cranebill. Father Berard noted that if the one-sung-over has no flint or shell to attach to the pouch, the phrase is omitted from the prayer.[25] The significance of the offering is very complex and is fully treated in Chapter Nine.

The description of the journey of the Holy Person from his home toward that of the one praying (P), is distinctive for these prayers. Although Gila Monster is addressed in but one known example of the prayer, the journey clearly recalls the arrival of one who possesses the knowledge and power needed for the restoration of health. This passage also seems to refer to the return journey of the powers of life to the one who is suffering. This may be seen for instance in the "Prayer to the Crane," wherein the names mentioned have characteristics which signal the return to life after an apparent loss of life. The cranes are named and their migratory habit represents the return and restoration of life. Changing Woman is named. It is her characteristic, as ordained in Blessingway, to work six months of the year and to rest the other six months. During her period of rest, the vegetation appears to die, things grow cold, and the earth appears to be dead. Yet, Changing Woman becomes young again, for she has the power of restoration, and life returns to the earth and its vegetation. Sun Carrier is named. He is associated with the sun which has similar cyclical patterns, both in its daily and annual paths. These cyclical patterns are obviously associated with the power of restoration of life. Pollen Boy and Cornbeetle (Ripener) Girl, who are named in every prayer as a closing blessing part, likewise represent this power. Thunder, which struck the young hunter, is likened to the cranes in that it travels away during the winter to return with summer. Thus, the journey passage terminating at the home of the one praying (P) may be seen as describing the return of life, as the return of those who most clearly exemplify this cyclical aspect of human life, and as the acquisition of the help of those who have the knowledge and materials with which to restore life.

Navajos utilize the crane and cranebill for the characteristics which may be abstracted for symbolic purposes. They have no misunderstanding about the cranes. In the songs they attribute the periodic disappearance to migration and not to death. What is being affirmed and communicated is the notion that it is the way of things to go away or to appear to die periodically without this necessarily being caused by the malintentions of others or one's own errors. It is simply the "way" things are. Flintway, as a Lifeway ceremonial, affirms this "way," but in the journey passage (P) it also attempts to hasten the cycle by calling for the return and restoration of the lost consciousness or vitality.

The association/identification passage of the prayer (G), follows the pattern discussed for blessing prayers. It is clearly an association with the forces of life. The catalog—feet, legs, body, mind, voice—is prominent. But in the Flintway prayers the emphasis is on the association/identification for the purpose of restoring life and health. Consequently, this passage is usually extensive and complex, using several phases to accommodate the association/identification for the restoration of health. This passage complements the journey passage preceding it by assuming that the life forces have returned and have effected renewal by their re-identification with the one praying.

This passage of renewal is followed by a description of the state which succeeds the restoration of health (U). Although somewhat ambiguous, the phrase, "With its aid . . . ," may refer to the presence of the cranebills. The passage goes on to describe the restored person as standing, walking, and in perfect condition.

In Flintway prayers the state of blessing (V) follows the restoration of health accomplished by the prayer act.

The sequence of changes of the Navajo verb tenses moving from future through the progressive concluding with the past tense suggests that the prayer act functions, in part, as a performative utterance, that is, that its very performance effects the desired conditions.[26]

Father Berard recorded only the description of the archetypical performance of Flintway and no actual performances of it, consequently, there is little at this point that can be said of how Lifeway prayer acts become specifically significant in response to explicit needs. About all that can be said on the basis of the information is that the prayer texts are adapted to some situations by naming those associated with the cause to which the suffering is attributed.

It is clear that Lifeway prayer acts are heavily dependent upon Blessing prayer acts and upon Blessingway ideology and practices. The prayer act would be far less intelligible and less significant were it not for an assumed Blessingway basis—the notions of the inner life form as the basis of life, the essential placement of the inner life form in all living things, the significance of the medicine bundle in human form as the source of life, the ranges of meaning of pollen and cornbeetle (ripener), and the kinship between having the proper relationships with things in the world and being healthy, blessed, and holy.

Wherein Blessingway is concerned with creation, with the establishment of the relationships which are basic to life, Lifeway and its prayer acts are concerned with restoration or re-creation on the occasions when imbalance and disorder result from the dynamic life processes.

NOTES

1. See Leland C. Wyman, "The Female Shooting Life Chant," *American Anthropologist* 38 (1936): 634-53 and Leland C. Wyman and Flora L. Bailey, "Idea and Action Patterns in Navajo Flintway," *Southwestern Journal of Anthropology* 1 (1945): 356-77.

2. Father Berard Haile, *Origin Legend of the Navaho Flintway* (Chicago: University of Chicago Press, 1943), pp. 7 and 28.

3. Wyman and Kluckhohn, *Navajo Classifications,* pp. 30-31.

4. Haile, *Flintway,* p. 39.

5. Ibid., p. 38.

6. Ibid., pp. 244-45.

7. Ibid., pp. 218-22, 225-29, 275-79, and 281-82. See also Father Berard's notes on the bath ceremonies, pp. 15 and 54.

8. Ibid., p. 218.

9. Ibid., p. 221.

10. Ibid., p. 58.

11. Ibid.

12. Ibid., p. 68.

13. Ibid., p. 69.

14. Ibid., pp. 104 and 106.
15. Ibid., p. 112.
16. Ibid., p. 2.
17. Ibid., p. 25.
18. Ibid., p. 244.
19. Ibid., pp. 22-23.
20. Ibid., p. 117.
21. Ibid., p. 118.
22. Ibid.
23. Ibid., p. 275.
24. Ibid., pp. 286 and 319 n.300.
25. Ibid., pp. 38 and 317 n.213.
26. For further development of this see Sam D. Gill, "Prayer as Person: The Performative Force in Navajo Prayer Acts," *History of Religions* 17 (1977): 143-57.

CHAPTER SEVEN

ENEMYWAY PRAYER ACTS

The class of prayer acts whose purpose is the expulsion of foreign malevolence (A) . . . (G) Ķ (V) has only a few examples all of which occur in Enemyway *(anaa'ji)*, a ceremonial once used to respond to the infection caused by contact with foreigners at times of war but more recently used for any infection thought to be caused by foreign contact. In either case the source of the malevolence is thought to come from a ghost *(ch'įįdii)*, the disembodied spirit of the dead foreigner. The many references to prayer in Enemyway mythology and ritual descriptions suggest that prayer is an integral and essential part of the ritual process, yet only a few of the prayers have been recorded. Several types of prayers may occur in the Enemyway ritual process. The recorded Enemyway prayers which are concerned with the expulsion of the foreign malevolence are set in several ritual contexts: the preparation of ritual objects, medicine and blackening rites, and special rites which may be added to Enemyway upon request.

Enemyway mythology, as it is recorded, is complex and often difficult to decipher. There are many ambiguities. There are notable differences between the archetypical ceremonial performances as described in Enemyway mythology and the recorded descriptions of actual performances. Enemyway mythology is related to other parts of Navajo mythology, with an apparent dependence upon Blessingway and especially upon a cycle of stories about the killing of the monsters by Monster Slayer and Born for Water, the twin sons of Changing Woman. This latter cycle is commonly known as Monsterway.

Enemyway, known also as the "Navajo War Dance" and the "Navajo Squaw Dance," is related to a wide range of Navajo ceremonials, but its ritual process and ideology are distinct, and it is usually considered as a separate ceremonial class. Wyman and Kluckhohn have indicated that Enemyway is used simply for "alien infection."[1] Father Berard's comments were more explicit. He found that historically Enemyway appeared to be primarily for the purpose of removing the effects of war and possibly in preparation for war. In postwar times it has been adapted to resolve problems associated with the disembodied spirit, or ghost, of a non-Navajo. This is quite often traced to an event when the sight of a foreigner's blood or death is witnessed.[2]

THE CONTEXTS AND COMPOSITION OF
ENEMYWAY PRAYER ACTS

The most outstanding prayer text in this class is recorded in one of the archetypical performances of the Enemyway ceremonial. Two such performances are described. One is sung for Young Man at Jarring Mountain who helped the corn people defeat the Taos Pueblos. His affliction is traced to the ghosts of the defeated enemy.[3] The situation in which the second archetypical performance is done is unclear, but the description is much clearer and contains the full text of the "Prayer to Shoulder Bands and Wristlets,"[4] which is perhaps the finest recorded example of a prayer of this class. It is said in the context of a series of complex ritual acts. As the preparations for these ritual acts were taking place, many animal figures arrived and contributed something to the medicine of Enemyway. Water was boiled and the medicine was added. Then the medicine concoction was put into a basket from which the one-sung-over drank. It worked as an emetic, and after the one-sung-over had vomited, the remainder of the medicine was applied to his entire body. Then

Immediately, it seems, the cornbeetle put its head to his ear and gave its call, "loooo lololo"; again on the other side, twice on both sides it did this. Directly, it seems, the figure in pollen of cornbeetle boy and cornbeetle girl was made, after which the same song was used in performing upon him here, as had been heard by the Changing Woman's boys, when they returned from the slaughter of big ye-ii.[5]

The shoulder bands were placed in his hands for the recitation of the "Prayer to the Shoulder Bands and Wristlets." He "stirred the medicine with his finger, took a taste of it, then sprayed the unravelers with it, which he had laid to the side."[6] The unraveling followed after which the tallow was prepared and applied to him in the blackening rite. All of the ritual acts were done to the accompaniment of song.

This archetypical performance corresponds to the ritual acts performed on the morning of the third day in a contemporary performance described to Father Berard after a recitation of the myth.[7]

A study of the prayer act for the expulsion of foreign malevolence should include the emetic rite, the recitation of the prayer, the unraveling rite, and the blackening rite. The prayer text gives focus and meaning to these components of the prayer act.

The Emetic Rite

There seems to be no precedent for the emetic rite in Enemyway or Monsterway mythology other than in the archetypical performance. This suggests that it may be a late addition to the mythology to align it with current ceremonial practice. The primary source for the meaning of a given act is usually found by considering the story associated with its first performance. Since such a story does not appear to exist, it is more difficult to understand the emetic rite beyond the obvious connotations of purgation. Still some understanding can be gained from studying how the rite is performed. From the archetypical performance of the emetic rite which is a part of Enemyway mythology, it appears that the one-sung-over drinks the emetic medicine, vomits, and applies the remaining medicine to his body. Then the cornbeetle (ripener) calls in his ear, and the pollen figures, cornbeetle (ripener) boy and girl, perform for him.[8] The ambiguities here may be resolved somewhat by considering the description of the actual ceremonial performance of the emetic. In this instance the water and medicine are prepared. Then

> in front of the basket, along the rear of the room, he [the singer] draws the figure of a cornbeetle [with pollen] and, in the very center of the emetic, he draws a pollen figure of the big fly. He then instructs the patient [one-sung-over], "You will kneel on the knees of the cornbeetle and rest your hands on its hands, then drink from the very center of the big fly figure!"[9]

The emetic follows the bathing of the hair which is approached in a manner very similar to the Blessingway bath ritual and appears to be an extension of it. The pollen figure of cornbeetle (ripener) is closely associated with Blessingway. In Monsterway mythology Changing Woman was signaled by the call of the cornbeetle (ripener) that her sons were returning from their father's house,[10] where they had been dressed and equipped to slay the monsters which were preventing the world from being a place where people could live. Throughout Navajo mythology, Big Fly is a messenger between the Holy People and the Earth Surface People. He informs the people of the appropriate way to approach Holy People so as to gain their attention and assistance. In Enemyway, Big Fly is among those who contributed medicine for the emetic. Upon presenting his medicine he said, "As for myself, if an enemy's ghost ever takes possession of a person's interior, my medicine will be of use in such cases."[11] This appears to refer to the emetic powers of the medicine.

In the songs sung during its preparation, the emetic is identified as food.

> *enaya* With a thrill, my grandchild, you have prepared a food
>   for yourself, with a thrill,
> My grandchild, you have prepared a food for yourself with
>   a thrill, my grandchild,
> You have prepared a food for yourself, *halaghai*.[12]

The songs sung during the application of the emetic medicine to the one-sung-over identifies him with Monster Slayer.

Monster Slayer now shakes a dark cloud from his soles,
    look, look,
Monster Slayer now shakes a dark cloud from his toetips,
    look, look.[13]

The emetic rite appears to be concerned with more than purgation, although this is the way it has usually been understood by scholars. It is
performed in a ritual manner similar to the Blessingway bath rite, but
the emetic element of the rite suggests that it is an act of expulsion via
contact with the medicine water rather than contact with the source
and power of creativity. The emetic medicine is associated with food
and with the weapons and powers of destruction which are characteristic
of Monster Slayer, for out of the dark clouds which surround the many
body parts of Monster Slayer come the destructive forces of lightning.
The emetic is drunk while the one-sung-over is on a platform which
physically associates him or her with cornbeetle (ripener) and pollen and
suggests blessing. The one-sung-over acquires that which will rid his
interior of the unwanted malevolence by drinking the Big Fly medicine.
There are two forces at work in the emetic rite. One is directed toward
the expulsion of malevolence; the other toward the aquisition of blessing.

The Prayer Recitation

Before the prayer is intoned, the songs which Changing Woman heard
on the return of her boys from the slaughter of Big Ye'ii are sung. These
songs begin

At the woman's place, at the woman's place, at the woman's
    place he is putting it into its former shape. . . .
I am the child of Changing Woman. . . .
At the center of the room of the turquoise home he is putting
    it in shape. . . .
Turquoise boy is [nicely] putting it in shape. . . .
As child of turquoise he is [nicely] putting it in shape. . . .
It is pleasant in front of him, when he [nicely] puts it in
    shape.
The child of long life and happiness is [nicely] putting it in
    shape.[14]

This song strikingly has the features distinctive for the prayer constituent which describes a state of blessing (V). It is concerned with things being put in their proper places and suggests the movement toward achieving a state of blessing.

The shoulder bands and wristlets which are held during the prayer recitation are made of yucca during the preparatory part of the ceremonial. The origin of the shoulder band is associated with Monster Slayer's killing of the Horned Monster after which he "filled the colon of the horned monster with its blood, and with this pack slung across his arm he was now walking along."[15] This blood-filled colon was consequently used to kill Rock Monster Eagle, thus instituting the practice of collecting blood-stained articles from the enemy and displaying them on the shoulder bands.[16] Slim Curly told Father Berard that the "patient is decorated with wristlets made of yucca, to represent the weapons of Monster Slayer in his campaign against the monsters."[17] In holding the shoulder bands and wristlets during the prayer recitation, one holds not only representations of the power of death, the weapons of Monster Slayer, but also representations of the power which made the earth a habitable place.

The "Prayer to the Shoulder Bands and Wristlets" is actually a prayer set composed of twelve prayers of identical constituent structure with two appended passages. The first eight prayers name Monster Slayer, Born for Water, Born at Yellow Mountain, Reared Underground, Sun, Moon, Talking God and Calling God. The prayers differ from one another in terms of name mention and certain alternations in line sequences and phrases. The first prayer which names Monster Slayer as "Who time and again kills monsters" is as follows:

B Who time and again kills monsters,

A He of "Waters flow together"!

His feet [legs, body, mind, voice] have become my feet
G   [legs, body, mind, voice] , thereby I shall go about,
   By which he is long life, by that I am long life,
   By which he is happiness, by that I am happiness,
   By which it is pleasant at his front, thereby it is pleasant
      at my front,

By which it is pleasant in his rear, thereby it is pleasant
    at my rear,
When the pollen which encircles sun's mouth also encircles
    my mouth, and that enables me to speak and continue
    speaking,

K You shall take the death of the upright, of the extended
    bowstring out of me! You have taken it out of me, it was
    returned upon him, it has settled far away!
Therefore the dart of the Ute enemy's ghost, its filth,
    by which it bothered my interior, which had traveled
    in my interior, which had absorbed my interior, shall this
    day return out of me! This day it has returned out of me!
The dart of the Ute enemy's ghost, its filth, that had
    traveled between my skin, that had absorbed my skin
    layers shall this day return out of me, therefore I am
    saying this. Because this day it has returned out of me,
    I am saying this.
The dart of the Ute enemy's ghost, its filth, by which it
    bothered my skin, which had traveled on my skin,
    which had absorbed my skin, shall this day move away
    from me, therefore I am saying this. Because this day it
    has moved away from me, I am saying this.
The dart of the Ute enemy's ghost, its filth, has turned away
    from me, upon him it has turned, far away it has returned.
Right there it has changed into water, it has changed into dew
    [while] I shall go about in peace.

V Long life, happiness I shall be, pleasant again it has become,
    pleasant again it has become, pleasant again it has be-
    come, pleasant again it has become, pleasant again it
    has become.

Prayers nine to twelve mention the names of White Corn Boy, Yellow
Corn Girl, Pollen Boy and Cornbeetle (Ripener) Girl. These prayers are
the same as the first eight except that the passage which identifies the
one praying with the Holy People (G) has a variation in wording.

Where white corn boy . . . rests his pollen feet, there I have
G   placed my feet,
Where he rests his hands in pollen, there I rest my hands.
Where he rests his head in pollen, there I rest my head,
His pollen feet [legs, body, mind, voice] have become my
     feet [legs, body, mind, voice], thereby I shall go about,
[continuing as in the other prayers].

Following the twelfth prayer, two short passages name Pollen Boy and
Cornbeetle (Ripener) Girl.

B Pollen Boy,

Nicely you shall put my foodpipe [windpipe, heart, nerves]
U   in its [former] condition again!
Nicely I shall walk about, without ailment I shall go about,
     unaffected by sickness I shall be going about!
Without monsters seeing me I shall be going about! Without
     beings which are evil seeing me I shall be going about!
With monsters dreading me I shall be going about!
With monsters respecting me I shall be going about!
Governed by this I shall be going about! After conquering
     monsters I shall be going about! After accomplishing this
     with monsters I shall be going about!

Pleasant again it has become. Pleasant again it has become.
Pleasant again it has become. Pleasant again it has become.
Pleasant again it has become. (EH # 1)

The Unraveling Rite

Medicine and pollen are applied to the unravelers while medicine songs
are sung. The unraveling follows. Slip knots are tied in strings. The number
of knots in each string and the number of strings are carefully prescribed.
While holding these unravelers at certain parts of the one-sung-over's
body, the slip knots are pulled out. Slim Curly told Father Berard that
these body parts are those

which are ordinarily not visible to the patient [one-sung-over], therefore at his soles, under the bent kneejoint, aside of the hipjoint, at the back of shoulders, the palms of the hands, on the cheeks, ears [or temples] and, either at the top of the head, or away from the patient's mouth, as the singer may choose. From these parts of the body the foreign ghosts are supposed to leave the patient, to whom they are invisible. Therefore also, after the last unraveling [from head or mouth], he is directed to "blow the ghost away."[18]

The unravelers are pulled at the mention of the words "extended bow string" and "queue" in the accompanying songs.

The keywords of the songs are (1) with my grandchild he extracts them, (2) with my grandchild he has extracted them, (3) he unravels it with you, my grandchild, (4) he has unraveled it with you, my grandchild (5) my grandchild, it has returned far from you, (6) my grandchild, it has returned upon him, and (7) my grandchild, it has returned far away. The full text of the fourth song is

> My grandchild, he has unraveled it with you, my grandchild,
>   he has unraveled it with you, my grandchild, he has un-
>   raveled it with you,
> Now Changing Woman has unraveled it with you, she has un-
>   raveled the dark cord with you, the extended bowstring has
>   unraveled it to their death with you,
> Now long life and happiness, my grandchild, has unraveled it
>   with you, my grandchild, she has unraveled it with you,
>   my grandchild, she has unraveled it with you, my grand-
>   child, she has unraveled it with you,
> Now Black God has unraveled it with you, the blue cord he
>   has unraveled with you, the wide queue has unraveled it
>   to their death with you,
> Now long life and happiness, my grandchild, has unraveled it
>   with you, my grandchild, he has unraveled it with you,
>   my grandchild, he has unraveled it with you, my grand-
>   child, he has unraveled it with you.[19]

This song, the ritual act of unraveling, and the prayer constituent, share the distinctive feature of the prayer constituent which is focused on the expulsion and dispersion of the foreign malevolence (K).

The words "extended bow string" and "wide queue" appear in the unraveling songs and in the prayer. They refer to important ritual objects of Enemyway. The extended bow ($\gtrless$|) represents the weapons which Monster Slayer used to kill the monsters and is his symbol. It is associated with him wherever he occurs.[20] The queue (χ) which is the symbol of Born for Water, Monster Slayer's twin brother, recalls Changing Woman. She tied her hair into a bundle, represented by the queue, when she was about to give birth to the twins.[21] These designs always appear with Monster Slayer and Born for Water or their influence.

When the unraveling is completed, medicine and pollen are applied to the body of the one-sung-over accompanied by the singing of medicine songs which begin

> Now at the summit of Huerfano Mountain
> [is] the real child of Changing Woman,
> the real child of Monster Slayer, whose
> feet are dawn, and because I now am
> long life and happiness, my child do
> come, come! my child come, come,
> do so![22]

Closely associated with Blessingway, this song indicates the establishment of an association between the one-sung-over and Changing Woman and Monster Slayer, and the acquisition of the life-sustaining powers represented as long life and happiness. Thus, the features of this song correlate with distinctive features of several prayer constituents: the establishment of a kinship relationship with Holy People (F), the association/identification with Holy People (G), and the resolution of all problems through these relationships and associations which put all things in their proper places (V)

The Blackening Rite

The blackening rite is the final part of the prayer act. In the archetypical performance of this rite, Black God, the Holy Person who conducted the rite, said, "Whenever enemy ghosts become bothersome to you and cause you to pale, and you rub yourself with it, your flesh will become whole again."[23] The blackening is accompanied by a set of thirty-four songs.[24] In the description of the tallow used as the blackening agent, each of the several ingredients is associated with some event in the killing of the monsters in Monsterway.[25] Upon the completion of the blackening, the myth explains, "Then he [the one-sung-over] was dressed up in the manner that Monster Slayer had used at the time."[26]

Given these factors, the blackening is a complex process of identifying the one-sung-over with Monster Slayer and his powers to slay the threatening malevolence. The one blackened, dressed as Monster Slayer, is prepared to conquer the foreign ghosts. The blackening rite concludes with the song which begins, "Monster Slayer is coming along."[27]

THE SIGNIFICANCE OF ENEMYWAY PRAYER ACTS

In returning to the prayer text in this prayer act we need to consider the constituents of the prayer as well as the changes among the various prayers which compose the twelve prayer set. The structural diagram for the prayer is 1) B_1AGKV to 11) $B_{11}AGKV$, 12) $B_{12}AGKV/B_{11}UV B_{12}$ UV. In the first eight prayers the name mention (B), invokes an association with eight different characters. The twins, Monster Slayer and Born for Water, are the protagonists of Enemyway and Monsterway mythology. Born at Yellow Mountain and Reared Underground are a pair who are associated, even identified, with the twins. Sun is the father of the twins, and he prepared them for the killing of the monsters. Moon is not well understood from the immediate mythological context, but appears to be a counterpart or complement of Sun. Talking God and Calling God are likewise complementary pairs. Talking God appears in the Monsterway myth as one opposed to war,[28] and both are associated with Blessingway as the inner life forms of the sacred mountains.

In the prayer all of these Holy People are located at a place referred to as "waters flow together," which is the last place where Monster Slayer was seen on the earth surface.[29]

The association/identification constituent (G) expresses the desired acquisition of Monster Slayer's weapons which are so powerful against malevolence. This prayer passage is parallel to the pattern of blackening, where the whole body is identified with that of Monster Slayer when he was prepared to slay the monsters. The associations with the other Holy People named are complementary to the association with Monster Slayer.

The prayer passage which describes the removal and dispersion of the foreign malevolence (K) follows the acquisition of the weapons and powers needed to do so. The passage is notable in its reference to the malevolence as an object, a dart. This concept of disease is rarely referred to in the literature, although Navajos have told me that techniques akin to sucking shamanism are sometimes used. To my knowledge there is little published record of this practice. Sucking shamanism involves a ritual curing technique in which an entranced figure removes, by sucking from a sufferer's body, a symbolic object that is identified as the cause of the illness. To conceive of disease as an object is consistent with the Navajo concept of the life principle as an inner life form representable by physical objects. The dart is recognized as an intrusion upon the inner life form resulting in an illness. The opening phrase in this passage refers to the extended bowstring and the wide queue. "You shall take the death of the upright, of the extended bowstring out of me!" This phrase is highly ambiguous out of the context of the prayer act. The reference is to the weapons, the club or staff, of Monster Slayer which rendered death to the monsters. The one praying identifies with the powers of destruction, and must accept the responsibility for the deaths which result from the use of these powers. Killing an enemy may incur an attack by the ghost of the dead one. The phrase asks that the consequences of the death which the one-sung-over has encountered be removed, that is, for the expulsion of the malevolent dart placed in the one-sung-over by the ghost. This passage is another example of one which contains a progression of verbs through several tenses, from future to past, attesting to the performative force of the prayer.

"Long life, happiness I shall be," when the foreign malevolence is removed, that is, when things are in their proper places, it shall become pleasant again. To expel the malevolent influence is to restore the condition of one's inner life form with the expected consequence of the acquisition of an environment of health and beauty.

The ideology made clear in Blessingway is central to these first eight prayers in the prayer set. The structure is bent upon the reacquisition of long life and happiness and the return of hózhǫ́. Yet the association/

identification passage (G) is used differently here than in blessing prayers, for it seeks an association with the powers of death rather than life.

In prayers nine through twelve in this prayer set, even though the constituent structure is unchanged, there is a shift in the significance of the prayer. In these prayers there is an association with the powers of creation and reproduction instead of with the powers of destruction. The one praying is associated, by means of the life-giving substance pollen, with White Corn Boy and Yellow Corn Girl, Pollen Boy and Cornbeetle (Ripener) Girl. Still the passage which describes the removal of the malevolent influence (K) remains unchanged in these last four prayers.

The two passages which conclude the prayer set name Pollen Boy and Cornbeetle (Ripener) Girl. They recapitulate the last two prayers but drop all but the passages which petition Pollen Boy and Cornbeetle (Ripener) Girl to put the insides of the one praying back into "nice" condition again (U) and which describe the resulting state of blessing (V). The interior parts of the body are emphasized: the foodpipe, the heart, and the nerves. The passages state that the interior restoration is due to the conquering of monsters who are now far away and remain in fear of the person.

A number of structural parallels in the prayer act make more explicit the significance of the prayer and its effect. The basic constituent structure of each prayer text is an association/identification (G) followed by the expulsion and dispersion of the malevolence (K) resulting in and concluding with a state of restoration and blessing (V). There is a parallel structure for the twelve prayer set of the "Prayer to the Shoulder Bands and Wristlets." Each of the first eight prayers is initially focused upon the association and acquisition of the powers of death and destruction, concluding with a description of the resultant state of blessing. In the last four prayers in the set, the focus shifts to the association with the powers of life and creation, while retaining the stated desire for the expulsion and dispersion of the malevolence (K). Even this concern with expulsion and dispersion is dropped in the concluding two prayer passages, where the focus rests upon a major petitionary statement seeking the restoration of one's interior and the acquisition of blessing. The structure of the prayer set is parallel to that of the constituent structure of the separate prayers which compose the set.

The parallel does not stop there. The emetic rite has a similar structure. The drinking of the emetic through the pollen figure of Big Fly makes an association with the forces which have the power to expel malevolence. The emetic is a medicine designed to expel the undesirable through vomiting. Even though the rite is noted for its powers of exorcism it has other powers. The one-sung-over drinks the emetic on his hands and knees which are placed in physical contact with a pollen figure of the cornbeetle (ripener). With this foot to foot, knee to knee, and hand to hand contact with the pollen figure of cornbeetle (ripener), the emetic is drunk through the pollen figure of Big Fly drawn upon the liquid medicine. Pollen, the substance of life and the food of the Holy People, is ingested along with the emetic. These factors, along with the structural similarity of the emetic rite to the bath rite, suggest that in the emetic rite there is a balance between the acquisition of the powers of expulsion and death and the acquisition of the powers of life and blessing.

The structural parallel is also apparent in the series of songs which begin after the emetic and proceed through the unraveling. After vomiting, the remaining medicine is applied to the body of the one-sung-over accompanied by songs which identify the various parts of his body with the weapon adorned body of Monster Slayer. This association/identification is parallel to the emphasis in the first eight prayers in the set. The songs which Changing Woman heard on the return of her boys from the slaughter of Big Ye-ii are sung just before the recitation of the prayer. These are set in the context of the aftermath of the utilization of the powers of death by Monster Slayer and affirm that the use of these powers will put things back into their proper order. The unraveling takes place following the prayer, and the seven unraveling songs are about the expulsion and dispersion of the malevolence. The sequence of songs sung from the emetic rite through the unraveling have a structure similar to that of the first eight prayers in the prayer set emphasizing the acquisition of the powers of destruction, yet they carry as a minor theme the state of blessing and health to which this acquisition will lead.

At the conclusion of the unraveling, medicine and pollen are applied to the accompaniment of songs which emphasize the acquisition of life and creation. The songs declare an identification with long life and happiness, "I am long life and happiness," but they retain as a minor theme the relationship with Monster Slayer when the one-sung-over says that he is the "real child of Monster Slayer." In these songs there is a correspondence with the structure of the last four prayers in the prayer set and the two additions which conclude it.

The ritual acts reflect the same composition. The application of medicine to the various body parts is a ritual act of association/identification. The pulling of the slip knots of the unravelers at the various body parts is an act of both association/identification and expulsion and dispersion.

The prayer act concludes with the blackening rite. As the emetic rite at the beginning of the prayer act embodies the full structure of the prayer act and serves as an initial summary of the prayer act, the blackening rite serves as a sort of recapitulation of the structure of the prayer act. Father Berard made no comment on the significance of the blackening rite beyond noting that it is a preparation for the attack.[30] Reichard indicated that in Enemyway, blackening "is a rite with almost exclusively exorcistic purposes."[31] But a further analysis of the prayer act shows that it may now be understood more fully. The blackening corresponds at one level to the prayer passage making an association with Monster Slayer and his powers of destruction (G). The prototype for blackening in Enemyway mythology concludes, "Then he was dressed up in the manner that Monster Slayer had used at the time."[32] First of all, the blackening is a means by which the powers of destruction and death may be acquired. There is also evidence in the same archetypical performance of the rite that blackening has medicinal value and actually adds to the acquisition of health and life. When Black God gave instructions about the composition and use of tallow during its preparation he said, "Concerning this tallow part, it is tallow of every kind of game. Therefore whenever an enemy's ghost has caused you to become pale and you rub one another with it, your flesh will thereby become moist." And after the tallow was prepared he said, "Whenever enemy ghosts become bothersome to you and cause you to pale, and you rub yourselves with it, your flesh will become whole again."[33] The structure of the blackening rite corresponds to that of the prayer act and serves as a visual representation of it.

The significance of this prayer act is in the interplay between the emphasis upon the acquisition of the powers of destruction and death on the one hand and upon the acquisition of the powers of life and health on the other. The analysis of the structure of the Enemyway prayer act shows that the Navajo see these concerns as interdependent.

The stories of Monsterway are the exemplars for all uses of the forces of destruction. In these stories each death caused by Monster Slayer was also an act of creation. Improper acts which cause death or mistreatment of the dead may result in illness. When the corn people and Young Man of Jarring Mountain discussed the reasons for their becoming weakened they decided that

it must be because of this saying, that the enemies shall die at the surface of the earth, [where] the coyotes shall eat them, and the buzzards and crows and magpies, shall carry them away, and because of the sounds entering the earth [woman], the mountain woman, and water woman. Before that [war] time we know that it was not thus, they had made their own rule about this.[34]

Father Berard confirmed the notion in his footnote on this rule, which he described as

a rule that the earth, mountains and water were not to be treated in this manner, by rejoicing in the enemy's death and allowing corpses to become the food of scavengers, and their blood to flow, without compensating these benefactors, the earth, mountains and water. These show their displeasure by weakening the people living in the mountains and waters.[35]

Death must not be inflicted except for creative purposes. When it is, as may occur in times of war, ill consequences may result which are ascribed to the ghost of the dead. Enemyway expels this ghost, but it may only do so by an act of creation. Until some creative act results from that death, the ghost can never be allayed.

NOTES

1. Kluckhohn and Wyman, *Navaho Classification,* p. 33.
2. Father Berard Haile, *Origin Legend of the Navajo Enemy Way* (New Haven: Yale University Publications in Anthropology, no. 17, 1938), p. 25. Enemyway has been the subject of a number of studies with diverse interests. Enemyway has as part of its character a social and public dimension that is perhaps not so obvious in most of the other ceremonials. For many observers Enemyway is a social occasion with religious overtones. In recent years Enemyway has retained and developed this social characteristic resulting in its being an important social occasion for

Navajo people. This exoteric and easily observed part of Enemyway has been the focus of most of the studies of Enemyway, while the religious dimensions have been largely ignored. For a discussion of the basic sources for the study of Enemyway see Sam D. Gill, *Theory of Navajo Prayer Acts*, pp. 217-19.

3. Haile, *Enemyway*, pp. 191-99.
4. Ibid., pp. 199-217.
5. Ibid., p. 207.
6. Ibid., p. 213.
7. Ibid., pp. 231-35.
8. Ibid., p. 207.
9. Ibid., p. 231.
10. Ibid., pp. 40 and 207.
11. Ibid., p. 207.
12. Ibid., p. 266.
13. Ibid., p. 268.
14. Ibid., p. 270.
15. Ibid., p. 117.
16. Ibid., p. 65.
17. Ibid., p. 73.
18. Ibid., pp. 70-71.
19. Ibid., pp. 270-71.
20. Ibid., p. 37.
21. Ibid., p. 59.
22. Ibid., p. 272. See Gill, *Songs of Life*, Plates X and XI for related iconography.
23. Ibid., p. 195.
24. Ibid., pp. 272-84.
25. Ibid., p. 197.
26. Ibid., p. 199.
27. Ibid., p. 284.
28. Ibid., p. 163.
29. Ibid., p. 179.
30. Ibid., p. 35.
31. Reichard, *Navaho Religion*, p. 624.
32. Haile, *Enemy Way*, p. 199.
33. Ibid., p. 195.
34. Ibid., p. 179.
35. Ibid., p. 255 n.102.

CHAPTER EIGHT

UGLYWAY PRAYER ACTS

The prayer acts which focus upon the expulsion and dispersion of native malevolence are in many ways similar to Enemyway prayer acts, but their concern with malevolence of a native source distinguishes these acts. The structure of the texts in this class of prayer acts is (A) . . . (F) M (N).

There are only a few recorded prayer acts of this type, and all of them occur in ceremonials conducted according to Uglyway ritual processes. A brief analysis of one of these prayer acts will illustrate the distinctive character of this class of prayer acts and distinguish it from the Enemyway prayer acts.

THE CONTEXTS AND COMPOSITION
OF UGLYWAY PRAYER ACTS

The best example of an Uglyway prayer act was recorded by Father Berard Haile and published in the *Legend of the Ghostway Ritual in the Male Branch of Shootingway* (1950).[1] The prayer act is performed when a native ghost is suspected of malintentions. The ceremonial is brief and involves making an offering at a charred tree.

In 1933, Gray Man told Father Berard:

You see if a person requests this thing and one agrees, one tells him that
the bark of a thunder-struck tree that has fallen on its north side should
be brought the length of four fingertips. This is brought from there, and
with it a very old sweathouse stone and charcoal are brought. This charcoal is ground and one strews it in a circle upon the said bark leaving an
opening at the growing end of the bark. Over this ashes are also strewn
in a circle, the aforementioned sweathouse stone is ground and again
strewn in a circle. The patient [one-sung-over] then places a jet jewel
exactly in the center, he adds a white bead, a turquoise and an abalone
chip, then adds another white bead to make it five. Then towards the
north side of hogan a very old charred tree burnt to the ground is located,
to which the patient [one-sung-over] carries the jewel container in his
left and places it on the farther side of the charred stump with its opening away [from the hogan]. Then he sits on the east side facing it, while
the singer sits on the west side of it facing the bark. Then he begins the
prayer:

      First deceased at the time of emergence,
B   woman chief, big ghost, ugly thing,

      Because you have thought of me in the
C   past by ugly means, and have bothered
      me with ugly intent as proven,
     I have made this sacrifice to you,
        I have made a sacrifice of a nice jet,
        a sacrifice of a nice white bead,
        a sacrifice of a nice turquoise,
        a sacrifice of a nice abalone!
     I have made you an offering of fine specular
       iron ore, an offering of fine blue pollen,
       an offering of fine pollen!
     Because of the witchery of the ugly one that
       existed in my interior I have made you
       this offering!
     Because of the witchery of the ugly one that
       was bothering my marrow [flesh, blood,
       body, moisture] I have made you this
       offering!

The witchery of the ugly thing that
M   formerly existed at the pit of my stomach began
to move up from there!
It moved along upward through my pleura,
    it began to move upward along my Adam's apple,
    all of it moved to the tip of my speech.
There wolf young man did not hesitate,
    with the dark bow and the white bead arrow he
    attacked it, below the north he held it up with
    [these weapons], then he placed it down with them,
    there it shouted its cry on that account, it cried itself
    to death, then it did not move, then it did not move.
[The ugly thing was attacked by other young men
    described by a repetition of the phrase mentioning
    wolf young man, making changes only in the names
    and the weapons used. The others were: mountain-
    lion with the mock orange bow and turquoise arrow,
    bobcat with the dark bow and gray arrow, cougar with
    the mock orange bow and spotted arrow, yellow bill
    with the dark bow and yellow arrow, big hawk with
    the mock orange bow and red arrow, black eagle
    with the dark bow and black arrow, and turkey buzzard
    with the mock orange bow and gray arrow.]

It is dead for good, . . . it is changed into ashes, . . .
N   may my winters be many, . . . I am safe, . . . (SMGH # 3)[2]

During the recitation of the prayer the one-sung-over holds the offering
and a ritual bow and arrow. When the prayer is completed the singer and
the one-sung-over return to the hogan stepping "over any yucca, or cactus,
or any other thorny plants along there."[3] They sing three songs while
they are returning. The ceremonial is concluded upon their return.

In spite of the brevity of the ceremonial, the meanings of the various
ritual acts, ritual objects, and words of the prayer are complex.

A story in Male Shootingway Uglyway will illustrate the motivation
for the offering. A young hunter on an excursion in search of food came
upon and killed four fine bucks. His father-in-law, Big Snake Man, with
whom he was hunting, possessed certain malevolent powers. Jealous of

his son-in-law's hunting success, he used these powers against him. Big
Snake Man

notified the one called dark thunder. And before very much time had
elapsed clouds darkened the sky, it began to rain, the stored away
venison was all scattered in various directions, walking became diffi-
icult for the two, incessant crackling noises were heard. "What has
happened, you are again getting this treatment at the instigation of the
old man himself! Go ahead, make an offering to it, to so and so by name!"
he was told. Immediately it seems he made the offering to [Thunder] of
jet, turquoise, abalone, white bead, and another abalone making it five.
Then of specular iron ore, blue pollen, flag pollen and ordinary pollen.
As soon as he had made this offering to it a rumbling noise was heard
high up. In this same manner this offering is now made to it when there
is a ghostway [Uglyway] ceremonial. For this reason, it was learned,
thunder was treating him so.[4]

On the basis of this story the offering is made to allay Thunder, the emis-
sary of an ill-intentioned native, at a charred tree in a container from a
thunder-struck tree.

The prayer names "First deceased at the time of emergence," which
refers to the first death. There are several accounts of the story of the
first death,[5] but the one recorded by Father Berard as part of Upward
Reachingway[6] is of particular importance since Father Berard believed
that Upward Reachingway was the exemplar for all Uglyway ceremonials.

In Upward Reachingway, the first death is that of Woman Speaker who,
with her husband, Bent Speaker, led the people out of the underworlds.
Woman Speaker died of a hemorrhage caused by the witchcraft of First
Man, and her children, First Boy and First Girl, buried her. After two
days the children returned to check on her grave, but they found her
sitting on a rock combing her hair. This had occurred because they had
failed to reverse her moccasins when they buried her. Bent Speaker
heard that his wife was still alive and went looking for her. Finding her
in the emergence place, Bent Speaker entered the underworlds to get her.
While there he learned of the nature of this forbidden place, but he was
unable to return to the earth surface which made it necessary for Talking God to rescue him. The meaning of the story of the first death is summarized at its conclusion.

The point of the entire story is, that First-man had caused the death of "woman speaker" and that First-woman had "talked" the husband, "bent speaker" down into the *xaži•nái* [emergence place] to follow her. Naturally, then, First-man and woman were much angered to see "bent speaker" return by the efforts of "talking and calling gods" and at once set out to thwart these beneficient efforts. Briefly, two wildcat youths are introduced to counteract their schemes and, when First-man dispatched his darts [arrows] at "bent speaker" the two youths caught them and instructed bent speaker to blow them back upon First-man with these formulas spoken to the arrow: . . . return upon him! . . . return to his interior! . . . return encircling him! and finally: . . . kill him himself in return! formulas, which are now common in *xóčǫ•ží* "ghost-way" songs and prayers. . . . This accounts for "over-shooting" in "ghostway of Upward Reaching-way" and the two archers, with small bows and arrows, must wear wristlets and shoulderstraps adorned with wildcat claws.[7]

THE SIGNIFICANCE OF UGLYWAY PRAYER ACTS

In the prayer, the naming of "First deceased at the time of emergence, woman chief, big ghost, ugly thing," evokes the story of the first death and its meanings. In this way reference is made to witchcraft, ghosts, ghostland or the land of the dead, the spheres of the underworlds and perhaps the one praying feels some association with Bent Speaker who had to be rescued from ghostland. The prayer passage which makes an offering (C) is greatly extended to describe the purpose for the offering and this purpose makes explicit the desires and the problems of the one praying. Here it is clear that there is a correspondence between the witchery *(be'iinzįįd)* of the "First deceased" and the pains suffered by the one praying. This suffering is believed to exist in the interior of the body where it bothers the marrow, flesh, blood, and body moisture. To rid one of the cause of the suffering is the reason for making the offering. The offering of jewels correlates with the description of the offering in the prayer act.

Having stated the reasons for making the offering, the next passage describes the manner in which the object of malevolence is expelled from the body and done away with (M). It moves up from the pit of the stomach finally reaching the "tip of my speech." Once outside the body it is attacked by eight figures whose arrows cause it to cry out and die. This sequence, called the "overshooting," has its model in the story of the first death.[8] It is a standard feature of Uglyway ritual. In the overshooting rite, the two people who are appointed to perform the overshooting move in opposite directions and shoot over the one-sung-over and they repeat the shooting over the ceremonial hogan. At the conclusion of several shootings a cry is heard signifying the death of the malevolent one. In the Upward Reachingway story the overshooters were identified as wildcat youths, while in the story in Shootingway they are not identified. The eight animal youths named as the overshooters in the prayer passage have not been found in any other place in recorded Shootingway mythology. Perhaps the eight youths are an elaborate representation of the overshooters specified in Upward Reachingway. All are animals of prey and have a kinship with the wildcat youths.

The concluding passage describes the state of safety resulting from the death of the malevolent one (N) who is now "changed into ashes."

As similar as the Uglyway class of prayer acts is to the Enemyway class, there are notable differences when the two are compared. It is difficult to point out any Blessingway influence in the Uglyway prayer acts. These prayer texts do not even conclude with the statement of regained beauty (V), a structural characteristic which is almost universal in the corpus of Navajo prayer texts. The arrows in Shootingway are traced to the twins, Monster Slayer and Born for Water, and in Reichard's account of Male Shootingway Holyway, the full Monsterway story is told as a preface to Shootingway proper.[9] But in this prayer act there is little to indicate that the story of the twins contributes to its meaning. The Uglyway prayer act appears to be almost totally exorcistic. The removal and killing of the malevolent influence is the primary concern. The jewel offering may have some association with the life-giving items in First Man's medicine bundle in Blessingway, but the prayer act does not substantiate this. Although First Man appears in Blessingway, he is more centrally associated with the events of the emergence. He is denied a significant role beyond the initial creative acts of Blessingway because he is believed to be the source of witchcraft practices.[10] In this prayer act it is only First Man's and First Woman's associations with witchcraft that are evoked.

Of all prayer acts considered to this point, the Uglyway prayers appear to have stemmed from a separate ideology. Still there are no unique prayer constituent units.

NOTES

1. Father Berard preferred to render the Navajo *hóchʠ́ʠ́'jí* as "ghostway" while Wyman, Kluckhohn, and others have rendered it as "evilway." I prefer "uglyway" on the basis of the analysis done by Gary Witherspoon "Central Concepts (I)," p. 54, and because it avoids the associations with the good-evil dichotomy of Western religious traditions.

2. Father Berard Haile, *Legend of the Ghostway Ritual in the Male Branch of Shooting Way* (St. Michaels, Arizona: St. Michaels Press, 1950), pp. 265-70.

3. Ibid., p. 271.

4. Ibid., pp. 41-42.

5. See Matthews, *Navaho Legends*, p. 77; Goddard, *Navaho Texts*, p. 138; and Haile, *Creation and Emergence Myth*, and "Navaho Upward-Reaching Way and Emergence Place," *American Anthropologist* 44 (1942): 411.

6. Haile, "Upward-Reaching Way," p. 411.

7. Ibid., pp. 413-14.

8. Haile, *Legend of the Ghostway Ritual*, pp. 145-53.

9. Gladys A. Reichard, *Navaho Male Shooting Chant (Holy)*, n.d., Manuscript 29-45, 46, Museum of Northern Arizona, Flagstaff.

10. For a survey of the role of First Man and First Woman in Navajo theology, see Reichard, *Navaho Religion*, pp. 433-38.

CHAPTER NINE

HOLYWAY PRAYER ACTS

The removal of malevolence of a native source is emphasized in, even distinctive of, two classes of prayer texts. When it does not refer to the removal of ghost or witch malevolence, it is concerned with disorder brought about by Holy People through their use of power *(ál'il)*. The class of prayers which calls for the removal of this power (M) and for a restoration of the affected one to his former condition has the structure (A) . . . (G) H M (U) (V).

Many prayers of this type have been recorded in their cultural and religious contexts. With only a couple of exceptions all of the prayers in this class are in the context of prayerstick rites. They all have the same constituent structure and vary only in the optional use of place designation (A) and the names which appear in the name mention (B).

THE CONTEXTS AND COMPOSITION OF HOLYWAY PRAYER ACTS

All prayerstick rites occur only in the context of Holyway ceremonials, *diyink'ehji* which Father Berard described as "when a ceremonial is accorded to holy (ones) or directed by them." That is, if there is evidence that an illness is due to the "anger of the holy ones" a Holyway ritual is chosen.[1]

The prayer act normally occurs during the morning of each of the first four days of the Holyway ceremonial which may be five or nine nights in length. Prayersticks are usually short hollow reeds which are prepared and decorated with particular Holy People in mind. The decorated prayersticks, along with offerings of bits of semiprecious stone, feathers, and other materials, are prepared and wrapped in cloth or cornhusk bundles. The one-sung-over holds these while the prayer is intoned in a litany lead by the singer. At the conclusion of the prayer, the singer takes the bundles and ritually presses them several times to the sacred parts of the one-sung-over's body. As songs are sung, an assistant takes the bundles outside of the ceremonial structure to deposit their contents in places appropriate to the Holy People for whom they are intended.

A prayer of this type from Beautyway goes:

A At the range set upon another [Hosta Butte]

B Big snakes, at whose front the earth sounds,
         youth chief.

C I have made an offering for you,
       I have prepared a smoke for you!

    This very day you must remake my feet for me,
H This very day you must remake my legs for me,
    This very day you must remake my body for me,
    This very day you must remake my mind for me.
    This very day you must remake my voice for me.

    This very day you must take your spell out of me
M   by which you are bothering me,
    This very day you have removed your spell from me
      by which you were bothering me,
    You have left to take it far away from me,
    You have taken it far away from me.

    This very day I shall recover,
U This very day my body is cooling down,
    This very day my pains are moving out of me!

With my body cooled off, I am walking about,
V With my body light in weight, I am walking about,
With a feeling of ease I am walking about,
With nothing ailing me I am walking about,
Immune to every disease I am walking about,
With pleasant conditions at my front I am walking about,
With pleasant conditions at my rear I am walking about,
As one who is long life and happiness I am walking about,
Pleasant again it has become,
Pleasant again it has become! (BFHW # 1)

This prayer is normally repeated several times changing only the name of the Holy Person and his attributes. This constitutes a prayer set.

While there are many interrelated elements in the prayer act, the focus is clearly upon the prayerstick. It is a major ritual symbol and the object of various ritual acts. The number of prayers in the prayer set correlates with the number of prayersticks prepared, and the names mentioned in the prayers correspond to the Holy People for whom the prayersticks are made. The significance of prayersticks, their preparation and offering, is essential to the understanding of the prayer act.

Prayersticks

The English rendering of the Navajo *k'eet'áán* as "prayerstick" arose because of the similarity of the Navajo ritual object to that of the Pueblo ritual object, *paho,* which is called a prayerstick in English, but it is not, as Father Berard noted, the best rendering of the word.

The compound noun *k'eet'ą́ą́n* eludes definite analysis, but it is suggested that *k'ee-* is related to stem *-k'ee'* "to make a single cut" and *-t'áán* or *-t'ą́ą́* recalls *-t'ą́* a joint as of bones, especially since reed joints are frequently used. Stem *-tt'ą́* or *-stą́ą́n* "feathered" as in *'aceebest'áán* tail feathered [arrow] is not very likely, though the Navajo prayerstick is very likely of Pueblo origin and this, we know, is feathered by Pueblo Indians. Downy feathers are usually laid aside of prayersticks when they are deposited in an offering. Cut [reed] joint is probably uppermost in the native mind, but usage among investigators has commonly adopted the term prayerstick which we retain from *k'eet'ą́ą́n.* [2]

The general explanation of the use of *k'eet'áán* has remained unchanged throughout the literature since Matthews, who called them cigarettes because they are reeds into which tobacco is placed, first explained that "they are messages to the gods."[3] He said that once offered, the "god examines and smells the cigarettes" to determine their acceptability. Reichard believed that the distinctive feature for all ritual objects which could be called *k'eet'áán* is the function of serving the "purpose of invoking supernatural aid," or as a Navajo explained to her, "They are just like a written invitation."[4] Reichard understood the *k'eet'áán*, properly prepared and offered, as compelling the recipient to respond.[5] But she understood these offerings to be part of a system of reciprocity, for she noted that "offerings are exchanges, tokens to curry deific favor. In Navajo religion no service is gratuitous, it is interchanged, measured, traded, the benefits being reciprocal."[6]

While this explanation is basically correct, further study will show that in the terms of the relationship that Navajos have with the Holy People, when an offering is properly made the Holy People are obligated to respond. It is necessary to review the uses of and statements about prayersticks that occur in Navajo mythology, including the emergence and creation stories and the Holyway mythology. An examination of prayersticks in the ritual process will yield further understanding, as will an investigation of the structure and composition of prayersticks.

To begin, Beautyway mythology will be examined since it is the story that goes with the prayer text quoted above. The protagonist of Beautyway is a girl who is tricked into marrying Big Snake Man. He is an ugly old man but he attracted the girl by changing himself into a handsome youth. When she discovered his true appearance, the girl fled but she eventually became a captive of her husband's kin, the Snake People. Every day the Snake People told her of certain things she was forbidden to do, but her curiosity quickly led her to do them anyway. Finally, Toad Old Man, in disgust at hearing her many acts of disobedience, acted against her causing her injury by shooting her with mudballs which pierced her body in many places.[7]

When the Snake People returned, they wondered how she had been injured, and Big Fly finally told them. He also told them that Toad Old Man himself was probably the only one who could help restore her. It was difficult to discover the proper way to approach Toad Old Man, but finally it was accomplished and he performed Beautyway for the girl and she was restored by it.

Crucial to our understanding of prayersticks is the process described in the myth through which those seeking aid for the one suffering were able to gain the help of the Holy Person whose angered action had caused the suffering. The process is fairly standard from one Holyway account to another. There is a detailed description given in one rather clear account of Navajo Windway.[8]

In Navajo Windway, Elder Brother is lost while Holy People are playing a game with him. After searching in vain for him it is learned that Black God might know where he is and could bring him back. In order to gain his favor and thus his help, they offer him first one "laced bundle," but they are ignored. Then they offer him two, three, and four laced bundles but again they are ignored each time. Bat appears to give assistance and asks a series of questions in order to ascertain that the offering is as it should be, for he knows that "If it be not like this, he will not recognize it, although ye may have made a gift [of it] to him!"[9]

Then Bat begins another line of questioning to determine if the prayerstick is properly prepared. Following Bat's instructions, Black God is properly presented with the appropriate offering.

When this was done he [Black God] smelled it. "Who but you would do this, you who flop about with the darkness!" he said, "You are the only one who knows my offering, I am positive of this!" he said. "Now there you are talking! As for me where do I ever go? You know that I spend all my days right here!" he said [to the Bat].

"Go ahead then, my grandchild, prepare me a smoke," he said. "You really should prepare me a smoke, my granduncle, since I am visiting you!" he [the offerer] said to him. Here he spread out a sewed fabric, they say, on top of which he placed the tobacco pouch which he had with him. "You also, my granduncle, put it down here," he said.[10]

When a smoke had been exchanged with Black God he said, "All right, my grandchild, what can happen to him [the one suffering] !". . . . "I will positively return with my grandchild."[11]

This is the archetype for the use of the prayersticks and offering bundle as an invitation and invocation to Holy People who are needed to perform a healing ceremonial. The nature of Black God's response justifies Reichard's understanding that the offering is obligatory or compelling. But it may now be seen that the Holy Person is obligated to respond only because he is properly and respectfully approached. By using the proper approach the Holy Person is engaged in a binding relationship. Kinship terms are used, and the response of the Holy Person is that of a grandfather to his grandchild. The response is not so much mechanical as social. Navajo singers are approached in much the same manner by the representatives of the one who has need of a ceremonial performance.

A review of all of the Holyway mythology reveals no reference to prayersticks other than in this context, and these references offer no clues to the significance of the choice of these ritual objects and their composition.

Something more can be learned by considering references to prayersticks in other portions of Navajo mythology. The emergence and creation mythology upon which Upward Reachingway is based is replete with references to prayersticks. This is unusual, since the associated ceremonial makes no use of prayersticks. An important reference to prayersticks occurs near the end of the creation story. The Holy People are preparing to leave the earth surface, and they give final instructions to those they have created.

This is the last time that you will see the Diyin, "the Gods," and since then these Gods have not been seen in the Blessing Rite. The Gods said, "You may continue your journey, and if anyone tells you that he has seen the Gods you will know it is not true, but when you hear small birds twitter you will know that we are near by; when you call on us, you must make our prayersticks and give offerings of jewels and collected spring water."[12]

At the end of the creation era the Holy People departed from the earth surface leaving instructions that whenever they were needed they could be contacted only by making prayersticks and by giving them offerings.

The significance of the prayersticks is revealed in the portion of this story which tells of the creation of the earth surface. In this story the prayersticks are the materials placed upon the floor of the hogan in connection with the acts of creation.[13]

Neither the composition and construction nor the origin of these prayersticks is found in this story, but it is clear that they are basic materials of creation equivalent to the medicine bundle items in the

Blessingway account. From them were created the generative organs representative of the life of the world. "The genitalia of man remained on the sky and the genitalia of woman remained on the earth [named Sky Man and Earth Woman S.G.]."[14] The prayersticks are thus homologous with the talking gods in Blessingway who were the personification of the materials of life, the basic elements of all creation.[15] Prayersticks are usually prepared with facial designation from which we infer that they are to be considered people. As talking gods they serve as mediators and messengers across the gap left at the end of creation between the earth surface and the domain of the Holy People.[16]

As for the jewel offering which accompanies the prayersticks, Changing Woman commented on its importance when she gave instructions in Blessingway.

And these Holy People are found in many places so, while those that are chiefs as it were stay in their homes, they have many messengers going out from there. These messengers [always on alert] sit facing you here while you plead [pray]. This news they bring back to the homes of their chiefs where they relate of you, "Clearly he is pleading when he says, I have made your sacrifice [offering]." Therefore you will treat it with every respect. Even for those places [for depositing jewels] this holds, do your pleading only with good jewels [because the messenger examines them].[17]

The messengers are the talking gods/prayersticks held in the hands of the one praying. The depositing of the prayerstick and offering after the prayer sends the talking gods to the homes of the Holy People if the offerings are properly prepared. Only the talking gods can go between the earth surface and the homes of the Holy People.

The composition of the offering and the decoration of the prayerstick corresponds with the significance, character, and attributes of the Holy Person with whom it is to be associated.[18]

Holyway Prayer Texts

The names of the Holy People mentioned as either the first or second constituent of the prayer text (B) usually refer to those who are active characters in the corresponding ceremonial origin myth. Big Snake Man who is named in the Beautyway prayer text quoted above is considered one of the agents who is causing the suffering and therefore a potential aide in relieving the condition. The place designations (A) are the usual habitats of the ones named.

The offering/smoke passage (C) which follows refers directly to the prayerstick and offering bundles in the immediate ritual context and to the prayerstick rite of which the prayer is a constituent. The significance of this prayer passage is illuminated by a knowledge of the mythological exemplar for approaching a Holy Person to aid in the restoration of one who suffers from his anger.

The words which name a Holy Person and announce that an offering and smoke have been made may thus be understood at several levels. In the limited context of the immediate ritual acts of the prayerstick rite they are simple descriptive statements which refer to the completed manual tasks of preparing the prayersticks and the offering bundles. The Navajo verbs used in these phrases—'ishła ("I have made") and nádįįhiłá ("I have prepared")—are in the perfective mode which designates completed acts.[19] But when seen in the context of the Navajo way of approaching Holy People on such occasions, these words refer not only to the manual acts, but also to the events in sacred history in which the procedure for approaching a Holy Person were established. The words of this portion of the prayer along with the associated ritual acts amount to the acts necessary to establish the kind of relationship with a Holy Person which obligate him to respond to certain requests made of him.

The next passage of the prayer amounts to an imperative to remake (H). "This very day you must remake my feet for me," and so on. It confirms the effectiveness of the preceding passage to establish a relationship with the Holy Person, for he is directly addressed in the imperative mood. The passage does not humbly ask a favor, it urges the Holy Person to remake the feet, legs, body, mind, and voice of the sufferer. The passage, as well as the ritual act of pressing the body parts with the prayerstick bundles, emphasizes the significance of the Navajo concept that life is dependent upon the proper alignment and placement of the inner life form within the physical body. The catalog in the passage and the accompanying ritual acts must be seen in the context of this Navajo concept of life and the processes of creation as discussed extensively in chapters four and five.

This request that the Holy Person act is understood as having a pragmatic effect since the following passage describes the progressive removal and dispersion of the inflicted spell (M). The Navajo verbal modes shift from the imperative, *shá'áádíídíí̜l* ("you must take it out of me") to the perfective, *shqhanéiníĺá* ("You have taken it out of me") and *dahnídinilá* ("you have taken it away"), indicating the completion of the act of removal.

The removal of the bothersome power is not sufficient for recovery as is attested in the next prayer passage which describes the recovery taking place (U). Again the verbal mode is telling. The Navajo verb *náádídeshdáá̜l* rendered "I shall recover" is actually in the iterative mode which means more nearly "I shall start right now to go again like I went before." It indicates that the action is beginning in the immediate present. The Navajo verb translated as "is cooling" *(hodínook'eet)* is in the progressive mode indicating that the body is cooling down as the words are being uttered.

The concluding passage of the prayer which describes a state of blessing (V) repeats the verb *naasháadoo*, rendered as "I am walking about." It is in the progressive mode with a continuative aspect which indicates that the action is in progress and that it will continue or endure. The prayer establishes in the one praying a physical state expressed in terms of coolness, lightness in weight, a feeling of easiness and a state of immunity and places the person in an environment of beauty and order *(hózhǫ́)* identified with long life and happiness, the forces of life. The prayer concludes with the conventional phrase "Pleasant again it has become."[20]

Holyway prayers are used in the treatment of a wide range of illness, yet they are standard formulaic prayers.[21] Several elements in Holyway prayer acts are adaptable to numerous situational contexts. The variable constituents are the decoration of the prayersticks, the composition of the jewel offerings in the prayerstick bundles, the name mentions in the prayers, and the places of deposit for the prayersticks. These are all interrelated with the Holy Person who is being approached. This scarcely limits the possibilities for responding to felt needs, since the number of combinations of prayersticks which may be chosen is enormous for any Holyway ceremonial. This is clearly documented in Father Berard's book, *Prayerstick Cutting in a Five Night Navaho Ceremonial of the Male Branch of Shootingway* (1947) which shows how prayersticks are selected in response to an assessment of the etiology of the illness suffered.

THE SIGNIFICANCE OF HOLYWAY PRAYER ACTS

The significance of Holyway prayer acts is at one with the purpose of Holyway ceremonials, that is to remove the powerful influence of an angered Holy Person and to reestablish the life-giving relationships. From the prayer act we can see that the process depends upon the reestablishment of kinship relationships with the irritated Holy People. This is effected through the offerings presented to the Holy People mediated by prayersticks representing talking gods.

Once the malevolent influence is removed the restoration follows the process of creation as set forth in Blessingway focusing on the vital body parts to establish the order and relationships upon which life depends.

NOTES

1. Father Berard Haile, "Navaho Chantways and Ceremonials," *American Anthropologist* 40 (1938): 648. See this cited article by Haile, pp. 648-52, and Wyman and Kluckhohn, *Navaho Classification*, pp. 7-18, for a discussion of the subdivisions of Holyway ritual.

2. Father Berard Haile, *Prayer Stick Cutting in a Five Night Navaho Ceremonial of the Male Branch of Shootingway* (Chicago: University of Chicago Press, 1947), p. 50.

3. Washington Matthews, *The Night Chant, A Navaho Ceremony,* American Museum of Natural History, Memoirs, vol. 6 (New York, 1902), p. 37.

4. Reichard, *Navaho Religion*, pp. 301-2.

5. Ibid., pp. 302 and 306.

6. Ibid., p. 307. Other basic sources about prayersticks may be added to the ones cited in this paragraph. They are Washington Matthews, *The Mountain Chant,* Bureau of Ethnology, 5th Annual Report (Washington, D.C., 1887), p. 419, and "Some Sacred Objects of the Navaho Rites," Archives of the International Folklore Congress of the World's Columbian Exposition (Chicago, 1898), pp. 237-48; and Franciscan Fathers, *Dictionary*, pp. 396-98.

7. Wyman, *Beautyway*, pp. 78-79.

8. Wyman, *Windways*, pp. 90-94.

9. Ibid., p. 93.

10. Ibid., p. 94.

11. Ibid., pp. 94-95. See also examples in Gladys A. Reichard, *The Story of the Navaho Hail Chant* (New York: Barnard College, Columbia University, 1944), pp. 37-39; Wyman, *Red Antway,* pp. 121-22; and Haile, *Flintway,* p. 63.

12. Mary C. Wheelwright, *Emergence Myth According to the Hanelthnayhe or Upward-Reaching Rite* (Santa Fe: Museum of Navajo Ceremonial Art, 1949), p. 60.

13. Ibid., p. 43.

14. Ibid., p. 45.

15. Further support for this is given in Gill, *A Theory of Navajo Prayer Acts,* pp. 282-289.

16. I think that in recent years this meaning has been obscured by a more simplistic rationale which Navajos have learned from anthropologists.

17. Wyman, *Blessingway,* p. 238.

18. A type of prayerstick referred to as *k'eet'áán yałtih* or talking prayersticks also exists. See a discussion of the significance of this type of prayerstick in Gill, *A Theory of Navajo Prayer Acts,* pp. 289-94. See also a discussion of the interrelationship between prayersticks and the medicine bundle *(jish),* Ibid., pp. 294-98. See Gill, *Songs of Life,* Plates XVII to XXI for prayerstick iconography.

19. The Navajo verb is capable of distinguishing as many as four different aspects and six different modes by alterations of the stem. The modes distinguished are: *imperfective,* indicating that the action is incomplete but is in the act of being accomplished or about to be done; *perfective,* indicating that the action is complete; *progressive,* indicating that the action is in progress; *iterative,* denoting repetition of the act; *usitative,* denoting habituality in performing the act; and *optative,* expressing potentiality and desire. The aspects are: *momentaneous,* action beginning and ending in an instant; *repetitive,* action repeated; *semelfactive,* action which occurs once and is neither continued nor repeated; and *continuative,* action which is continued. See Robert W. Young and William Morgan, *The Navajo Language* (Salt Lake City, Utah: Deseret Book Co., 1972), p. 42.

20. A more extensive analysis of this kind of prayer may be found in Gill, "Prayer as Person."

21. Based on dozens of examples, I have found the Holyway prayer acts performed in conjunction with the offering of prayersticks to be the most formulaic of all Navajo prayers. It is notable that a text recorded in 1957 by David McAllester (SMHM #1) in a prayerstick offering to Snake differs significantly from Holyway prayer structure; indeed, it has neither of the constituents distinctive of Holyway prayers. This text has only recently been published and it will be interesting to investigate what may explain this notable variation.

CHAPTER TEN

LIBERATION PRAYER ACTS

Prayers in one class, with texts of impressive length and complexity, are recited to recover, return, and reassociate the lost means of a healthy life to persons who are suffering. The distinctive complex journey sequences by which the lost means of health are rescued (Q) and returned (S), account for the bulk of the prayer texts, whose structure is (A) (B) Q R S (T) (G) (V). The prayer acts amount to a shamanic style liberation of the inner life form of the one suffering from its bondage in some remote and dangerous place.

The two Navajo terms which may be used to designate these prayers are *ha'ayátééh* and *ch'ééhóyátééh*. Father Berard was the first to consider the meaning of these terms which he did in his discussion of Upward Reachingway.

The *ha'ayátééh* "talking (to return) upward or out of a lower place," a liberation prayer in Upward Reaching-way, is recited by the singer who holds the *'azee* "medicine" or *dziłeezh* "mountain soil" bag during the prayer and instructs the patient [one-sung-over] to repeat it verbatim. The purpose of this technique is to "talk the ghost down into ghostland and then to lead the patient [one-sung-over] upward restored from its spell." Here the ghost is called *chahałheeł naaldohi'* "moving mass in or of darkness" and *chahałheeł 'oołmąsii* "whirling mass of darkness" and is talked down into *hook'eedghan* "nobody's home." But the patient [one-sung-over] who believes himself subject to its influence is "talked" or prayed out of that home. . . .

Other chantways prefer to call their liberation prayers: *ch'ééhóyatééh* "praying or return-talking-out-of-a-place." . . . the purpose of either type of prayer is, primarily, not to leave a patient [one-sung-over] in the home of the source of his ailment, but to talk this factor by prayer back to its home, then to return the liberated patient, restored perfectly, to his own fireside.[1]

Liberation prayers were discussed with several Navajo singers. They tend to distinguish these prayers on the basis of the location and direction of the journey and to base this upon the etiology of the disease suffered. The *ha'ayatééh* is a journey into the lower worlds to liberate one from the domain of ghosts. The *ch'ééhóyatééh* is a journey to each of the cardinal directions on the earth surface to liberate one from some malevolence, commonly witchcraft.[2] Frank Goldtooth expressed it differently. He said that *ha'ayatééh* "goes all the way down to the underworld. There are some people living there and you have to talk to them in this prayer. There are two parts to the prayer, *ha'ayatééh* goes down and *ch'ééhóyatééh* comes back up." Both Andrew Woody and John Billy agreed that *ha'ayatééh* "goes down" and *ch'ééhóyatééh* "stays on this world."[3]

Several other important points were raised by Navajo singers with respect to these prayers. Both Andrew Woody and Frank Goldtooth associated *ha'ayatééh* with the Earth's Prayer (The Prayer to the Earth's Inner Forms) which was discussed in chapter 5 as a Blessing prayer. Andrew Woody recited the major segments of the several prayers which compose *ha'ayatééh* and they closely match the names mentioned in the Earth's Prayer in Blessingway, although Andrew Woody's prayers included a second part in which he mentioned the names in reverse order. The first part, he explained, goes down through the lower worlds and the second part comes back up. He noted that the prayers are said in litany fashion while the one praying holds the talking prayersticks. He explained that the talking prayersticks go along with you on the journey

into the lower worlds as helpers. They are referred to in the prayer passage,
"I shall be walking with someone's feet, [mind, life]."

Father Berard's rendering of *ha'áyatééh* as "upward-return prayer"
affirms that it is a postemergence prayer. The structure of the prayer
and the description of the journey places the home of the one praying
upon the earth surface, but the structure of the prayer text is based upon
the existence of an underworld and in part upon the ideology of the
emergence process. In Upward Reachingway the origin of the *ha'áyatééh*
prayer is connected with the appearance of pillars of light upon jewel
baskets in the four directions.

Right there is the beginning of the *hanetnehee,* Moving-Up-Rite [Upward
Reachingway], which, therefore, too, has . . . the "prayer out of the
east, out of the south, out of the west, out of the north, out of the zenith,
and out of the nadir."[4]

The prayer, but mentioned here, is described in greater detail at a later
point in the emergence process. Herbal medicines are introduced, and
their use is taught to those people present. Then they are told that

Whenever these medicines just enumerated prove ineffective on men and
women, young and old, a prayer, the *hatc'e yaathee'ii* (lit. which prays
out from below) is employed. It is recited by the singer with the patient
[one-sung-over], wherein they together travel to the homes of the super-
naturals below the east. The patient [one-sung-over] repeats each phrase
as pronounced by the singer.

After reaching the home of the divinity in the east and placing their
petition there, the prayer makes the return by reversing each step of the
journey until the starting point has been reached again. Step by step the
evil is removed and the patient [one-sung-over] restored to his former
condition. This accounts for the name "to pray it out." Pollen is then
placed upon the tongue and head of the patient [one-sung-over] and
otherwise is used freely by the singer. The same prayer is repeated to the
holy ones dwelling in the south, in the west and north. The prayer to the
nadir (below) must be said with great care as the evil ones have their
homes in this region. The return part of this section of the prayer to the

zenith removes every vestige of their influence. A short petition is then added to a circle in the center, another to a second enlarged circle and so on to four circles, one always larger than the preceding one. This *tc'e yaatxee'ii* is used, as said, whenever the prescribed medicines prove ineffective.[5]

From these accounts in Emergence mythology it appears that the *ha'áyátééh* and *ch'éého'yátééh* prayers were once two parts of a set of prayers. This may account for the introduction of other terms such as *ada'háyátééh* which Andrew Woody said is the same thing as *ch'éého'yátééh* and *ha'áyátééh*.

Ha'áyátééh and *ch'éého'yátééh* prayer acts have been found in Lifeway, Uglyway, Holyway and Blessingway type ceremonials, providing a notable break with the close correlation between classification of prayer acts and ceremonial classification.[6] These prayer acts can be most effectively analyzed by considering the two types of Liberation prayers separately to show how the particular structures serve the needs motivating each.

HA'ÁYÁTÉÉH PRAYER ACTS

The story of the first death which is part of Upward Reachingway mythology contains a prototype of the *ha'áyátééh* prayer.[7] When Bent Speaker pursued his wife into the land of the ghosts, the underworlds, he had to be rescued by Talking God and Calling God.

They were coming to enable the husband to "reach" the present world again. Spider man must have hinted at this purpose in his prophetic announcement: "Whenever you hear or see *ghé'ii* 'fearful ones' it spells misfortune. A certain prayer alone will remedy it." This prayer is then introduced and describes the entrance to *hook'eeghan* "nobody's home" as curtained with *dládd* "lichen" of various colors, which the two gods left with the *yotgaigish* "white bead cane" of talking god. Leaving this forbidden place the man is made to stand on a rainbow, talking god takes the lead while calling god, with his two *k'eet'áá yátti'* "talking prayer-sticks" tied together, *ha'áyátééh biniighé* for "talking out purposes," makes up the rear.[8]

Undoubtedly the prayer referred to here is the *ha'áyátééh* prayer. The *ha'áyátééh* prayers all describe a rescue journey to the home of the ghosts described by various phrases, such as "nobody's home."[9]

Washington Matthews recorded an example of this prayer in a special prayer ceremony performed by a singer to avoid the illness which might result from his venturing into the dangerous and forbidden underworlds which he had done as part of the act of narrating the Emergence myth.[10] Here the prayer ceremony appears to have contained no ritual acts other than the long recitation of the prayer by the singer holding no ritual objects. However, the variety of situations in which this prayer is used is matched by widely varying ritual components in the prayer act.

There are several *ha'áyátééh* prayer acts in Big Starway. A study of one of these will broaden our understanding of Liberation prayer acts. The "Prayer of Invocation and Liberation from the Myth of the Great Star" is said while sitting on a buckskin with a sandpainting of Pollen Boy or Cornbeetle (Ripener) Girl drawn upon it.

In the myth of the Big Starway, the use of the *ha'áyátééh* prayer is explained. "This prayer is all-powerful: it can take you down under the earth, up to the sky, and back to the earth again. It is in two parts, one goes down to the Spirits under the earth, and one up to the sky. It is used when all else fails in a ceremony."[11] While it is all powerful it is not integral to the ritual process of Big Starway or other ceremonials. The Navajo singer who recited the prayer as it occurs in Big Starway said, "This prayer, you see, is not spoken at every chant, but when a person asks for it at any time it is then said."[12] It appears, then, that the *ha'áyátééh* prayer in this Uglyway version of Big Starway is used when an illness which is caused by native ghosts does not respond to normal treatment.

The prayer text is very long with much repetition of extended passages at each step of the liberation journey. The prayer begins with the journey of Monster Slayer, armed with his dark staff and lightnings and carrying his rock crystal and talking prayersticks, as he searches through mountains, clouds, mists, mosses, and waters for the means of health which had been abducted and is being detained in the home of the ghosts in the lower worlds (Q). Then the recovery of the one lost is described (R), followed by the return journey to replace the lost one back at his home on the earth surface (S). The return journey includes stops at the mountains of

Soft Stuffs, Jewel, Pollen, Cornbeetle (Ripener), and Old Age as well as at the sacred mountains in the four directions. Once the earth surface is reached, the final approach to the home of the lost one is conducted by Talking God. Upon reaching the most interior, and thus the safest, place in the home, Talking God reunites the lost one with the things with which he had been formerly associated (T). Then Talking God bestows blessing upon the person who has been put back into his former condition through the announcement of an association/identification of himself and his means of blessing with the restored person (G). The prayer concludes with the announcement of a state of blessing (V).

It is clear that the means of health and life is conceived as being in human-like form. The one praying suffers from the loss of this inner vital form. The *ha'ayátééh* prayer is used because it is surmised that the inner form has been removed to the home of a malevolent one in the regions of the lower worlds. This prayer has the power to enter this dangerous territory to liberate and recover the lost inner life form.

Monster Slayer's and Talking God's roles in the Liberation prayer are more clearly understood in the context of the relationship of Liberation prayer acts to the Uglyway prayer acts to expel and disperse native ghosts. Native ghosts are identified with the monsters which were slain in sacred history so that the rescue of the means of health from the home of the ghost is homologous with the many journeys Monster Slayer made to the homes of the monsters to slay them. On this journey he carried talking prayersticks which perhaps represent Talking God and Calling God, and they are certainly a source of the knowledge and power essential to such a journey. Once safely returned from ghostland, the weapons and warrior powers of Monster Slayer are no longer needed. Talking God, the active power of the Holy People, performs the acts of reassociation necessary for full recovery. The last portion of the prayer, the restoration of the one praying and his association with Talking God to obtain a state of blessing (T, G, and V) are strongly oriented to Blessingway ideology, confirming the need for re-creation and reassociation as well as the return of the lost inner life form.

Many Navajos stress that the recitation of the prayer is the performance of the acts described. The prayer becomes an active force itself upon being uttered. Frank Goldtooth, Andrew Woody, and Doc White Singer all referred to the prayer as a person. Frank Goldtooth said, "he [the prayer] knows everything that is going on down at the bottom of the earth. So no white or Navajo knows anything about it. It's in the ground. The prayer is the only way you can reach down underneath."

CH'ÉÉHOYÁTÉÉH PRAYER ACTS

The *ch'ééhoyátééh* prayer is normally uttered in the hoop transformation ceremony which is performed to accomplish the retransformation of the one suffering back to his former self.[13] The suffering is attributed to his being transformed into a snake or a coyote. In Navajo Windway, Older Brother is transformed into a big snake because he broke hunting restrictions. In the several stories in which the protagonist is transformed into a coyote, the setting is one of hunting as well, but the motivation of Coyote to perform such a disabling deed often stems from sexual jealousy. Coyote desires the wife of a hunter but is degraded and rejected by the hunter and his wife. When Coyote "blows his skin" on the hunter he in turn obtains the outward appearance of the hunter so that he can approach the hunter's wife. His lack of skill in hunting and his smell of coyote urine betray that he is not the hunter. Consequently a search is made for the hunter and he is found in a miserable state "curled up on top of driftwood, . . . lying as a coyote usually does with his nose stuck in his anus."[14] Unable to speak he could only wiggle in response to the questions of Younger Brother who found him. The process of restoration is then performed by the hoop transformation ceremony.

The ritual process of the hoop transformation ceremony is a complex composition of ritual acts, ritual objects, and ritual speech acts, involving the one-sung-over moving through a series of hoops set in one of the cardinal directions on each of four consecutive days. A *ch'ééhoyátééh* prayer is intoned inside the ceremonial hogan at the conclusion of the rite each day. The prayer and the various constituents of the ritual process of the hoop transformation ceremony enjoy complex interrelationships. To again show how the prayer text is highly dependent upon the ritual environment for its significance, we will carefully consider both the ceremony and the prayer text as constituents of an act of prayer.

Father Berard recorded a prayer text in the ritual context of Shootingway according to Uglyway ritual, although it was narrated rather than performed.

The preparation for the hoop transformation ceremony is preceded by the bathing of the clothes and belongings of the hunter who has been transformed into a coyote. His clothes and belongings, which were taken over by the coyote, are defiled and smell of coyote urine. When the coyote smell is finally gone, the attention is turned to the preparation for the hoop transformation ceremony. The hoops are meticulously prepared.

For this, you see, four white hoops are prepared making it five with the wild rose hoop. Of these hoops two have foreheads, while on the other two their faces are merely cut out. Their faces are blue, their head tops black, their chins streaked yellow, their foreheads streaked white. In four places pairs of black lines are drawn around, four bundles of spruce are tied to them, on top of which four white down feathers are also tied. On the leading one the figure of the sun is drawn, his eyes at the growing end, his mouth toward the white butt end. One red circle is drawn around it. Out from either side of the sun figure a dark snake lies, on which there are [deer] hoof marks, squares and hooks [crescents]. Their borders are white, their necks blue with four pairs of red lines drawn across. A red spot is placed on the top of their heads, their tongues are yellow. Both snakes are [made] exactly alike. Where the hoop ends cross each other the unraveling cord is tied. And on the next three that are set up only a pair of snakes lie facing each other. They are all of one pattern with the wild rose [hoop] last in line. The latter only is fuzzed with spruce and four turkey downs are attached to it. When all are in readiness they are merely laid aside for the time being.[15]

When the hoops are set up and the trail is made, the ceremony begins. Refer to Figure 1 for a diagram of the setup.

[A] The singer then ties the headplume on the patient [one-sung-over] and places the pouch parts, tail feathered, yellow tail feathered arrow, talking prayerstick, the leading bow, and groaning stick into his hands. [B] The patient [one-sung-over] then walks outside and goes on the north side of the line of hoops and sits down in a straight line with and facing the hoops. The singer then sits here in the rear of the room in a straight line with the patient [one-sung-over] whom he faces from here. [C] He then puts the locust [mixture] in his mouth and walks out, steps over the feathers that are stuck in crossing each other, and sits down, facing the patient [one-sung-over], at the last hoop [at this end].

[D] With the locust [mixture] just mentioned he blows four times in through the hoops and, while he too carries a pair of talking prayersticks in his hand he goes through the said fuzzy hoop, and stepping over each mountain he continues on through all of them to the farther end where he steps out to the north side [of one-sung-over]. [E] In the usual sunwise fashion he then moves the talking prayersticks around the patient [one-sung-over] and places them into his right hand. [F] Then [the latter] proceeds on over the said snakes and mountains and through the hoops, all the while being covered with a buckskin. As he passes through each hoop the singer draws the robe back a little, and [G] removes it from him as soon as he has passed through the fuzzy one. He then steps over all the pairs of feathers to the doorway which he enters. [H] He then steps with his right foot first on the footprints there, then with his left, then right and left foot. [I] And after encircling the sun figure in the customary sunwise fashion he sits down on the north side of it. [J] The said hoops are then brought inside and, after covering the sun with a buckskin, they are laid on this [in a circle], into which the patient then steps. He sits with his chest facing the east, while the singer sits in front of him then begins the prayer for him.[16]

The prayer is a *ch'ééhóyátééh* prayer set in four parts, one part is said on each of the four consecutive performances of the hoop transformation ceremony. Each part has the structure, Q R S T S T V. (SMGH # 1)[17]

In light of the hoop transformation ceremony which is an integral part of the prayer act, the significance of the prayer text is much illuminated. The structure of the ritual acts which are involved in passing the one-sung-over through the hoops is clearly parallel to a major portion of the prayer text. The prayer describes the journey of Talking God over the obstacles which guard the home of the ugly one as he moves to rescue the life form of the one suffering from its captivity there. The return journey is directed to the home of the one suffering. Its conclusion will result in a return to health and blessing. In the hoop ceremony a parallel journey of recovery is performed by the singer, moving over feathers, through hoops, over mountains, and finally over snakes to reach the one-sung-over who sits behind the snakes. All of these objects are obstacles

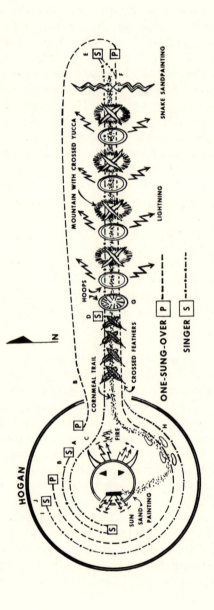

FIGURE 1

Diagram of Hoop Ceremonial Process

to the one-sung-over's returning home. The singer enacts a gesture of recovery which gets the one-sung-over on his feet and oriented in the direction of return. Then during the return the one-sung-over is transformed back to his former condition signified by the progressive removal of a cloth or hide covering as he proceeds through the hoops.

There are a number of further things suggested by the prayer text in the context of the ritual acts of the hoop ceremony. While the prayer text and the hoop transformation acts are parallel, they are not simply two expressions of the same event. The prayer text is not a step by step description of the act of going through the hoops. The prayer does not appear to be the score or script of a drama nor is it recited while the ritual acts are being performed. The prayer text is part of the constituency of the hoop transformation rite and as such provides a unique contribution to the significance of the ceremonial.

In the ritual process the transformation is effected by a complex set of elements. The one-sung-over is presented as a captive in the home of some evil one, by being positioned behind the snakes whose crossed bodies serve as ominous door guards. All of the mountains, hoops, feathers, and other materials are seemingly uncrossable obstacles to the pitiable sufferer. The singer, approaching through the channel provided by the path of cornmeal, encounters the series of obstacles. The singer stops and blows a mixture of locust medicine through the hoops. With medicine and the talking prayersticks, the singer is able to cross the obstacles and rescue the one-sung-over. Upon the return the obstacles have become transformed from the ominous objects they were to benevolent objects that are essential to the transformation.

The ceremony is repeated a total of four times, with the recitation of each of the four parts of *ch'ééhoyáteeh* corresponding to the four directions. Each journey concludes with the one-sung-over sitting in the ceremonial hogan with the hoops stacked around him as he recites the prayer. The prayer recapitulates and describes the rescue journey enacted through the ritual acts. But upon careful observation the prayer describes a journey to the four directions and to the home of "the one first to die at the time of emergence, the ugly thing, the ghost,"[18] which is in the lower worlds. The prayer enacts a rescue from the lower worlds and associates witchcraft with these regions by explicitly describing the barriers to the home of the ghosts as "the witchery of the ugly thing" but the entrance to these lower regions is found not in the center of the world but at its rim in each of the four directions.

The hoops surrounding the one-sung-over during the prayer recitation may represent the levels of the lower worlds through which the prayer "talks" the one praying. This interpretation recalls the earlier suggestion of an interrelationship between the *ha'áyátééh* and *ch'ééhóyátééh* prayers. It suggests that the transformation enacted in the hoop prayer ceremony is modeled upon the emergency paradigm of the transformations which were experienced in sacred history as the way was made to the earth surface. The hoops would be homologous with the reeds and columns through which the emergence was made, as well as with the designation of world levels.[19]

The hoops and the talking prayersticks appear to be essential to the hoop transformation ceremony. The wide range of meanings associated with the hoops has heretofore been largely ignored by students of this ceremony.[20] Yet in the context of the third day of Shootingway, Reichard indicates that the blue hoops represented the Yellow Snake People and the red willow hoops represented the Black Snake People.[21] In her comparative material from Big Starway she indicates that the hoops "represent conveyances and stars."[22] Beyond this, a survey of the mythology reveals a variety of associations with hoops. The significance of the decorations of hoops is very complex, perhaps on an order similar to the prayersticks. The decorations include faces that identify the hoops as "Holy People" who are probably connected with the relevant mythology.

The hoops are prepared by tying long withes into circles with cords explicitly called unraveling cords. At the conclusion of the hoop ceremony the hoops are unraveled.[23] The associations of this act with release, liberation, and exorcism have been discussed at length in chapter 7.

The wood of which the hoops are made is specified for each day of the ceremonial performance. In some mythological accounts the varieties of wood are identified with the four trees or bushes under which the protagonist slept on each of the four nights he was in the form of a coyote.[24] With this association the hoops recall the pitiable condition of the lost person before the retransformation and the shelter and protection he had found.

The other primary ritual object is the talking prayerstick bundle.[25] The talking prayersticks provide the power of movement in the prayers bridging the gap between the earth surface and other worlds. Without the talking prayersticks the singer could not pass through the hoops to rescue the one-sung-over, nor could the one-sung-over pass back through the hoops to be retransformed. They represent the power of movement and of action, a fundamental necessity of this class of prayer acts.

This analysis of the *ch'ééhóyátééh* prayer act has shown that it is an act of transformation, but that the transformation is actually a retransformation designed to realign the outer and inner forms of the one suffering so that health and a state of blessing may be restored. The prayer text and the ritual acts are divided into two parts to accomplish these necessary elements. The text describes a rescue and recovery journey (Q, R, and S) while the ritual process enacts an outward transformation to rid one of the foreign influence. Then the reintegration is described in the prayer (T, G) while the ritual enacts the association of the one-sung-over with Sun. The prayer text and the ritual process conclude with all things in their proper places, enjoying a state of blessing.

It is significant that Coyote is so strongly associated with the hoop ceremony for he is the one whose place in the world is not fixed. Ambivalent at best he runs both at night and day. Coyote was associated with the month of October during the creation of months since it was half in summer, half in winter.[26] During the emergence events Coyote was able to transform himself into any color so that he could take on any disguise and, therefore, go any place.[27] Coyote is often depicted in ceremonial occasions as standing near the door so that he may ally himself with either side.[28] The name given to Coyote, *mą'ii,* "roamer," was given to him because he has no particular place.[29] Throughout Navajo thought Coyote presents a threat to order, health, and beauty, but this threat is essential to life, health, and beauty.

It has been shown that the structure of *ch'ééhóyátééh* prayer acts differs little from the *ha'ayátééh* prayer acts. The retransformation, for which the prayers are characteristic, retains the basic structure of the rescue journey. In the prayer act it is the ritual context of the prayer text that transforms the rescue journey into an act of retransformation.

The degree to which the significance of the Liberation prayer is adaptable to a variety of pragmatic situations without radically changing its structure can be readily demonstrated in a *ch'ééhóyátééh* prayer which was recorded in Blessingway in the story of the abduction of the children of

Rock Crystal Talking God by Changing Wóman when she took them to her home to teach them Blessingway. Rock Crystal Talking God utilized ceremonial means to attempt to gain their liberation and this included the recitation of a *ch'ééhóyátééh* prayer in making an offering at the place where he found the footprints of his children.[30] The journey sequence in this prayer begins at the home of Rock Crystal Talking God and proceeds to the center of the cornfield to the footprints of the children. The prayer does not effect a rescue and liberation but rather the delivery of an offering in anticipation of an act of reciprocity which will result in the liberation and return of the children.

The journey is not only to be restorative to the children, but to Rock Crystal Talking God as well, for upon his return to his home the prayer says,

> Since Talking God, my granduncle, says so
> I have definitely returned to my feet,
> I have returned to my legs,
> I have returned to my travel power,
> I have returned to my body,
> I have returned to my mind.
> I have returned to my voice.[31]

This appears to extend the function of the prayer beyond the rescue and return of the lost means of health to the person suffering. Here the person is not looking for his own means of life, the instanding one, but that of his offspring, the product of his powers of generation. This tends to expand the notion of health as presented in prayer beyond the concern for physical health to the concern for the powers of creation. This is very consistent with Blessingway ideology.

In this very brief discussion of the Blessingway Liberation prayer act, we observe that while the prayer text retains the same basic Liberation prayer structure, it can address the very specific needs of a wide variety of situations in which it may be performed.

The structure of the prayer act remains identified with a rescue journey which is inseparable from connotations of the lower worlds, of ghosts, and of death. But these associations simply add to the significance of the prayer, for were it not for the return of the children who bring with them the knowledge of Blessingway the entire world would remain forever in disarray, since no means for the acquisition of blessing, of putting things in their proper places, would exist.

CONCLUSION

The notable characteristics of Liberation prayer acts are their shamanic journey structure, their length and elaborateness, their adaptability to almost any ritual context, and their recitation occurring only in times of most dire need. Surely they stand as one of the most significant events in Navajo oral tradition or in that of any other people.

An analysis of the relevant mythology has indicated that the events which surround the first death in the postemergence period provide the basis for the general structure of the prayer. In this analysis it was suggested that the basic division between *ha'áyátééh* prayers and *ch'éébóyátééh* prayers stems from an original prayer set with a two part structure. Further, it was found that all of the prayers of this class are characterized by a journey of rescue, distinctive to the prayer class structure, and that this journey is practically inseparable from connotations with the rescue of one lost in the lower world homes of the ghosts.

In the ceremonial and mythological contexts, this rescue from the homes of the ghosts was found to be an exceptional use of the prayer, and is not found as an integral part of any ceremonial practice. It is used on special request and then only when all medicines and other practices have failed. When used, the prayer is surrounded with precaution and Navajos consider it to be among the most powerful ritual acts which can be performed.

The Liberation prayer adapts the journey of rescue from the land of the ghosts to the ritual of the hoop transformation ceremony in order to return the sufferer to his former condition. The journey takes place in horizontal directions to the world's rim where entrance is gained to the homes of the malevolent ones below the rim. The emphasis is shifted from rescue to transformation. The theme of the rescue, which is strongly oriented toward Uglyway practices, is transformed to a focus upon the expulsion of the malevolence as represented by the skin of coyote. In this shift some Holyway ideology is introduced in the notion that the Holy People represented by the hoops assist in the transformation.

Finally, ideology akin to Holyway and Blessingway can emerge in this class of prayer acts when they are adapted for the Blessingway context. The prayer is used to make an offering to Holy People to gain the return of the lost children. The journey sequence is still retained but is accompanied with the acquisition of blessing at every step in both directions. This prayer results in the adaptation of the journey sequence to communicate a Blessingway message. While the journey retains the appearance of the rescue of the children, it is clear throughout that the children are in no real danger unless their father fails to show the proper respect for Changing Woman by giving her an offering of jewels. Furthermore, Rock Crystal Talking God is aware from the outset that his compliance with the system of reciprocity will benefit him by both the return of his children and by the acquisition of the knowledge and control of Blessingway.

NOTES

1. Haile, "Upward-Reaching Way," pp. 417-18.

2. Leland C. Wyman and Flora L. Bailey affirmed this distinction in their discussion of the Upward Reachingway ceremonial, *Navaho Upward-Reaching Way: Objective Behavior Rationale and Sanction*, University of New Mexico Bulletin, Anthropology Series, vol. 4 (Albuquerque, 1943), pp. 42-43.

3. This information was obtained from singers on the western side of the Navajo Reservation during field research in the summer of 1973.

4. Haile, *Creation and Emergence Myth*, p. 6.

5. Ibid., pp. 37-38.

6. See Gill, *A Theory of Navajo Prayer Acts*, pp. 310-16 for a description of the contexts.

7. See a discussion of this event in chapter 8.

8. Haile, "Upward-Reaching Way," p. 413.

9. Ibid.

10. Washington Matthews, "The Prayer of a Navaho Shaman," *American Anthropologist* 1 (1888): 149-70.

11. Wheelwright, *Great Star Chant*, p. 52.

12. Ibid., p. 56.

13. For further examples and discussion of the hoop transformation rite see Haile, *Legend of the Ghostway Ritual*, pp. 70-71 and 83-89; Wyman, *Red Antway*, pp. 136-60; Reichard, *Navaho Religion*, pp. 649-57; Wyman and Bailey, *Upward-Reaching Way*, pp. 27-32; Leland C. Wyman, "Snakeskins and Hoops," *Plateau* 39 (1966): 4-25; and Haile, *Creation and Emergence Myth*, p. 120. See Gill, *Songs of Life*, Plates XXII and XXIII for related iconography.

14. Haile, *Legend of the Ghostway Ritual,* p. 64.

15. Ibid., p. 84.

16. Ibid., pp. 86-88.

17. Ibid., pp. 106-24.

18. Ibid., p. 93.

19. This does not contradict Reichard's interpretation that the hoops stacked in a flat position "restrict territory to a manageable space, a zone of safety" (*Navaho Religion,* p. 546), since the emergence reeds were the original zones of safety.

20. See Gill, *A Theory of Navajo Prayer Acts,* pp. 355-56.

21. Reichard, *Navaho Religion,* p. 656.

22. Ibid., p. 657.

23. For example, see Wyman and Bailey, *Upward-Reaching Way,* p. 33.

24. Ibid., p. 31, n.65.

25. See the discussion of prayersticks in chapter 9.

26. Wheelwright, *Navaho Creation Myth,* pp. 65-66.

27. Wheelwright, *Emergence Myth According to the Hanelthnayhe,* p. 4.

28. Reichard, *Navaho Religion,* p. 423.

29. Wheelwright, *Emergence Myth According to the Hanelthnayhe,* p. 45.

30. Wyman, *Blessingway,* pp. 266-67.

31. Ibid., p. 268.

CHAPTER ELEVEN

PROTECTION PRAYER ACTS

One class of prayer acts is distinguished for its purpose of procuring protection against an attack upon the health of the one praying. The Navajo term for the texts in this class is *ach'ah sodizin,* and they have the structure (A) . . . (G) L (N).

While the largest incidence of these prayers occurs in special prayer ceremonies performed outside of major ceremonials, they may still be associated with Holyway, Uglyway, and Lifeway ceremonials through the identification of the kind of impending danger for which protection is being sought.

Protection prayer acts are part of the Holyway and Uglyway ritual processes, where they are used to prepare and place ritual objects. Protection prayers are uttered at the ritual collection of sticks in preparation for the fire poker rite during which the participants step over poker sticks pointing in each cardinal direction radiating out from the central fire. Protection prayers are also said in Holyway ceremonials in a ritual "facing around" of sacred objects on an earthen mound constructed outside the ceremonial hogan. On four consecutive days ritual objects representing Holy People are placed on this mound. The first three days they are placed facing the ceremonial hogan, but on the fourth day they are turned around to face away from the ceremonial hogan. At the setting-out of these objects on the fourth day a Protection prayer is intoned.

Protection prayer ceremonies are enacted in numerous cultural situations. Any recognition of the violation of a taboo or restriction, any of a number of warning signs or omens, and certain dreams or imaginations may suggest to a person that he is subject to attack which would cause suffering. Such a situation would require the immediate performance of protective measures.[1] The associated mythology is extensive.

PROTECTION PRAYER AT THE COLLECTION OF POKERS

White Singer told Father Berard of the poker collection in Male Shootingway Holyway.

Somewhere in the Jemez range Thunder had shattered him [Holy Young Man] to pieces and that same Thunder had restored him to life again. At the time a five-night ceremonial was planned for his benefit and the various plants were chosen for the emetic, and various sticks for the pokers. The latter were broken off from the cardinal points of a tree, at the base of which a jewel offering had been placed with this prayer:

B	Who drops down with clouds, dark thunder, young man chief,

C	I have made your offering, I have prepared a smoke for you;

F	This day I have become your child, this day I have become your grandchild; Just as I say to you, you shall act, just as you say to me, I shall act;

L	You will watch over me, you will stand up to protect me, you will raise your hand to protect me, you will speak up to protect me; may no harm come to me from streams under trees; may no harm come to me from under plants;

may no harm come to me from passing winds; may no
harm come to me from passing rains; may no harm come
to me from passing lightning;

V
May dew continue to form for me; may pollen continue to
form for me; may paths at my front be pleasant, may
paths in my rear be pleasant; may I be long life, may I be
happiness;
Pleasant again it has become, pleasant again it has become.

[Three parallel prayers follow naming, "With whom water drops time and
again, blue thunder, young woman chief," "With whom mist drops time
and again, yellow thunder, young man chief," "With whom summer drops
time and again, glittering thunder, young woman chief" with certain
phrase alterations associated with the second and fourth prayers.]
(SMHH # 1)[2]

The pokers are important ritual objects to a fulfillment of the desires
stated in the Protection prayer. The pokers are associated with the
Thunders named in the prayer and with the cardinal directions. Beyond
these poker associations are others which contribute to the significance
of this prayer act. These may be revealed in an examination of the fire
poker rite.

On the morning of the first day of the Shootingway ceremonial, after
the ritual objects are placed upon the mound outside the hogan, emetic
materials are prepared and the fire is ceremonially started. The emetic
pot is placed on the fire, and at each of the cardinal directions on the floor
surrounding the fire a snake sandpainting is prepared. Each one is distinct,
but all four have their heads toward the fire.[3]

The singer then gives a pinch of thunder charcoal to the one who had
brought the pokers. This he puts in his mouth, stands along[side] the
entrance and the singer then intones:
He who encircles the earth has arrived, him I obey,
the earth I am encircling, I am holy.
The assistant sticks the poker intended for the east side into the fire, then
blows upon it with that thunder charcoal, places it alongside south of the
snake lying along the east, then stands along the west.

He who encircles the mountain has arrived, him I obey,
I am encircling the mountain, I am holy.

Then again he pokes it into the fire, blows that thunder charcoal on its surface, then places the stick on the snake's north side and proceeds to the south side. [This procedure continues on through all four sides.] [4]

As the one-sung-over and the others enter, they step over the snake figures and pokers before taking their seats in preparation for the emetic rite. [5]
    Father Berard noted that

Some legends explain that snakes in the form of beautiful young men and women enter the hogan and lay [sic] at the fireside with their heads toward the fire. The pokers [and figures if any] represent these snakes. [6]

A Navajo told Kluckhohn and Wyman that the "pokers represent men who chase evil away,"[7] and with reference to the ritual act of stepping over the snake figures and pokers they report:

The patient [one-sung-over] and then every participant, individually, walks around the fire four times . . . stepping over the pokers [and snake paintings] right foot first. In the beginning a participant who stepped over left foot first stumbled, and as a result he sickened and died, so now the right foot comes first . . . moreover evil spirits step left foot first. . . . Evil spirits cannot cross the pokers and so the participant gets away from them.

On evidence from Big Starway, Hailway, and Shootingway, Gladys Reichard found that "pokers are symbols of the danger line in the sweat-emetic rite."[9] She discussed this danger line, 'ach'qh hoodzoh (literally, line of protection) as an important concept in the ceremonial aspects of war. Lines were drawn upon the ground representing lightning and other weather-related phenomena to prevent the enemy from crossing into Navajo territory.[10]
    Against this understanding of the protection value of pokers and their ritual use in Navajo ceremonials, it is clear why protection should be sought in the prayer act at the collection of the poker sticks. The pokers become "lines of protection" strongly associated with the active powers of the Thunders and weather-related phenomena, so that they are not

only boundary lines, but armed lines of defense. In the origin myth for Shootingway, Holy Young Man had learned Shootingway after being subjected to the shattering power of Thunder, who upon restoring him gave him the knowledge of Shootingway and consequently the powers held by Thunder. The collection, placement, and act of stepping over the pokers all carry out the intentions of the Protection prayer which is said at the collection of the pokers. It asks the Thunders to accept the offering made to them and in return to provide the one praying with protection from the threatening dangers. The pokers represent that protection and their placement around the fire establishes the requested "line of protection." The ritual of stepping over the pokers serves to place the one-sung-over on the proper side, the side of protection.

PROTECTION PRAYER AT THE "FACING AROUND" OF THE UPRIGHT SET-OUT

The other major occasion for a Protection prayer act in the rites of preparation is on the occasion of the "facing around" of the ritual objects at the mound constructed outside the ceremonial hogan. Father Berard has recorded a description of this rite in Navajo Windway.[11]

The "facing around" occurs on the fourth and last day of placing the objects on the mound. The ritual objects representing Holy People are faced east, away from the ceremonial hogan. The placement is done to the setting-out songs.

According to this I go about, guided by earth I go about,
    chief long life, chief happiness are my guide as I go about.
Sky [is my guide] , chief long life, chief happiness is my guide.
[Continuing as above naming Mountain Woman, Water Wom-
    an, Darkness, Dawn, Talking God, White Corn, Yellow
    Corn, Pollen, Ripener and ending as follows.]
In my rear it is pleasant, at my front it is pleasant,
    below me it is pleasant, above me it is pleasant,
    in all my surroundings it is pleasant, my speech
    extends out beautiful. As I am chief long life,
    chief happiness.

Then after sprinkling pollen or cornmeal upon the ritual objects, the Protection prayer is said.

B Dark Wind youth chief, who stands upon the dawn,

L This day you shall stand in my protection, you shall hold your hand out in my protection, at your rear I shall [always] be spared.

F This day, as you speak, I shall act right according to that! This day, right as I again speak to you, you shall act right accordingly! This day I shall act right according to your way of thinking about me! This day you shall act just in accordance with what I think about you! This day I have become your child, this day I have become your grandchild!

G This day [the means] which cause fear to extend from you, those same shall cause fear to extend from me! This day [the means] which make your surroundings dangerous, those same shall [also] make my surroundings dangerous! This day [the means] which make you at ease, those same shall also make me at ease! This day [the means] which make your body cool, those same shall also make my body cool! This day [the means] which cause pleasant [conditions] in your front, those same shall also make it pleasant at my front! This day [the means] which cause pleasant [conditions] in your rear, those same shall make it pleasant in my rear!

V Pleasant again it has become, pleasant again it has become!

[It is repeated three times naming "Blue wind maiden chief, who stands upon the dawn," "One who goes along licking pollen, youth chief," and

"One who goes along shaking pollen, maiden chief," with the last prayer being concluded with an elaborately expanded Unit V passage.] (WNW #6)[12]

An important point in the performance of this setting-out rite is the change which is effected in the ritual process of the first three performances of the rite. At this fourth setting-out the changes are the reversal of the directional orientation of the ritual objects, the singing of a different song, and the added recitation of the Protection prayer.

In Navajo Windway the mound is called "dawn mountain," hence the phrase "who stands upon the dawn" in the prayer, and the ritual objects, which are four wide boards (tsin 'iisteel), represent the Dark, Blue, Yellow, and White Winds. Talking prayersticks representing the Snake People are placed between them. Father Berard discussed the significance of changing the directional orientation of the ritual objects in his notes on Male Shootingway Holyway.

Gray Man does not explain why this is done. However, if we consult the text of White Singer, especially the ceremonies of the fourth morning . . . , we may glean the importance of this "facing around" procedure. Singer and patient [one-sung-over] alone perform this final performance at the improvised mound. The song which the singer intones on this morning is a so-called twelve word song with the significant burden: . . . this [or these] is my guide in life, this guides me as I go about. . . . The patient [one-sung-over] is dependent on them [those named in the song] for his well being, no matter where he travels.[13]

Thus the "facing around" serves to garner the powers upon which a person depends for his health and life as he prepares to leave the ceremonial environment and travel forth into the world.

This interpretation may be extended by considering the Protection prayer uttered at the "facing around." It names the ones represented by the wide boards and calls for them to "stand in my protection," forming a "line of protection" facing toward the attacking enemy. The song of the setting-out identifies those who are one's guides in life, while the prayer calls upon them for protection.

PROTECTION PRAYERS IN SPECIAL PRAYER CEREMONIES

Protection prayer acts commonly occur as special prayer ceremonies. They occur before the anticipated onset of illness and the subsequent need for a major ceremonial. Several of these prayer ceremonies were recorded by Father Berard in connection with the mythology of Male Shootingway Uglyway. Generally these prayer acts emphasize the armor of the Holy People who are called upon to form a "line of protection" for the one praying. The ritual process of these prayer ceremonies is adapted from the larger ceremonials with which they are associated.

The distinctive aspects of these prayer acts can be shown in an example of a special prayer ceremony associated with Male Shootingway Uglyway called the "bath below a thunder-struck tree."

When a request is made for the *bath below a thunderstruck tree,* one collects herbs around a thunderstruck tree, which are put into an ordinary clay pot of water. For this unraveling also is done on the same side [of the tree] towards the hogan, with a collection of herbs ordinarily employed by unravelings. One blade of wide leafed yucca is added to each bundle, of which any number, either five or seven, are employed. In this case unraveling is done first. After all is finished the unraveling bundles are laid below the said thunderstruck tree on the side away from the hogan. Now finally one applies the above mentioned foot liniment to him, then the patient [one-sung-over] drinks some and bathes himself with it. Then he dresses himself again and now the singer begins a prayer [while the one-sung-over holds a branch from the tree].

B Dark thunder young man chief,

E today I desire your assistance,

With your dark flint shoes you will rise in my defense,
L with the zigzag lightnings that have two dark flint points and flash out with these from the tip of your toes you will rise in my defense.
With your dark flint leggings . . . from the tips of your knees. . . .

With your dark flint garment . . . from the tip of your
   body. . . .
With your dark flint hat . . . from the tip of your head. . . .
You will rise in my protection with your mind that terrifies,
   you will rise in my defense with your voice that terrifies!
With your dark shield that is white dotted in the center and
   through which dark thunder lies you will rise to defend
   me! With lightning crashes that surround it in four places
   you will rise to defend me! With the dark hail that slides
   around it in four places you will rise to defend me.

Then the witchery of the ugly thing, its dart, its magic power

N   shall not reach me, and it did not reach me!
The witchery of the ugly thing has gone from me, its witchery
   has gone back upon it, its witchery has returned down into
   its interior.
It was lockjawed right there with its former witchery, it closed
   its eyes with its witchery, it became motionless with its
   former witchery, it did not move, it did not move, monster
   missed me, monster missed me,
I am safe, I am safe, I am safe, I am safe at last, may my winters be many!

[Three other prayers parallel to this one name Blue thunder young woman
chief, Yellow thunder young man chief, and Pink thunder young woman
with corresponding changes in color designations. (SMGH # 4).]

Following the prayer recitation, in a direction toward the hogan at some
distance feathers are stuck up in four places crossing each other with
fronts turned away from the hogan. Over these the patient [one-sung-
over] steps, right foot first, then also all others in turn step over them,
the singer last, and back of him again the one that swings the groaning
stick continues to swing it as he steps over them and picks them up right
there. And while the singer sings a song all enter the hogan. That finishes
that ceremony again.[14]

   The prayer act focuses upon the acquisition of protection against specific dangers, in this case the "witchery of the ugly thing." This prayer is

concluded with a statement of acquired safety (N) and not the common statement of acquired blessing (V), as was the case in the Holyway Protection prayers. Here the structure of the prayer is transformed to accommodate its association with the Uglyway context. The purpose of the Protection prayer is modified or tailored to specifically meet the needs of the situation at hand, which is to prevent the attack of a native ghost. The focus shifts to maintaining a state of blessing rather than regaining one already lost.

CONCLUSION

The several texts examined in this class of Protection prayers are similar in constituent structure. They share the purpose of preventing illness by the acquisition of protection. The analysis of several Protection prayer acts has shown how extensively the significance of this prayer act can change, with little alteration in the structure of the prayer text, when it is recited in a variety of accompanying ritual and mythology.

NOTES

1. Leland C. Wyman, Willard W. Hill, and Iva Osanai, *Navajo Eschatology*, University of New Mexico Bulletin, Anthropology Series, vol. 4 (Albuquerque, 1942), pp. 25 and 35.
2. Haile, *Prayer Stick Cutting*, pp. 77-80.
3. Ibid., pp. 113-22.
4. Ibid., pp. 123-25.
5. Ibid., p. 126.
6. Ibid., pp. 43-44.
7. Kluckhohn and Wyman, *Navaho Chant Practice*, p. 84.
8. Ibid., p. 86.
9. Reichard, *Navaho Religion*, p. 581.
10. Ibid., pp. 545-47.
11. Wyman, *Windways*, pp. 202-5. See Gill, *Songs of Life*, Plate XXIV for set-out iconography.
12. Wyman, *Windways*, pp. 202-5.
13. Haile, *Prayer Stick Cutting*, p. 73.
14. Haile, *Legend of the Ghostway Ritual*, pp. 271-76.

CHAPTER TWELVE

REMAKING PRAYER ACTS

The rather surprising purpose of one class of prayer acts is to remake, redress, and restore Holy People (I). This class has the structure (A) (B) I (J) (T) (U) (V). These prayer acts occur in remaking rites, *análnééh*, which include the carving and depositing of a figurine. On the basis of the analysis of the prayer constituent structure alone, it seems that the prayer utterance is motivated by the belief that the predicament suffered is due to an injury inflicted upon a Holy Person. The reparation is made by remaking, in the form of a figurine, the life form or vitality of the afflicted Holy Person and returning it to the Holy Person.

In a monograph entitled *Navaho Sacrificial Figurines*, Father Berard described the remaking rites in detail, including thirty-two variations of the figurine rite and the accompanying prayer texts.[1] Nearly all of these versions are associated with animals. In general, he described the rite as a "minor ceremonial, at which the figure of a doll, but chiefly of animals is reproduced."[2] He said that it is performed in order to right misdemeanors which "generally refer to injuries inflicted upon animals, . . . [and that the] figurine complex seems again to emphasize that the offender has not so much injured or abused the animal form as he has the human or super-natural form of the animal in question."[3] This is corroborated by the more recent statement of Hosteen Jimmie who said that the mechanism of transmission of the illness is "the supernatural within whom and under whose direction the doll or animal exists."[4]

The remaking rite is primarily interested in the inner life form, or life principle, of animals which is conceived as being in human-like form. Consequently all figurines are carved in human-like form and decorated with jewels, fabrics, and paint in order to give them specific identity.

Father Berard's book is largely composed of the texts of the prayers said in the figurine rites. While he presented over fifty prayer texts, he devoted but half a page to the interpretation of these prayers.[5]

PRAYER ACT TO REMAKE THE RATTLESNAKE

During the summer of 1973, a situation was related to me which involved a diagnosis calling for the "remaking rite" *(análnééh)*, which can be used as the basis for an analysis of the prayer act. A twenty-three year old Navajo man in the Cow Springs area of the Navajo Reservation had been suffering from pains in his back for some time. He attended peyote meetings occasionally with his family, although he was not a regular peyotist. In one of these meetings his trouble was diagnosed as stemming from his having killed a rattlesnake a couple of years previously. He indicated that he had cut off the rattles and carried them for some time. He said that during the peyote meeting the diagnosis was clear when a rattlesnake moved around the room above the heads of the people. He said that although he could only hear it, others could see it. It stopped above his head. Those present interpreted this for him and recommended that he have the traditional Navajo rite to "remake the snake" sung for him.[6]

Father Berard described a remaking rite for the rattlesnake, differing from other remaking rites only in detail. The figurine and its accompanying prayerstick are prepared as a part of the ceremony during which a set of songs is sung.

> For young man traveler on rocks one has recently laid it down.
> A dark stick one has just laid down for him,
> A fine jet one has just laid down for him,

Fine small birds one has just laid down for him,
A fine down one has just laid down for him,
A fine cotton cord one has just laid down for him,
Fine pollen one has just laid down for him,
It's the earth surface young man whose feet, whose legs,
    whose body, whose mind, whose voice shall be exchanged
    for them, [therefore] one has just now placed these for him.

This song is repeated for young woman traveler on rocks. Then it is repeated for each of the pair totaling finally nine verses. The other verses
incorporate the following phrase changes: (2) Recently one is preparing
it for him, (3) Recently one has prepared it for him, (4) Recently he has
picked it up, (5) Recently he held it up, (6) Recently they have carried
it away for its benefit, (7) They have put it down for it, (8) He came
upon [found] it, (9) He is glad [satisfied].[7]

When the figurine and prayerstick are prepared, the singer strews
pollen upon them while saying a pollen prayer. He hands them in a cloth
to the one-sung-over, who holds them while he recites with the singer
the prayer for the figurine.

B Who travels with his body, young man,

Properly I have restored your former condition,
I   Your feet . . . [legs, body, mind, voice] I remade for you.
I have made white bead to be your feet . . . [legs, body,
   mind, voice] again.
I have redressed you in a fine white bead. . . . [turquoise,
   abalone, jet, variegated jewels]
Into pollen I have remade your feet . . . [legs, body, mind,
   voice, headplume],
Because of pollen you are invisible, thus I have remade you.
In collected waters . . . [water's child, dark cloud, he rain,
    dark mist, she rain, zigzag lightning, straight lightning,
    sunray, rainbow, reflected sunred] I have redressed you.
Collected water pollen, with this I have remade your intestines,
By this means alive again I have made you.

By this means you have moved again,
By this means you took leave.

From my home's rear corner you took leave,
J At the center of the room in my home you took leave,
In my home at the fireside you took leave,
At the side corners of my home you took leave,
At my home's entrance you took leave,
At the trail that starts away from my home you took leave,
At trails leading away from my hogan you took leave,
Along a trail on rainbow, along a trail on pollen you took
    leave.
Where your home first came into view you have arrived,
At your home's entrance you have returned.
Into the blue rock home you have returned.
Into the blue rock room you have returned.
Into the trail where pollen lies here and there you have re-
    entered, yonder in the rear of the room upon a floor of
    pollen you have returned.

To your father you have returned, to your mother [brothers,
T sisters, neighbors, chief] you returned, thanks that you
    returned to us you were told.
Your father reclaimed you as a relative, you reclaimed your
    father as a relative. . . .

Here on our side whatever conditions there are on earth,
U dark clouds that come from time to time, he rains that
    come at times, of these you told them, tobacco that
    originates from time to time, its dew, its pollen that forms,
    of these you told them.
They on their side, whatever conditions are on earth, of this
    you were told, of dark mists that form, of the rains that
    form, of these you were told, of tobacco that comes into
    being, of its dew and pollen that form, of these you were
    told.
In that event he shall recover, what previously bothered him
    right there it shall disappear, right there it shall fade away.

Conditions are identical on both sides, that's clear, now in
   peace he shall continue to live,

Pleasant again it has come to be, pleasant again it has come
V   to be, pleasant again it has come to be, pleasant again it
   has come to be. (SFH #21)[8]

Following this prayer another must be said for the prayerstick. It is identical in structure to the prayers which are recited in the prayerstick rites of Holyway ceremonials discussed in chapter 9.

In the Remaking prayer the name of the rattlesnake (B) is given as "who travels with his body" *(bits'íís yee nagháhí)*, the name of the inner life form, rather than "rattlesnake," *(tł'iish' áníníígíí),* the ordinary reference to the snake form. The remaking and redressing passage (I) begins by telling the snake that it has been restored to its former conditions by a process of remaking its feet, legs, body, mind, and voice, which is then described in detail. First, as described in the prayer, the body form is made of white bead. The details of the human form are designated by the placement of various jewels at the critical parts of the body of the figurine. Then, the prayer goes on to say, the form is made invisible by an application of pollen. This corresponds to the ritual act of covering the carved figurine with pollen. Finally, the prayer describes the dressing of the figurine with a number of weather-related phenomena. This corresponds to the placement of jewels (other than the ones associated with the powers of movement), fabrics, and paint upon the figurine.[9]

The emphasis of this passage is upon the re-creation of the former condition of the inner life form of the snake, an act which requires an exemplar in mythology. The Navajo, Tom Ration, suggested that the paradigm for making the inner form of the doll lies in the clan origin myth which describes the first Navajos arising as corn people from human-like forms of cornmeal prepared by the Holy People.[10] The creation acts in clan origin myths are a part of Blessingway mythology. They are largely modeled upon the acts of creation which took place after the emergence from the lower worlds in the first no-sleep ceremony which was performed for the purpose of making and placing the inner life forms of things which were to exist on the earth surface.[11] The ritual process of creating and preparing the inner life forms which is described in the

Blessingway creation stories is quite similar to the ritual process of carving, dressing, and depositing the figurine and to the prayer passage (I) which describes this process. The primary difference is that in the remaking rite the concern is with *re*storing, *re*making, and *re*dressing to provide a restoration to a former condition.

To this point in the analysis of the prayer act, the inner life form of the Holy Person (the rattlesnake in this case) is prepared and given back the power of life and movement by the process of remaking and redressing on the pattern of creation mythology. In this way the inner life form is readied to return to its domain. This return corresponds to the deposit of the carved figurine. The Navajo term for deposit in the case of figurines is *naa'iinii*, which means "to return to its place of origin any item of trade or value,"[12] which supports the next passage of the prayer describing the journey by which the Holy Person returns to his home (J).

The prayer text ends with a passage concerning the equality and identity of both "sides" (U) and the resulting return of "pleasantness" (V). The prayer text clearly links the movement of the inner life form of the Holy Person back to its proper domain with the reinstatement of an identity or stasis between the domain of the Earth Surface People and the domain of the Holy People. The prayer text further states that this identity is necessary and sufficient for the sufferer to recover his health and for peace to come to him again. This suggests an interesting aspect of a notion which has been found to underlie most Navajo prayer acts. It is that health and blessing are not only dependent upon all things being in their proper places as ordained in the creation events of sacred history, but that they also depend upon maintaining an identity or association between "our side," the earth surface, and "their side," the domain of the Holy People. Since the inner life form, the instanding one, is closely related to the Holy People, this demonstrates the necessity of maintaining the proper relationship between the inner and outer forms.

The relationship between the figurine and the prayerstick which accompanies it may now be considered. The ceremony focuses upon the figurine, but the prayerstick is essential, and one corresponds with every figurine. The objective of the ritual process as described in prayer and in ritual action is to get the figurine or that which it represents to the "other side." As shown in Holyway prayers in chapter 9, the movement between sides is not open to all. The talking gods, represented primarily by prayersticks, have this power of movement and also the extraordinary power of speech. Thus it may be concluded that the prayerstick conveys the figurine to the "other side."

On the basis of the analysis, the purpose and meaning of the prayer act may be stated more precisely. The etiological theory holds that the sufferer is thought to have caused, or to have somehow been related to, a disorder in the proper placement of the inner life form of certain Holy People, resulting in an inequity between "sides"—the earth surface and the domain of the Holy People. The consequence of the inequity is manifest in the predicament suffered. The killing of a rattlesnake is seen as an unnecessary act. When a Navajo friend was asked why one should not kill a rattlesnake while it is acceptable to kill sheep, he responded that his mother had explained that rattlesnakes are not used for food or any other purpose by Navajos and, therefore, the killing of the rattlesnake should be avoided. The killing of the snake is recognized as a disruption of the "way" of the world, of the identity of the sides, and the one who is responsible for this disturbance may suffer as a result. The prayer act in the remaking rite communicates the intentions of the one praying and beseeches the one to whom he prays to make the proper response. The desired result, as communicated in the prayer act, is a reestablishment of the right order in the world and the consequent restoration of health and peace. There is clearly no exorcism in the true sense, which has been the only interpretation heretofore made of these prayers. The prayer act describes a positive act of remaking and redressing, not removing or expelling. The remaking rite is an act of creation, or re-creation, on the model of the original creation.

Father Berard's many descriptions of the figurines and prayersticks, the prayers for the figurines and the prayersticks, and the accompanying songs show how effectively this prayer act may be adapted to meet a wide range of situational needs.

HISTORICAL CONSIDERATIONS

The consensus has been that the remaking rite has had very strong Pueblo influence if it is not actually of Pueblo origin.[13] This argument rests on several points—the deposit of the doll figurine near ancient ruins, the use of a language for some songs in the ceremony which is not modern Navajo (although not identified as Pueblo), and the Pueblo use of *katcina* dolls and *tihu* figurines.[14] The argument based on the place of deposit cannot be conclusive, since the many figurine rites of the animals recorded by Father Berard designate a place of deposit associated with the animal. For example, the rattlesnake figurine is deposited "at the base of a greasewood bush or at a hole in the ground."[15] The argument based on language is not conclusive since the language could be ancient Navajo or a non-Pueblo language. Finally, there is clearly a basic difference in the purposes for making *katcina* dolls and *tihu* figurines and those for making Navajo figurines, since traditionally the Pueblo objects were made as baby dolls for children to play with and served pedagogical interests as well.

There is further evidence, on the basis of the religious ideology, for believing that even if the remaking rites have been influenced by Pueblo practices they bear a distinctive Navajo stamp. Navajos entered the predominantly agricultural American Southwest only a few centuries ago. Before that they were among hunting cultures who lived in the western Canadian region. In a study by David Brugge, it was shown that while Navajo people had become widely influenced by Puebloan cultures, in the mideighteenth century they rejected much of this influence and, in a nativistic movement, reasserted practices from their ancient Athapascan heritage. According to Brugge the formation of Blessingway was at the core of this effort.[16] Since it has been established here that the remaking rites are strongly dependent upon the creation paradigm of the mythology of Blessingway, then, if Brugge is correct, we may consider that the remaking rites are in continuity with this more ancient tradition. This insight into the history of Navajo thought suggests that the Navajo recognition of the inner life form as the power and means of life is basic to Navajo religious tradition and predates Pueblo influence. Further support for this notion is gained by examining a prayer act performed by Navajo hunters at the conclusion of the hunt. This assumes that the prayer stems from the Athapascan, as opposed to Puebloan, hunting traditions. This prayer contains a passage describing the return of the animal spirit to its home (J) which is parallel to a distinctive prayer passage in Remaking prayer texts. Before uttering the prayer the hunter breaks all of the bones of the first deer killed. He attaches a jewel to the horns of the deer and deposits these remains at the base of a cliff rose, a favorite food of the deer. Then he prays.

In the future that we may continue to hold each other with
F   the turquoise hand

Now that you may return to the place from which you came
J   In the future as time goes on that I may rely on you for food
To the home of the dawn you are starting to return
With the jet hoofs you are starting to return
By means of the zigzag lightning you are starting to return
By the evening twilight your legs are yellow
That way you are starting to return
By the white of dawn your buttocks are white and that way
    you are starting to return
A dark tail be in your tail and that way you are starting to
    return
A haze be in your fur and that way you are starting to return
A growing vegetation be in your ears and that way are you
    starting to return
A mixture of beautiful flowers and water be in your intestines
    and that way you are starting to return
May turquoise be in your liver and abalone shell the partition
    between your heart and intestines and that way are you
    starting to return
May red shell be your lungs and white shell be your windpipe
    and that way you are starting to return
May dark wind and straight lightning be your speech and that
    way you are starting to return
There you have returned within the interior of the jet basket
    in the midst of the beautiful flower pollens
Pleasantly you have arrived home

Pleasantly may you and I both continue to live
V   From this day you may lead the other game along the trails
    that I may hunt
Because I have obeyed all the restrictions laid down by your
    god in skinning you
Therefore I ask for this luck that I may continue to have good
    luck in hunting you. (SWH # 2)[17]

This prayer of the hunter is said to assure an abundance of game. The hunter's continuing supply of food is dependent upon the return of the animal's power and means of life to its home so that it will reproduce and continue to live. The return of this life force to its home is described in the prayer (J) including the association of its various body parts with jewels, weather-related phenomena, and vegetable matter. The successful return of the animal spirit and the future supply of game animals is dependent upon the hunter's careful observance of hunting practices and on properly dressing and using the game. This hunting prayer act shares with the figurine prayer act not only surface features but an underlying ideology, the identification of the power of life and movement with the association of jewels to vital body parts. The return of the power and life of the animal to its home is essential to the continuing health and life of the hunter. All but one of the remaking rites described by Father Berard are concerned with animals, yet none of these are game animals. It seems likely that the remaking rite grew out of the older Navajo hunter tradition which was not only concerned with the proper way to kill and skin game animals, but also with avoiding injuring or killing animals which were not considered game.

NOTES

1. The rite involving the figurine carving was previously described only in the Franciscan Fathers' *Dictionary*. Two articles, one by R. E. Kelly, and one by R. W. Lang and H. Walters, were published together as a booklet in 1972. This booklet renewed the interest in these rites by making available the compilation and summary of the descriptive data on figurines which have been found, new evidence concerning the use and practice of the rite, and an interpretation of the function and significance of the figurines and the rituals in which they appear.

2. Father Berard Haile, *Navaho Sacrificial Figurines* (Chicago: University of Chicago Press, 1947), p. 1.

3. Ibid., pp. 3-4.

4. R. W. Lang and Harry Walters, "The Remaking Rites of the Navaho: Causal Factors of Illness and Its Nature," in *Navaho Figurines Called Dolls* (Santa Fe: Museum of Navaho Ceremonial Art, 1972), p. 40.

5. Haile, *Sacrificial Figurines*, p. 99. Kelly presents the full text of the doll figurine prayer and its associated prayerstick prayer, yet he is concerned with the interpretation of the prayer in only one paragraph which is largely quoted from Father Berard (p. 29). Lang and Walters present the same interpretation, again

stemming from Father Berard, in a single paragraph (p. 60). For a fuller critical review of these works see Sam Gill, "The Prayer of the Navajo Carved Figurine," *Plateau* 47 (1974): 59-69.

6. From a number of conversations that I have had with Navajos, it seems that the use of peyote meetings to diagnose illnesses to be treated by traditional ceremonials is increasingly common. The interrelationship between peyote and traditional ceremonialism has been inadequately studied, although some attention is given to the area in the recent research of Roland M. Wagner, "Some Pragmatic Aspects of Navaho Peyotism," *Plains Anthropologist* 20 (1975): 197-205.

7. Haile, *Sacrificial Figurines*, pp. 11-12.

8. Ibid., pp. 31-32.

9. Two prayers in Enemyway are found to have representation of the prayer constituent, Unit I, which is distinctive for the class of prayers for the remaking of a Holy Person. They are associated with the preparation of the rattle stick and the water pot drum, both of which are basic Enemyway ritual objects. The major theme in both prayers is the expulsion and dispersion of foreign ghosts, remaining consistent with other prayers in Enemyway. The significance which appears to be communicated by the inclusion of Unit I is the identification of the ritual objects as Holy People. The prayer used in the preparation of the rattle stick begins:

B Staff of Monster Slayer, staff of extended bowstring,

Of pollen I have made your feet, of pollen I have made your legs,
I   of pollen I have made your voice,
Invisible on account of pollen I have made you. . . . (EW # 2) (Haile,
Enemy Way, p. 215).

10. Lang and Walters, "Remaking Rites of the Navaho," p. 69.

11. See the discussion of creation events in chapter 4.

12. Kluckhohn and Wyman, *Navaho Chant Practice*, p. 89.

13. This is a view shared by the Franciscan Fathers, Father Berard, Kelly, and Lang and Walters.

14. A variety of these are pictured in the publications by Kelly and Lang and Walters.

15. Haile, *Sacrificial Figurines*, p. 32.

16. David M. Brugge, *Navajo Pottery and Ethnohistory* (Window Rock, Arizona: Navajoland Publications, 1963), p. 22.

17. Hill, *Agricultural and Hunting Methods*, pp. 128-29.

CHAPTER THIRTEEN

POETRY, PERFORMANCE, AND CREATIVITY

This study began with propositions derived from Gladys Reichard's analysis of Navajo prayer; these are that Navajo prayers can be described in terms of their structure at levels both internal and external to the prayer texts, and that the structure of prayers is significant. The analysis and description of the constituents or building blocks of which prayers are constructed was done. Then the classification of prayers on the basis of their structures led to the more far-reaching contextual studies of types of prayer acts. This discussion included a great portion of Navajo religious culture, especially its ritual and mythology. These contextual studies of prayer acts illuminated much of the nature and character of Navajo religion, its premises, categories, and principles.

Perhaps this study has confirmed Reichard's understanding that prayer is "the compulsive word" although much of this work was bent upon disproving this. If compulsion suggests magic in the sense of a mechanical response to an unintelligible formula recitation, and Reichard leaned toward this understanding despite the notable implications of her work, then the present study shows that this is at best an inadequate appreciation of Navajo prayer. Still, in many instances Navajo prayer is compulsive in that it effects certain spiritual relationships which can be relied upon more completely than any others. These relationships provide life. The element of compulsion is based in Navajo religious practice and belief and need not be stated in mechanical terms.

Another important point is the degree to which this study of Navajo prayer acts shows how the Navajo ceremonial system is a masterful vehicle by which the Navajo people may creatively bear responsibility for maintaining the world as it was created and presented to them. The religious system is at once rigidly formulaic and infinitely creative. It is rigidly formulaic in that variance is not tolerated within certain constituents of the ritual process, and the principles by which the ritual constituents are ordered are inviolable. Yet this religious system has the potential to be infinitely creative because the principles which underlie the ritual process are in the service of meaningful expression. Perhaps the creativity within the Navajo ritual process can be likened to the creativity in music or language where the constituents (notes or intervals and words) are finite in number and where principles of composition must be followed. It is common knowledge that despite these constraints music and language are infinitely open to new constructions. There are, by my analysis, but twenty distinct constituents with which to compose a prayer text, yet as this study has shown Navajos are able to utter prayers that address an immense range of concerns.

This point suggests other frames of reference in which Navajo prayer should be considered: oral poetry and the study of prayer in the history of religions. First, prayer as oral poetry.

NAVAJO PRAYER AS ORAL POETRY

For a long time Navajo ceremonialism has been cited as one of the most impressive examples of the capacity of nonliterate societies to learn and recite oral narratives. Perhaps the most often quoted statement is that of Clyde Kluckhohn who likened the task of the Navajo singer to the memorization of a Wagnerian opera including all of the instrumental and vocal parts.[1] This is an impressive feat of memory, but the study of Navajo prayer acts has shown that this is to a degree incorrect, and at the same time, too modest an appraisal of the Navajo. Certainly, the singer must have great knowledge to perform a ceremonial, and many elements of his oral presentations are committed to memory. The recitation of myths and stories are from memory. Yet the study of Navajo ritual processes focused upon the prayer acts has shown that the singer is not a performer of formulaic recitations invariable from one occasion to another, but rather that he is a master composer and that his performance is his moment of composition. It is in the performance of the ceremonial that the singer, using formulaic techniques, composes the songs and prayers upon which Navajo life depends. His prayers, songs, and ritual objects are ordered and interrelated in the performance so that they bear the message appropriate to the situation. This is more like composing an opera while performing it.

This should not be too great a surprise to us given the pioneering studies of Homeric epic and Yugoslavian epic songs by Milman Parry (1930, 1932) and Albert B. Lord (1960), from which has come the theory that oral composition is possible during performance by the poet's reliance upon formulaic style and themes. Lord used field studies of Yugoslavian poetry to develop the theory which he applied to Homeric epic poetry to establish that it has a characteristically oral style. These studies have immensely influenced the study of oral poetry. Notable are the works of Dell Hymes, Barre Toelken, and Dennis Tedlock on Native American oral traditions.[2]

In a review of a number of studies of oral poetry but rare mention of prayer has been found, yet by most definitions prayers should be considered as poetry, and in the Navajo case it is certainly a part of the oral tradition of a nonliterate people. Further, it seems that while the study of oral poetry has begun to recognize the elements of performance, this can rarely be done in any systematic way due to inadequate data on these nontextual elements and to the subtle variables which constitute a performance situation. These nontextual elements of performance are often nearly impossible to define, much less to correlate with the composition of the poetry as a response to the peculiar situation at hand. In the Navajo case, Barre Toelken has considered some of these performance factors in his study of Navajo coyote stories.[3]

On the basis of this study it is possible to suggest something of the nature of Navajo prayer as oral poetry and perhaps to suggest something of the character of oral poetry more generally. It was shown in chapters 2 and 3 that even with little regard for context, the description of the constituency and structuring principles of Navajo prayers yield considerable understanding of Navajo religion. However, despite their significance, the words of the prayer and in the text are but a part of the prayer when performed. To account for this, the notion of the prayer act was posited so that interrelationships between elements in the performance context could be systematically described and accounted for. This demonstrated that at least for Navajo prayer, performance is a complicated affair that involves more than just words. It includes song, ritual gestures, ritual objects, and a group of performers and assistants. The performance is far more than an oral experience; it engages all of the senses. While many of these elements have been incorporated in this study, the surface is hardly scratched—so many of the elements of the performance have either had to be ignored or have been indeterminate from available records. No mention has been made of the voice quality and the style of the singer, the character and rhythm of the musical accompaniment, the nonvocable elements in the songs, and the many fine details of the ritual processes and objects. These are all factors that, if accounted for, would enhance our understanding of the prayer performances.

The performance of Navajo prayers acquires another level of importance when seen in light of the role it plays in Navajo ceremonialism. As an act of speech prayer moves beyond the description of an event. Its primary concerns are to evoke a milieu of symbols and to provide an effect, to perform an act. The principles of aesthetics and composition are consequently tied to the religious world view. The evocative and performative aspects have been noted for the prayers considered. These aspects can also be seen in relationship to elements of style. For example, the performative aspect of a prayer is keyed to a movement through time effected by the change of tenses within the prayer text. This serves the performative needs of prayer in moving from a plea for expected future actions to a description of the actions taking place and concluding with the description of the results enjoyed by the accomplished actions. The transition from tense to tense is important when considering the aesthetics of composition. This is commonly accomplished by enjambment between constituents as a transitional device giving continuity even with a radical break in rhythm and tense. This treatment of time which signals a performative act also is carried into the ritual process of the prayer act. The prayer recitation is often the transitional ritual phase between temporal orientations. Prior to the prayer recitation the activities are commonly of a preparatory nature with a degree of anticipation, while those following are either performative themselves or rites of blessing.

Even in English translation it is clear that rhythm and repetition are essential elements of style in Navajo prayer. The common catalog construction is one principle of style involved here. A phrase is often repeated many times with the alteration of a single word. The sequence of alterations of words through the passage provides a pattern to the passage. Looking at the prayer diagrams, it is astonishing how complex and sophisticated the patterning can become. The repetition and patterning within a prayer constituent may recur at the level of composition within a prayer. Within prayer sets a very elaborate parallelism is basic to the patterns. Within some sets of prayers several days may be required to unfold the parallel pattern. Again, it has been shown that the base for these constructions is to be found in Navajo religious thought. Repetition and patterning occur throughout the ritual process. Even in the recitation of prayer there is a rhythmic character. Many of the prayers are said as litanies by the singer and the one-sung-over. They sit together on the floor of the hogan. The singer closes his eyes. His head remains more erect than bowed. The singer begins the prayer recitation phrase by phrase in an audible but not loud voice with but a short pause between phrases. This pause is not sufficient time for the one-sung-over to repeat the entire phrase. The result is an echo effect with the prayer being said twice, the second recitation echoing the first and overlaying it. The prayers are intoned with little emphasis or change in pitch apart from the normal tones in Navajo language. This permits the patterning of the words and of the character of the language itself to establish the audible effect which is complexly rhythmic.

NAVAJO PRAYER IN THE HISTORY OF RELIGIONS

Prayer is among the most peculiarly remarkable of human phenomena. It is foremost, and undeniably, religious. Yet prayer has received so little attention in the study of the history of religions, by both anthropologists and students of religion. Wherever prayer has been studied as a general religious phenomenon, a fundamental problem has emerged which has stifled the conclusions. The problem is in how to explain or reconcile the difference between the appearance of prayer as a formulaic, repetitive, redundant, and trite verbal act and our idea that prayer is a highly spontaneous, creative, and extemporaneous conversation between human beings and gods about heartfelt concerns.

This problem has been very much in evidence since E. B. Tylor's ten-page discussion of prayer in *Primitive Culture* (1873) where he was clearly distressed that prayer did not appear to conform to his evolutionist hypthesis. He found no clear way to show the evolution of prayer from "primitive" to "advanced" cultures because he discovered in what he considered to be the more advanced world religions, that rosaries, liturgical prayer, and prayer wheels are as rigidly formal as the prayers of non-literate peoples, whom he considered as less advanced or primitive. Tylor could only suggest that it must have been the processes of civilization which forced worship, and consequently prayer, into a mechanical routine needed to regulate human affairs by fixed ordinance. Still he did not give up his idea of prayer as "a means of strengthening emotion, of sustaining courage and exciting hope."[4]

Frederick Heiler's *Prayer* (1932), which is the only extensive study of prayer as a general religious phenomenon, was not much of an advance beyond Tylor.[5] Heiler held, as did Tylor, that prayer is "the address of personal spirit to personal spirit," yet he was forced to deal mainly with prayer texts which had the appearance of anything but extemporaneous, heartfelt communication. Still, Heiler would not give up the idea that the truest prayers are those spontaneous outpourings of the human heart uttered in times of great emotional fullness due to situations of need, awe, and thankfulness. But few, if any, of his textual data seemed to support this position. From his view, highly formulaic prayer could be seen only as a degradation of true prayer.

Reichard's study of Navajo prayer was a new chapter in this story. As noted, she had the idea that even the highly formulaic character of prayer is significant, but then she fell to an analysis of prayer as magically compulsive and ignored, for the most part, even the significance she had attributed to the form of prayer by her interpretation of content and the correlation of structure with context.

While the study of prayer has remained largely ignored, several recent studies have made advances. For example, Dennis Tedlock recently considered prayer in his study of Zuni speech acts.[6] His concern, however, was limited to the identification of inflectional patterns as a code which indexes aspects of the intent of the Zuni speaker. This clearly moves the study of prayer into the performance context and identifies an aspect of its form with its meaning, but it is not concerned with the whole act of prayer. The recent study of Chamul prayers by Gary Goosen is also notable.[7] He uses the approach formulated by Victor Turner to explain ritual symbols. In this way, Goosen shows that certain sets of time-space categories are symbolically encoded in these ritual speech acts, but he is concerned primarily with prayers as encoding certain cultural categories and not with the prayers as religious acts of culture.

Even with these recent contributions, the study of prayer, as a religious phenomenon, remains in a relatively primitive state. There appears to be no study which successfully addresses the disparity between the formal or formulaic appearance of many prayer acts and the idea that prayer is a creative act of divine-human communication motivated by heartfelt needs.

This study of Navajo prayer has something to contribute to the general study of prayer as a religious phenomenon. What it has shown is that the difference between the highly formal character of prayer and our idea of prayer as a creative human act is not really a problem after all; it has only appeared to be one. The hypothetical problem arises, in part, from the difference between viewing prayer as an isolated text and viewing prayer as a complex human act, that is, from the difference between prayer considered only as words and prayer considered as a performance which engages a wide religious and cultural context in association with the words. Not only is this apparent disparity not a problem but in appreciating the different aspects of prayer we come to achieve an understanding of how prayer is at once a meaningful and efficacious human act.

Based on the study of Navajo prayer we can offer a general description of prayer which should apply wherever ritual or formal prayers are found. First, while we can describe the message or information encoded in a prayer text at several levels, there is little indication that in the prayer performance this information is particularly unique or informative. While it is not irrelevant to the situation, the message of the prayer is highly redundant and the encoded information is well known. The style of the performance and the physical and emotional aspects of the performance seem to greatly overshadow any concern with message. Secondly, the extent of repetition, the elaboration of the text, and the ritual and mythological contexts are greatly out of proportion to the extent of the message which is borne in the prayer texts. We must not fail to ask the obvious question, Why are such complex and elaborate acts required to convey a simple message? We must ask why the information conveyed seems to be given such little attention. We must ask if there is not much involved in prayer which has little to do with the referential meaning in the text, or at least much that moves well beyond it. We must ask to what extent the meaning of prayer arises from aspects of prayer which are beyond the referential information it conveys.

That prayer serves much more than the conveyance of ordinary messages requires no proof. The sound, the setting, and the occasion of prayer are distinctive and signal that the act being performed is an act of prayer. The act is thus framed in the minds of those present so that they are prepared to receive it as an experience of prayer. They do not engage in debate about the compatability of the language of prayer and their ordinary understanding of the empirically known world. The symbolic aspects of the language of prayer are not measured against the encyclopedic knowledge of the empirical world and dismissed because they do not fit. The repetitions are not rejected because the message is redundant. The performance characteristics of prayer permit those present to experience it as prayer, as an experience of the symbolic evocation of images which are, in Tylor's words, capable of "strengthening emotion, of sustaining courage and exciting hope." It is precisely because the performance elements of prayer signal that a special frame of interpretation should be engaged by those present that we can speak of prayer as being symbolic in nature. To explain prayer only in terms of the information it conveys is to ignore the question of why it should be symbolic in the first place instead of a simple nonredundant uttering of a message we can decipher. But, on the other hand, to explain prayer only in terms of its evocational powers attributed to some mechanical principles of magic is to ignore the obvious aspect of even the most highly symbolic elements in the prayer performance, that is, that they convey messages and express feelings in terms we can clearly state.

Let me restate this matter. Seen in one way, an act of prayer is clearly an intelligible communication between human beings and higher powers. It is a language act open to translation, interpretation, and analysis. But seen in another way an act of prayer is mythopoeic and highly symbolic and seems to be far less concerned with communicating information than with evoking a network of symbols related to sense experiences, moods, emotions, and values. This evocational aspect is borne not only in the form of rhythmic repetition and the symbolic language of the text, but also, and perhaps to an even greater extent, in the context and texture of the ritual act of prayer—the sounds, sights, smells, stories, songs, ritual gestures, and dance movements which inform the experience.

A peculiarity of prayer is that while it is a practical and intelligible act of speech which seeks pragmatic results, it is also a ritual act which engages and coordinates numerous contextual spheres in the creation of a network of highly symbolic images. Based on this study of Navajo prayer, the conclusion is that while these aspects of prayer may seem disparate, and this has been the problem which has constantly vexed the study of prayer, they are in fact interdependent, indeed of the same fabric. The highly symbolic levels of the prayer act serve the pragmatic concerns of prayer by engendering the powers of evocation which can transform moods, reshape motivations, muster courage and present meaning-giving images. This means that while an act of prayer communicates an intelligible message with an expected pragmatic effect, it also engages the processes which serve to achieve the desired results.

Consequently, we can see that the performance of a prayer act can be creative and responsive to heartfelt needs while the words of the prayer are utterly formulaic. The relevance and immediacy and the creativity and freedom of a prayer are not fully apparent at the level of simple reference, but they become so when prayer is considered also as a highly symbolic religious act which incorporates much more than the words of the prayer. This study of Navajo prayer has shown not only the extent to which contextual elements are relevant, it also has described the structuring principles which underlie Navajo prayer acts. This study has shown that the ordinary information conveyed by the words of the prayer, the categories of thought and culture which are encoded in many aspects of the prayer act, and the whole network of images and symbols and their associated emotions which are evoked by the prayer act, are interconnected in a single complexly hierarchical structure.

The criteria for a further study of prayer is thus clear. It is exemplified in this study of Navajo prayer. We must be able to analyze the referential and deeper symbolic levels of prayer texts. This requires an analysis of both the content and the formal structure of the prayer texts. But we must also be able to analyze prayers as performances of religious acts which are ritual in character, and in doing this we must be able to construct a description of the network of symbolic images the performances may evoke. We must be able to evaluate the efficacy and meaning of these images. This requires the systematic analysis of the structures of prayers in their contexts of ritual (gesture, processes, and songs), mythology, and the pragmatic circumstances motivating the particular performances of the prayer acts.

We can thereby understand liturgical and other formulaic types of prayer as very complex acts which, when seen in a limited way, have an internal tension between their pragmatic and their mythopoeic or symbolic aspects. But when considered in the wider frame of their performance, this internal tension is recognized as the source of their vitality and potency in creating meaning and affecting the world. Thus only when we extend the frame in which we consider prayer to include all of the dimensions its performance calls into play, yet without losing track of the minute symbolic constituents in each of these dimensions, do we achieve an understanding of any prayer act.

NOTES

1. Clyde Kluckhohn and Dorothea Leighton, *The Navaho* (Garden City, New York: Doubleday Company, Ltd., 1962, rev. ed.), p. 229.

2. I do not feel it would contribute much to recount this history here, but one may find an excellent critical account in Ruth Finnegan, *Oral Poetry: Its Nature, Significance and Social Context* (New York: Cambridge University Press, 1977). A valuable collection of essays which deals with the interest by folklorists in the study of the meaning of oral poetry is Dan Ben-Amos and Kenneth S. Godstein, eds., *Folklore: Performance and Communication* (The Hague: Mouton, 1975). Along with an introductory article, which recounts the background and history of the issues dealt with in this volume, are excellent articles by Dell Hymes and Barre Toelken. Further bibliographies may be found in these articles. A special issue on "Oral Cultures and Oral Performances" was published in *New Literary History*, 1977. A valuable introduction to this area is Richard Bauman, "Verbal Art as Performance," *American Anthropologist* 77 (1975): 290-311. See Michael Foster, *From the Earth to Beyond the Sky: Ethnographic Approach to Four Longhouse Iroquois Speech Events* (Ottawa: National Museums of Canada, 1974). Not men-

tioned among these articles, but one that should not be overlooked, is Dennis Tedlock, "Verbal Art," *Handbook of North American Indians* (Washington: The Smithsonian, 1980), vol. 9, chapter 50.

3. Barre Toelken, "The 'Pretty Languages' of Yellowman: Genre, Mode, and Texture in Navajo Coyote Narratives," *Genre* 2: 3 (1969), 211-35 and "Ma'i Joldloshi: Legendary Styles and Navaho Myth," in *American Folk Legend,* ed. W. Hand (Berkeley: University of California Press, 1971), pp. 203-12.

4. Edward B. Tylor, *Primitive Culture* (London: John Murray, 1873), vol. II, pp. 364-74.

5. Frederick Heiler, *Prayer: A Study in the History and Psychology of Religion,* (New York: Oxford University Press, 1932). Robert H. Lowie pointed out that Heiler's study was little advance to Tylor's. See Lowie, *Primitive Religion* (New York: Liveright Publishing Corp., 1972), p. 322.

6. Dennis Tedlock, "From Prayer to Reprimand," in *Language in Religious Practice,* ed. William J. Samarin (Rowley, Massachusetts: Newbury House Publishers, 1976), pp. 72-83.

7. Gary H. Goosen, "Language as Ritual Substance," in *Language in Religious Practice,* ed. William J. Samarin (Rowley, Massachusetts: Newbury House Publishers, 1976), pp. 40-62.

CRITIQUE OF REICHARD'S ANALYSIS OF PRAYER

This review of Reichard's study of Navajo prayer attempts to systematically analyze the approach she used in her book, *Prayer: The Compulsive Word*. The critique is based in part upon applying her own principles to the full prayer texts which were not published in her book, but which were consulted in preparing this critique, and in part upon the significance of her approach.

REICHARD'S NOTION OF THE COMPOSITION OF PRAYER

While Reichard did not formally propose a structure for the composition of prayer, one may be found in her discussion of prayer. Although a number of her components are subject to question, she suggested a hierarchy into which these components may be organized, indicating her appreciation for the complexity of the prayer texts and their use in Navajo ceremonials.

At one level, Reichard discussed the symbolic elements which are components of prayer. This discussion of symbolism is similar to that found in her book *Navaho Religion*. The primary symbolic components which she discussed are color, direction, number, place, motion, light, sound, and repetition.[1] The basic unit of form in prayer is the line, according to Reichard. The designation of line boundaries was determined on the basis of the analysis of rhythm or sound sequences.[2]

In Reichard's chapter "Content of Prayer," some components of prayer are distinguished by their symbolic content. Some of these components were supported by examples from prayer texts. (1) "an address to deity," (2) "the reason for his [deity] coming to the patient's aid," (3) a description of "the symbol which he [deity] carries," (4) "the behavior of the deity and its concern for the patient," (5) "the concern the deity feels for the patient," and (6) "monotonous repetitions of ritualistic acts taken up motion by motion and advancing step by step."[3]

At another level, Reichard identified "three main divisions: the invocation, petition and benediction."[4] She did not indicate how she identified the "invocation" division, but she discussed the problems of distinguishing between petition and benediction. She resolved this problem by placing "under 'petition' the lines which show what the patient wants and under 'benediction' what he gets."[5]

Reichard formally proposed prayer classifications only on the basis of the structure of repetition and length of the prayer texts, but there is considerable evidence that she recognized some classes of prayers on the basis of their use and message. She indicated only two classifications on the basis of form. One class, which she identified as Type I, was described as a "single unit within which there are various line and line-grouped repetitions."[6] The other class, identified as Type II, was described as being "made up of repetitions of such units [Type I], any one of which may be nearly as complicated as the single unit of the first group."[7]

Upon considering Reichard's components of prayer, it appears that she did have an underlying notion that several levels of constituents, hierarchically organized, are basic to the system of Navajo prayer.

CONTENT VERSUS FORM

In Reichard's understanding of the components of prayer, there is a clear division between components of form and components of content. Only the "main divisions" of invocation, petition, and benediction are considered by Reichard as components distinguishable by both form and content. This distinction between content and form is further evident in the titles of two of her main chapters on prayer, Chapter Four, "Content of Prayers," and Chapter Five, "Structure of Prayers." In the chapter on content, Reichard discussed the symbolic components. In the chapter on structure, she described the components of line, the main divisions, and the two classes of form.

REICHARD'S ANALYSIS OF FORM

Reichard's interest in the analysis of the components of form in Navajo prayer stems from her interest in the rhythmic repetition in plastic art. In 1922 she published the results of her study of the repetition of the designs of the beadwork and embroidery made by the Thompson River Indians. She wanted to discern the principles underlying the color patterning in the beadwork and embroidered designs. Upon becoming familiar with Navajo religion, she extended this interest in rhythmic repetition to the musical and speech forms of the Navajo songs and prayers. She approached the analysis of Navajo prayer structure very much as she had the analysis of beadwork. She chose a basic unit of structure and assigned alphabetic characters to distinctive units in order to prepare a diagram of repetitions in prayer texts for ease in analysis.

As a data base for her analysis of the form of prayer, she selected a sample of twenty-five prayer texts from a wide range of ceremonials. She did not indicate her sampling process, but she did discuss how a sample might be selected, were this kind of analysis to be done more comprehensively.[8] Reichard provided a list of the prayer texts used in the analysis,[9] but only one prayer text is given.[10]

The only way of checking the accuracy of Reichard's data is to compare the texts in Reichard's sources with the symbolic representations of their structure which appear in her Figures 1 to 25. Upon making this comparison for all twenty-five prayer texts, ten of Reichard's diagrammatic representations were found to be significantly in error. Six of the first thirteen prayers which Reichard considered as Type I prayers, having only a single unit, were found to be Type II prayers, being composed of prayer sets. Other errors consisted of the omission of lines in the diagrammatical representations, the failure to designate parallel parts within prayer texts, and the failure to indicate sections as "optional additions."

Reichard's analysis of form was approached by developing diagrams to illustrate rhythmic repetitions. She did not define her method or terms clearly, but she did describe how she constructed the diagrams.

The figures which represent the analysis of the prayers were prepared so as to bring out primarily two phases of the rhythmic pattern. The letters represent the kind of word, phrase or sentence in a line, primes indicating a change of some phase of the line, often of only one word. The arrangement shows how lines of this type are grouped, that is, repetitions of a unit having more than one line.[11]

For the very simplest prayer, the diagram appeared as follows:

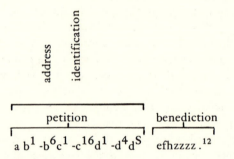

$$\text{a } b^1 \text{ -}b^6 c^1 \text{ -}c^{16} d^1 \text{ -}d^4 d^S \quad \text{efhzzzz.}^{12}$$

Two terms were given special alphabetical designations, summary (S) and increment (I). These terms are poorly defined. "Two features which designate the climax are, summary which is usually very short, and increment which may be very long."[13] Reichard prepared diagrams for all twenty-five prayers. Each one begins with the designation of the first line by the letter "a" and continues sequentially through the alphabet, using "z" for the concluding lines. Above the alphabetic representation, Reichard indicated her designation of the "main divisions" and above that she indicated such things as address, identification, description, god description, place description, exorcism, and offering.[14]

Through this process Reichard compiled a concise representation of extensive and complex materials. But the alphabetical designations reflect nothing, beyond style, of the content. They are based on a somewhat arbitrary formal analysis of lines. The line designation in an oral utterance is likewise dependent upon form rather than upon native designations. A further difficulty arises since the formal analysis is only partially transferable from one prayer to another, since the alphabetical designation of line constituents begins new with each prayer.

The primary purpose for which Reichard utilized these diagrams was to describe the pattern of rhythmic repetition of the prayer texts, for example, "Fig. 8 is interesting in that an oft-repeated benediction composed of forty-six units of three elements each, follows the invocation."[15] Some of these descriptions reach very complex proportions.

In Fig. 13 the large numbers 12 and 27 are a total of couplets having much tedious variations, nevertheless composed in similar lines. They are separated by three lines and followed by four of the same type; this relationship is indicated by a broken curved line underneath. The second part of the prayer differs greatly from the first. It is interesting for various reasons: the use of summary enters into intricate combination, the most astonishing of which is the summary of the m-series which refers back to seven lines. . . . Finally, the combined numerical groups come out 52-52 with the group totalling 52 made up of 26 plus 26 (not twice 26 since the two units are different). This seems almost too neat to be true, but the summaries leave no doubt that the parts are so considered.[16]

The complex prayer which Reichard analyzed as Figure 13 has three other parallel prayers for which Reichard did not account. Another problem with the analysis of the text diagrammed in Figure 13 is that she included as continuous with the prayer text a very lengthy passage which is indicated in the source as an "optional addition."

Beyond this descriptive analysis of the patterns of rhythmic repetitions, Reichard considered a number of the prayers in her sample for another type of analysis. Reichard charted by ceremony or rite the occurrence of both forms of prayer—Type I and Type II. Two entries are reproduced, in part, to illustrate her analysis.[17]

Rite or ceremony	Type I	Type II
Male Shooting Chant Evil	Figure 25	Figure 13
Male Shooting Chant Holy	Figure 5	Figure 16
	Figure 12	
	Figure 6	
	Figure 7	
	Figure 9.	

Based on this chart, Reichard made some interpretive comments. She noted "that a prayer of the first class which I shall call Type I is used with one of the second, Type II. This seems to hold for the prayers of the Male Shooting Chant Evil, of the Rain Ceremony, of the Rite on Buckskin, of the First Dancers of the Night Chant and of the general distribution of prayers available for the Male Shooting Chant Holy."[18] But Reichard did not feel the interpretation was conclusive. "The comparison seems quite suggestive but it does not include enough information about the purpose of the prayers to establish conclusively the reason for the types."[19]

The errors in her material invalidate even her tentative results. First, it may be noted that for Male Shooting Chant Evil, the Type I prayer Figure 13 and the Type II prayer Figure 25 are reversed in the chart, which is of no particular consequence to Reichard's interpretation. But, of serious consequence is that Figure 13 should actually be classed as a Type II since it has four parallel prayer parts, resulting in no Type I prayers in Reichard's sample for Male Shooting Chant Evil. The errors to be noted in the analysis of the prayers of Male Shooting Chant Holy are even more extensive. All of the prayers classified as Type I except the prayer represented by Figure 12 should be classified as Type II prayers.

Reichard made other observations on the significance of the two classes of form. "Prayers to get a person out of danger, that is, exorcistic prayers, and those to deities most difficult of persuasion seem to have the greatest elaboration."[20] This supports Reichard's contention that it requires more effort to expel evil than to attract good. The other remark was offered "merely as a suggestion." "It will be noted that only one prayer of Type I has exorcistic lines. This may mean that Type II is more closely identified with exorcism than Type I, but the remarks and classifications already made seem to show that the occurrence is fortuitous rather than real."[21]

While these observations and generalizations are without base due to the error in Reichard's data, it is nonetheless important to note the ingenuity of her method and its purpose. She was attempting to discover the significance of the form of the prayer texts, both individually and in general. She developed a constituent analysis of the prayers, she proposed a classification based upon this constituent analysis, and then compared the classification with what she understood to be the purpose of the prayers. She believed that "the form of the prayer may be considered subordinate to its purpose."[22]

NOTES

1. Reichard, *Prayer,* pp. 19-21 and 26-30.

2. Ibid., pp. 37-38. In comparing Reichard's translations of prayers with those made by Father Berard, there is a striking difference in the understanding of line boundaries. One of Father Berard's lines will usually encompass a number of Reichard's lines. Reichard did not explicitly state her criteria for determining line boundaries.

3. Reichard, *Prayer,* pp. 22-25.

4. Ibid., p. 41.

5. Ibid.

6. Ibid., p. 39.

7. Ibid., p. 40.

8. Ibid., p. 48.

9. Ibid., p. 97.

10. Ibid., pp. 58-93.

11. Ibid., p. 37. By "prime" it appears that Reichard intended "superscript."

12. Ibid., Figure 1.

13. Ibid., p. 36.

14. Below these diagrams Reichard reduced the pattern of rhythmic repetition to a numeric representation. For her Figure 1, which has been used as an example in this work, this representation is $-6\ 16\ ^{4}5^{S}\text{---}4$.

15. Ibid., p. 42.

16. Ibid., p. 47.

17. Ibid., p. 40.

18. Ibid.

19. Ibid., p. 41.

20. Ibid.

21. Ibid.

22. Ibid., p. 36.

THE CLASSIFICATION OF NAVAJO CEREMONIALS

The classification of Navajo ceremonials has played an important part in the understanding of Navajo religion and culture. Not only does a classification account for the extent of the ceremonial practices, it reveals some of the basic categories in the Navajo world view. The classification is the basis for distinguishing the various ceremonials and is essential to an understanding of them.

Several students of Navajo religion developed ceremonial classifications, each from a perspective corresponding to his or her distinctive approach to the study of the religion. The Franciscan Fathers presented a list of ceremonials in their ethnologic dictionary giving corresponding Navajo and English names with a brief note concerning their purpose and frequency of performance.[1] Father Berard Haile published an article, "Navajo Chantways and Ceremonials," which presented a classification of the ceremonials as well as a basic classification terminology on the basis of his linguistic analysis of the Navajo ceremonial names.[2] Leland Wyman and Clyde Kluckhohn coauthored a work, *Navaho Classification of Their Song Ceremonials*, which presented a ceremonial classification on the basis of field research.[3] A number of brief articles following these publications discussed the details and discrepancies. Gladys Reichard in her major work, *Navaho Religion*, offered a third important classification schema, weighted significantly by her experience gained by participation in ceremonials.[4] Her position was irreconcilable with that of Father Berard, primarily because he did not witness the ceremonials as she did. She felt her method was essential to complement linguistic analysis.[5] Finally, Kluckhohn wrote an article which in many ways synthesized and reconciled the discrepancies of Reichard and Father Berard with the position stated by himself and Wyman. This was later reviewed and restated by Louise Lamphere.[6] A comparative discussion and analysis of these classifications follows.

FATHER BERARD'S CLASSIFICATION (1938)

Father Berard's approach was based on an analysis of the Navajo ceremonial terminology. His classification proposed a hierarchic structure which may be illustrated diagrammatically, as shown in Figure 2.

FIGURE 2

Father Berard's Ceremonial Classification Schema

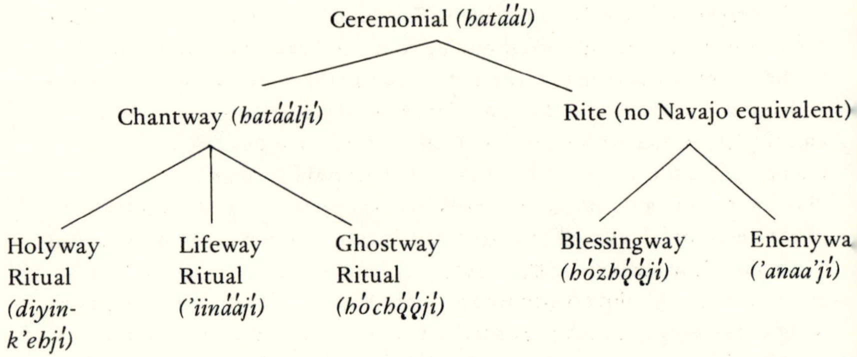

Ceremonial (*hatáál*)

Chantway (*hatáálji*)   Rite (no Navajo equivalent)

Holyway   Lifeway   Ghostway   Blessingway   Enemywa
Ritual   Ritual   Ritual   (*hózhǫ́ǫ́ji*)   (*'anaa'ji*)
(*diyin-   ('iináaji)   (*hóchǫ́ǫ́ji*)
k'ehji*)

The highest level categories within Father Berard's classification of ceremonials are "chantway" and "rite." The major category, "chantway," is designated as "only such ceremonials [as those] in which the songs are accompanied with a rattle instrument *('agháál)*."[7] He also indicated the distinctive features of "rites" by the ritual objects which accompany or are held during a song. The mountain soil bundle is held during Blessing-way songs, and the pot drum accompanies Enemyway singing.[8] Father Berard proposed that each chantway could be conducted in several "manners" which he also called "rituals," distinguished "by the attitude of the holy ones, who happen to be etiologically concerned in a given case."[9] In the analysis of chantway names, Father Berard discovered a hierarchy of variables which must be accounted for in the classification of chantway ceremonials.

a) a chantway may have multiple names
b) a chantway may have nicknames
c) a chantway may have both male and female branches
d) chantways may be combined
e) there is not a one-to-one relationship between the chantway names and etiological factors
f) the etiological factor may be a part of the chantway name
g) multiple "characterizations" are possible, such as prayersticks, sandpaintings, and jewel offerings
h) a chantway may have a combination of constituents
i) a chantway may have optional constituents
j) a chantway may have optional concluding constituents.[10]

On the basis of his analysis, Father Berard developed a hierarchical classification which focused on an appreciation of the complexity of the ceremonials as they respond to various needs.

The terminology which he developed has certain notable problems. The major classification term is "ceremonial" *(hatáál)*, a subclassification of which is "chantway" *(hatáálji)*. In the discussion of the various names of chantways, Father Berard repeatedly referred to the constituents of these chantways as "ceremonials."[11] His term "rite," used to distinguish the nonchantway ceremonials, is not a good choice of terms because the meanings generally associated with the word would suggest a ceremonial constituent rather than a classification of ceremonials. The same objection may be raised for the term "ritual" which designates the "manner" by which the chantway ceremonial is performed—Holyway, Lifeway, and Ghostway.

WYMAN AND KLUCKHOHN'S CLASSIFICATION (1938)

Based on their field research, Wyman and Kluckhohn, with the cooperation of Gladys Reichard, developed a classification of ceremonials using the native grouping and subgrouping of ceremonial names. Wyman and Kluckhohn indicated that they found a remarkable agreement among natives across a considerable geographic area.[12] The schema of classification takes the form of groups and subgroups, as indicated in Table 4.

TABLE 4

Wyman and Kluckhohn's Ceremonial
Classification Schema

I.   Blessing Way

II.   Holy Way (7 subgroups)

III. Life Way

IV.   Evil Way (2 subgroups)

V.   War Ceremonials (Enemy Way)

VI.   Game Way

To account for the complexity that is observed within the ceremonial performances, Wyman and Kluckhohn noted that

While the ceremonials listed are differentiated and given distinct names by the Navajo, there is, of course, considerable intertwining. The origin legends of certain ceremonials are highly similar up to a certain point and then, as the Navaho say, "they branch off." Certain songs, sandpaintings, and ceremonies as well as ritual elements are common to several, and sometimes to many ceremonials.[13]

Wyman and Kluckhohn indicate that the distinction between groups is based, in part, on the ritual process.

The ceremonials in each of the first four groups (at least) are characterized by a certain ritual, i.e., by certain rules or customs which must be observed in conducting ceremonies, in singing songs, reciting prayer words, preparing cut stick offerings, making sandpaintings. Since most ceremonials include a part which is conducted according to the ritual of the Blessing Way rite, it is placed first in the table.[14]

To support their classification, Wyman and Kluckhohn included "Supplementary Notes" which indicate for each group and subgroup a short description, the distinctive features, and the known uses.[15]

COMPARISON OF FATHER BERARD'S AND WYMAN AND KLUCKHOHN'S CLASSIFICATIONS

A brief comparison will help to make both of these classifications clearer, as well as to establish a background for Reichard's and Kluckhohn's later classifications.

It appears that Father Berard was more concerned with the classification schema, the reasoning and principles behind the classifications, then were Wyman and Kluckhohn, who appear to have been primarily concerned with the presentation of field-collected data. Father Berard presented an ordered hierarchy of categories, even though he was forced into inventing terms which had no Navajo equivalents. He was attempting to generalize upon the information he gained from the analysis of the Navajo names associated with ceremonials. Wyman and Kluckhohn did not include any interpretation of their own and carefully indicated when they had to make certain choices not based on field data, such as the ordering of the groups.

Father Berard was overtly interested in developing terminology which might be used to indicate various levels and positions within the hierarchic classification schema, although this language was largely inadequate. Wyman and Kluckhohn made no attempt to introduce terminology.

Father Berard based his classification primarily on the analysis of the Navajo language which is relevant to ceremonial names and categories.

Wyman and Kluckhohn depended largely upon the native classifications obtained in field research.

REICHARD'S CLASSIFICATION (1950)

Reichard presented a classification of ceremonials which provided both a general hierarchic schema and the details.[16] She explained her approach

Instead of starting with the comprehensive view, which assumes that each chanter understands the religion as a whole, I began with the details. Proceeding from the specific to the general, I find myself with a vast number of details—mythological episodes and incidents, rites, color, sound, directional symbols, ritualistic acts, and the like—bound together in a complex organization. Any one of these parts may be slipped from one context to another with ease and with what the Navaho considers complete consistency.[17]

Reichard was concerned with resolving problems arising out of the use of terminology, and discussed a number of terms on the basis of both a linguistic analysis and field research.

The result of Reichard's classification was a schema for organizing the groups and subgroups of Wyman and Kluckhohn's classification.[18] This schema is shown, in part, in Table 5.

At the base of Reichard's classification schema is the distinction between good and evil. Of these she said,

All things in the universe, materialistic and abstract, are viewed in terms of their effects on man. If he knows about them and can control them, they are good; if not, they are evil. Some things under only partial control are good when susceptible to that control; otherwise they are bad. Therefore, the fundamental subdivision—good and evil—which are not absolute, overlap. The good in all things must be attracted; hence ceremonial control invokes good in Blessing rites or "chants-according-to-holiness." The evil remaining outside ritualistic control must be driven off; hence the "evil-chasing ceremonies" with emphasis on exorcism, but from which attraction of good is by no means absent.[19]

TABLE 5

Reichard's Ceremonial Classification Schema

Good	Comprehensive	Evil
Rites of instruction	Prayer Chants	Rites of instruction
Blessingway	Dark-circle-	Hunting
House Blessing	of-branches	War
Girl's Puberty		. . . .
. . . .		War Ceremony
Lifeway		Male Shooting Chant
War Prophylactic		Evil
Chants According-		Female Shooting
to-Holiness		Chant Evil
Night Chant		Edurance Chant
Male Shooting Chant:		. . . .
Branches:		
. . . .		

Reichard presented a schema of classification based on her evaluation of the fundamental categories involved in the selection of the ceremonials, while retaining the detail of the classification presented by Wyman and Kluckhohn. The major problem, of which Reichard was well aware, was the difficulty in distinguishing between what the Navajos conceive as "good" and "evil," which ultimately undercuts any clear distinctions in her classification schema. She resorted to the utilization of the same kind of criteria which Father Berard used, the presence or absence of certain ritual objects, which she called "chant symbols."[20]

KLUCKHOHN'S CLASSIFICATION (1960)

Kluckhohn, noting the often documented Navajo propensity for categorization and systematization, felt that there should be a "master scheme" which would be more distinctive than Reichard's sweeping statement that "thus Navaho dogma connects all things." He chose, therefore, as his purpose in an article entitled "Navaho Categories" to examine in some detail standard Navaho categories in various spheres, trying to discover the criteria, explicit and implicit, applied in each area and seeing the extent to which some criteria tend to pervade all or many areas.[21]

The classification of ceremonials was, therefore, of concern to him, but unlike the classification which he developed with Wyman in 1938, Kluckhohn, in this article, was interested in "criteria, explicit and implicit," in other words, the schema of classification. By placing his categories and subcategories in diagrammatic form, his schema for ceremonial classification may be illustrated as shown in Figure 3.

FIGURE 3

Kluckhohn's Ceremonial Classification Schema

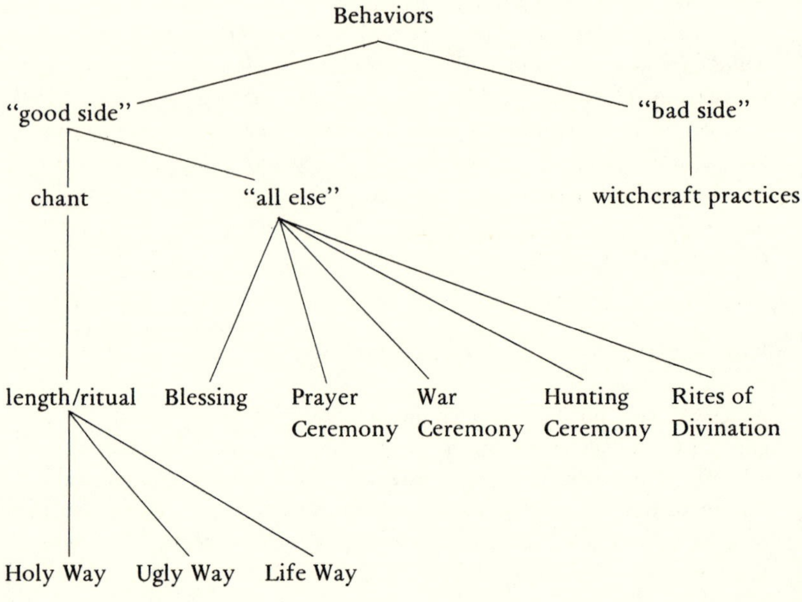

Kluckhohn's term, "behavior," is the rendering of a Navajo word, which he understood to mean, "an organized attempt is being made to influence the course of events by supernatural techniques."[22] Noting what he considered to be a general distinction between the "good side" and the "bad side," Kluckhohn discussed the various aspects of each category, finally arriving at the satisfactory distinction, "evil magic and ceremonialism."[23] He discussed the "bad side" at some length in his book, *Navaho Witchcraft* (1944). These subclassifications have not been placed in the diagram.

On the "good side" Kluckhohn distinguished between "chant" and "all else" on the same basis as Father Berard did: the presence or absence of the rattle accompaniment to singing.[24] Again, it can be noted that "all else" appears to lack a basis in native terminology and makes this category ambiguous. Within the "chant" category, Kluckhohn noted that both length and "ritual" were major variables and indicated the three categories of "ritual" as Holy Way, Ugly Way, and Life Way.

COMPARISON OF KLUCKHOHN'S CLASSIFICATION WITH THE OTHERS

It appears that Kluckhohn had a different understanding of Reichard's "fundamental subdivisions—good and evil," which made him designate categories of classification quite different from Reichard's. Kluckhohn's term "good side" is equivalent to Father Berard's term "ceremonial" and the subclassifications within "good side" are the same as within Father Berard's "ceremonials," with revisions in terminology and the expansion of the subclassifications of "all else." Kluckhohn's schema succeeds in finding a "master scheme," but suffers some of the problems noted in Father Berard's classification—the use of ambiguous terms to designate classifications which are not made in Navajo language and the selection of classification terms whose usage conflicts with general use.

CRITICAL OBSERVATIONS

There appears to be no disagreement on Wyman and Kluckhohn's classification of ceremonials based on Navajo information. The problem is in discerning the criteria, explicit and implicit, for the native classification of ceremonials. There have been apparent differences between groups of ceremonials, but the distinguishing criteria have not been clearly discerned. To distinguish ceremonial classifications on the basis of the presence or absence of certain ritual objects is simply indexical and does little if anything to increase our understanding of these Navajo class distinctions.

These problems have been largely overcome in this study of Navajo prayer and religion. It has produced a ceremonial classification schema, and it has done so in a manner that illuminates those Navajo perspectives that make the classification significant.

NOTES

1. Franciscan Fathers, *Dictionary*, pp. 361-66. While this is not a true classification, it does represent the first attempt to account for all Navajo ceremonials.

2. Haile, "Chantways and Ceremonials," pp. 639-52.

3. A corrigenda and addenda to this classification was made in an appendix to Kluckhohn and Wyman, *Navaho Chant Practice*, pp. 181-90.

4. See Reichard, *Navaho Religion*, pp. 314-38.

5. Ibid., pp. 315-16.

6. Kluckhohn, "Navajo Categories," pp. 65-98. Lamphere attempted a reconsideration of Kluckhohn's classification of 1960 by reworking his data in light of recent developments in anthropological method. See Louise Lamphere and Evon Z. Vogt, "Clyde Kluckhohn as Ethnographer and Student of Navaho Ceremonialism," in *Culture and Life, Essays in Memory of Clyde Kluckhohn*, eds., Walters W. Taylor *et al.*, (Carbondale: Southern Illinois University Press, 1973), pp. 94-135. A critique of Lamphere's work would not contribute greatly here, and I have already made comment on related aspects of her work, especially her discussion of color symbolism, in "The Color of Navajo Ritual Symbolism: An Evaluation of Methods," *Journal of Anthropological Research* 31 (1975): 350-63.

7. Haile, "Chantways and Ceremonials," p. 639.

8. Ibid.

9. Ibid., p. 647.

10. This list is a summarization of material presented in Haile's "Chantways and Ceremonials," pp. 639-47.

11. Haile, "Chantways and Ceremonials," p. 646.

12. Wyman and Kluckhohn, *Navaho Classification*, pp. 5-7.

13. Ibid., pp. 4-5.

14. Ibid., p. 8.

15. Ibid., pp. 18-36.

16. See Reichard, *Navaho Religion*, pp. 314-37.

17. Ibid., p. 314.
18. Ibid., pp. 322-23.
19. Ibid., p. 320.
20. Ibid., p. 334.
21. Kluckhohn, "Navaho Categories," p. 66.
22. Ibid., p. 67.
23. Ibid.
24. Ibid., p. 68.

PRAYER STRUCTURE DIAGRAMS

A register of the prayer structures presented in diagrammatic form, as described in chapter 2, for Navajo prayer texts is given in Table 7. The prayer text is identified by an alphanumeric designation which identifies the ceremonial, male or female branch, and ritual type where any of these are relevant and known. This alphanumeric designation also provides the reference for the prayer text. The list of the alphabetical designations is found in Table 6. The page numbers for the text are given with the diagrams in the "register," Table 7, so that reference to any prayer may be made by using Table 6 for the publication information and the "register," Table 7, for the page numbers. A brief contextual note is added where it is known. Finally, a numeric indication of the prayer act classification (third column headed "C") is also given for each prayer, if it can be determined. The numbers correspond with the classifications in Table 2.

Note that an "e" subscript to an alphabetical constituent unit designation indicates an *extended* constituent compared to corresponding examples of the same constituent in the same prayer set. A slash (/) indicates that the constituents following are optional. A question mark (?) indicates that one of the designated constituents cannot be clearly identified. For a description of the distinctive features of the constituent units refer to chapter 2 and the summary in Table 1.

TABLE 6

Alphabetical Designation of Prayer References

Designation	Description	Source
BFa	Blessingway, House blessing	Frisbie, "House Blessing"
BFb	Blessingway, House blessing	Frisbie, "Ritual Drama"
BFHW	Beautyway, Female, Holyway	Wyman, Beautyway
BGH	Big Godway, Figurine Complex	Haile, *Sacrificial Figurines*
BH	Blessingway	Hill, *Agricultural and Hunting Methods*
BS	Blessingway	Sapir & Hoijer, *Navaho Texts*
BSGW	Big Starway, Evilway	Wheelwright, *Great Star Chant*
		Haile, *Big Starway* [m.s.]
BSGH	Big Starway, Holyway	Wheelwright, *Great Star Chant*
		Haile, *Big Starway* [m.s.]
BW	Blessingway	Wyman, *Blessingway*
CW	Coyoteway	Luckert, *Coyoteway*
EH	Enemyway	Haile, *Enemy Way*
EMM	Emergence Myth	Matthews, *Navaho Legends*
FH	Flintway	Haile, *Flintway*
GW	Gameway	Luckert, *Navajo Hunter Tradition*
HH	Hunting Ceremonies	Hill, *Agricultural and Hunting Methods*
HR	Hailway	Reichard, *Hail Chant*
MFH	Mountaintopway, Female	Haile, *Female Mountainway*

212

MMH	Mountaintopway, Male	Haile, *Sacrificial Figurines*
NH	Nightway	Haile, *Head and Face Masks*
NMa	Nightway	Matthews, *Navaho Legends*
NMb	Nightway	Matthews, *Night Chant*
NMc	Nightway	Matthews, *Myths, Prayers, and Songs*
NS	Nightway	Stevenson, *Hasjelti Dailjis*
PCL	Prayer Ceremony	Luckert, "Navajo Theories"
PCM	Prayer Ceremony	Matthews, "Navaho Shaman"
PP	Protection Prayer	Luckert, *Navajo Mountain*
PW	Prostitutionway	Haile, *Love-Magic*
RCH	Rain Ceremony	Hill, *Agricultural and Hunting Methods*
RCS	Rain Ceremony	Stevenson, *Hasjelti Dailjis*
RMGW	Red Antway, Male, Evilway	Wyman, *Red Antway*
RMHW	Red Antway, Male, Holyway	Wyman, *Red Antway*
RR	Rainbow Prayer	Luckert, *Navajo Mountain*
RRP	Rain-Requesting Prayer	Luckert, *Navajo Mountain*
SFH	Sacrificial Figurine Complex	Haile, *Sacrificial Figurines*
SGH	Salt Gathering	Hill, "Salt Gathering"
SH	Suckingway	Haile, *Legend of Ghostway Ritual*
SMGH	Shootingway, Male, Evilway	Haile, *Legend of Ghostway Ritual*
SMGRa	Shootingway, Male, Evilway	Reichard, *Male Shooting Chant Evil*
SMGRb	Shootingway, Male, Evilway	Reichard, *Prayer*

TABLE 6—Continued

Designation	Description	Source
SMHH	Shootingway, Male, Holyway	Haile, *Prayer Stick Cutting*
SMHM	Shootingway, Male, Holyway	McAllester, "Shootingway"
SMHR	Shootingway, Male, Holyway	Reichard, *Male Shooting Chant Holy*
SWH	Stalkingway	Hill, *Agricultural and Hunting Methods*
UR	Upward Reachingway	Reichard, *Chant of Waning Endurance*
WCW	Windway, Chiricahua	Wyman, *Windways*
WH	Wolfway	Hill, *Agricultural and Hunting Methods*
WNW	Windway, Navajo	Wyman, *Windways*

TABLE 7

Register of Structure Diagrams of Prayer Texts

Alphanumeric Designation	Page No.	C*	Structure Diagram	Context
BFa #1	29-30	1	1) $A_1 G_1 V$ ...... 12) $A_{12} G_{12} V$	House blessing (four verses #1, 4, 7, and 12 are published)
BFb #1 - #11	183-84	1	V	Informal house blessing
BFb #12	184-85	1	B A G V	Text not given but described, a house blessing
BFb #13 - #14	185	1	V	Informal house blessing
BFb #15	186-87	1	V B A G V	Prayer for dedication of Gallup Stadium, 1940. Collected by Reichard
BFHW #1	95-96	5	1) $A_1 B_1 C H M U V$ 2) $A_2 B_2 C H M U V$	Prayerstick rite
BFHW #2	103	5	1) $B_1 C H M U V$ .... 4) $B_4 C H M U V$	Prayerstick rite
BFHW #3	105	5	1) $B_1 C H M U V$ .... 6) $B_6 C H M U V$	Prayerstick rite

*C refers to the classifications in Table 2.

TABLE 7—Continued

Alphanumeric Designation	Page No.	C*	Structure Diagram	Context
BFHW #4	107	5	1) B_1 C H M U V . . . . 8) B_8 C H M U V	Prayerstick rite
BFHW #5	141-42	5	1) C A B_1 C H M H M U V 2) C A B_2 C H M H M U V 3) C A B_3 C H M H M U V	Said at end of narration of myth
BFHW #6	95	1	G	Pollen prayer, application of pollen during prayer
BGH #1	90-99	8	B I J T U V	Figurine rite
BGH #2	90-99	5	B C H M U V	Prayerstick in figurine rite
BGH #3	90-99	8	B I J T U V	Figurine rite
BGH #4	90-99	5	B C H M U V	Prayerstick in figurine rite
BGH #5	90-99	8	B I J T U V	Figurine rite
BGH #6	90-99	5	B C H M U V	Prayerstick in figurine rite
BGH #7	90-99	8	B I J T U V	Figurine rite

216

BGH #8	90-99	5	B C H M U V	Prayerstick in figurine rite
BGH #9	90-99	8	B I J T U V	Figurine rite
BGH #10	90-99	5	B C H M U V	Prayerstick in figurine rite
BGH #11	90-99	8	B I J M U V	Figurine rite
BGH #12	90-99	5	B C H M U V	Prayerstick in figurine rite
BH #1	71	1	V	Rain and seed blessing
BS #1	98-99			Nonceremonial
BS #2	398-401			Nonceremonial
BSGW #1	57-64	6	1) Q R S T G V .... 4) Q R S T_e G V	Uglyway prayer said on special request, recited on a pollen figure
BSGW #2	71-77	6	1) Q R S T G V .... 4) Q R S T_e G V	Special no sleep ceremony. Not part of Big Starway, said on figure on buckskin
BSGW #3	78-80	7	1) B L U N .... 16) B L U N 17) B L U N $G_1 G_2 G_3 G_4$ N .... 20) B L U N $G_1 G_2 G_3 G_4$ N	May be used with or without ceremonial, added in evening after other rites, said with or without painting

TABLE 7–Continued

Alphanumeric Designation	Page No.	C*	Structure Diagram	Context
BSHW #1	64-70	6	1) Q R S T G T V .... 4) Q R S T G T V [Recorded by transformation rules from BSGW #1]	Said on painting, part of Big Starway, perforated stone placed on center of painting
BW #1	131-37	1	$[(G_{(ab)})V_{(ab)}G_{(ba)}V_{(ba)})V]^9$ ab represents a pair of inner forms of Holy People	No sleep ceremony at creation of inner/outer forms
BW #2	167	1	$(G^{HP}V)12V$, HP 1=1 Holy person	Puberty rite of Changing Woman
BW #3	186-87	1	$B V (F_V^{HP})45 G V$, HP 1=1 Holy person	No sleep ceremony for Changing Woman
BW #4	204-6	1	1) $B_1 G V$ ..... 4) $B_4 G V$	Mating of Corn
BW #5	223-24	1	$E F E C (G_a V G_b V)^4$	Offering of jewels and pollen to earth
BW #6	224-25	1	same as BW #5 Units G and V differ slightly	Offering of jewels and pollen to earth

218

BW # 7	265-69	6	$B\,Q_{FGV}R\,S_{FGV}{}^T\,V$	Rock Crystal's children return return from Changing Woman
BW # 8	272-74	1	$(G^{HP}{}_V)^{12}V\,G\,V$	House blessing
BW # 9	272-74	1	$B(G\,V)^{16}{}_{G(E^{HP})}7V$	To begin return journey of two boys after learning Blessingway
BW # 10	297-99	1	1) $A_1B_1G\,V$ .... 4) $A_4B_4G_e\,V$	Preparation of soil bundle at cornfield, act of creation
BW # 11	299-300	1	$(G^{HP}{}_V)^8V$	Eight word prayer
BW # 12	300-1	1	slightly longer version of BW # 11	Eight word prayer
BW # 13	306	1	V	Seed blessing
BW # 14	314	1	V	Pollen application
BW # 15	336-37	1	$(G^{HP}{}_V)^{12}V\,G\,V/V$	Ceremony for expectant mother
BW # 16	441	1	V	Changing Woman's morning prayer
BW # 17	441	1	V	First Man's morning prayer
BW # 18	442	1	V	Salt Woman's morning prayer
BW # 19	487	1	V	Pollen prayer
BW # 20	491-92	1	V	Heroes depart for Holy People
BW # 21	612-16	1	$B(G_{ab}V)^{16}{}_G\,U\,V$	Remaking/redressing mountains

TABLE 7—Continued

Alphanumeric Designation	Page No.	C*	Structure Diagram	Context
CW #1	65-67	5	1) B_1 C H M U V/V .... 4) B_4 C H M U V_e/V	Prayerstick rite
EH #1	207-13	3	1) B_1 A G K V .... 11) B_{11} A G K V 12) B_{12} A G K V/B_{11} U V B_{12} U V	Said on pollen figure of Corn-beetle Girl or Pollen Boy, while holding shoulder bands
EH #2	215-17	3	1) B_1 I G K V 2) B_2 I G K V	Preparation of rattle stick
EH #3	309-12	3	1) $B_1 A_1$ G K V .... 5) $B_5 A_5$ G K V	Optional, may be said in part
EH #4	213	1	V	Preparation for making rattle-stick
EH #5	217	3	1) B_1 I G K V .... 6) B_6 I G K V	Preparation of pot drum
EMM #1	109	1	V	Pollen prayer

220

FH #	Page	No.	Text	Description
FH # 1	92-93	2	1) $B_1 CP_1 G U V$ 2) $B_2 CP_2 G U V$ 3) $B_3 CP_1 G U V$ 4) $B_4 CP_2 G U V$ 5) $B_5 CP_3 G U V$ 6) $B_6 CP_3 G U V$	Restoration of thunderstruck hunter, broken taboo Prayers 5 and 6 are called blessing prayers
FH # 2	191-92	2	same as FH # 1	Prayer of return from buffalo home
FH # 3	214-15	1	1) $B_1 G_1 V$ 2) $B_2 G_2 V$	Hat talks to Holy Young Man as he returns from buffalo home
FH # 4	221-22		B T G.	Pollen application after bath
FH # 5	226		B C V	Collection of yucca for medicine, jewel deposit
FH # 6	230		No text	
FH # 7	244-53	2	same as FH # 1 with 10 prayers	Pouch held by one-sung-over, applied to him after prayer
FH # 8	253-67	7	1) $B_1 CP L M V$ . . . . $\overline{8}$) $B_8 CP L M V$ 9) $B_9 CP G V$ 10) $B_{10} CP G V ? V$	Independent prayer said on special request, ritual context unknown
FH # 9	275-78	2	1) $B_1^1 C\ H G U V$ 2) $B_2^1 C\ H G U V$	Collection of yucca for medicine

TABLE 7–Continued

Alphanumeric Designation	Page No.	C*	Structure Diagram	Context
FH # 10	284-85	2	same as FH # 1 with 6 prayers	Prayer to Sun, said on Sun figure
FH # 11	285	2	same as FH # 1 with 6 prayers	May be said any time
FH # 12	285-86	2	same as FH # 1 with 6 prayers	May be said any time
FH # 13	286	2	same as FH # 1	May be said any time
FH # 14	286	2	same as FH # 1	Not described
FH # 15	286	2	same as FH # 1	Injury due to rocks
FH # 16	286	2	same as FH # 1	Injury due to falling tree
FH # 17	287	2	same as FH # 1	Injury due to horse
FH # 18	287	2	same as FH # 1	Not given
FH # 19	287	2	same as FH # 1	Not given
FH # 20	287	2	same as FH # 1	Injury person to person
FH # 21	287	2	same as FH # 1	Injury by fall on ground
FH # 22	288		No text	

FH # 23	288		No text	
FH # 24	288		No text	
FH # 25	276		No text	
GW # 1	109-13		1) B_1 $?_1$ V_1 $\cdots\cdots$ 5) B_5 $?_5$ V_5	Prayer taught to hunters by which to call game
HH # 1	136	4	B M	Jewel offering at pinyon tree or at deer track
HH # 2	137	1	B G V	Mush fed to dog while praying
HH # 3	137-38		No text	
HH # 4	137-38	1	G	Offer feather to crow while standing on dead tree
HH # 5	141		1) L_1N 2) L_2N	Drinking and application of herb medicine
HR # 1	10		No text	
MFH # 1	4-5		1) B_1GN $\cdots\cdots$ 4) B_4GN	Prayer in myth directed towards Pueblo enemies
MFH # 2	118-19	5	1) B_1CHMUV 2) B_2CHMUV	Prayerstick rite—First Day
MFH # 3	120	5	same as MFH # 2	Prayerstick rite—First Day

TABLE 7—Continued

Alphanumeric Designation	Page No.	C*	Structure Diagram	Context
MFH # 4	120	5	same as MFH # 2	Prayerstick rite—First Day
MFH # 5	120	5	same as MFH # 2	Prayerstick rite—First Day
MFH # 6	120	5	same as MFH # 2	Prayerstick rite—First Day
MFH # 7	120-21	5	same as MFH # 2 with 6 prayers	Optional with prayerstick rite
MFH # 8	121-22	5	same as MFH # 2 with 6 prayers	Prayerstick rite—Second Day
MFH # 9	122	5	same as MFH # 2 with 6 prayers	Prayerstick rite, last two prayers added if Meal Strewer present
MFH # 10	123-24	5	same as MFH # 2 with 6 prayers	Prayerstick rite
MFH # 11	124	5	same as MFH # 2 with 4 prayers	Prayerstick rite
MFH # 12	124	5	same as MFH # 2 with 6 prayers	Prayerstick rite
MFH # 13	125	5	same as MFH # 2 with 2 prayers	Prayerstick rite
MFH # 14	125	5	same as MFH # 2 with 2 prayers	Prayerstick rite
MFH # 15	125-26	5	same as MFH # 2 with 4 prayers	Prayerstick rite
MFH # 16	127-28	5	same as MFH # 2 with 8 prayers	Figurine prayerstick rite
MFM # 1	395	1	V	Prayer to deer head

MFM # 2	420		B C H V	Prayerstick rite
MMH # 1	53-55	8	A B I J T U V	Figurine rite
MMH # 2	55-56	5	A B C H M U V	Figurine prayerstick rite
MMH # 3	56	5	same as MMH # 2	Figurine prayerstick rite
MMH # 4	60	8	same as MMH # 1	Figurine rite
MMH # 5	62	5	same as MMH # 2	Figurine prayerstick rite
MMH # 6-15	62-70	5	same as MMH # 2	Figurine prayerstick rite
NH # 1	113-22		1) B_1? G_1? V 2) B_2? G_2? V	First Dancers prayer
NMb # 1	297-99	5	1) B_1 C H M U V 2) A_1B_2 C H M U V 3) A_2B_3 C H M U V 4) B_4 C H M U V	Prayerstick rite
NMc # 2	47-53		1) P T V . . . . . . 4) P T V	On sandpainting, second day
NMb # 3	300-1	5	1) A_1B_1 C H M U V 2) A_1B_2 C H M U V 3) A_2B_3 C H M U V 4) A_3B_4 C H M U V 5) A_1B C H M U V 6) A_2B C H M U V	Prayerstick rite

TABLE 7—Continued

Alphanumeric Designation	Page No.	C*	Structure Diagram	Context
NMc #4	54-58	5	1) A_1B C H M U V 2) A_2B C H M U V	Prayerstick rite
NMb #5	301-2	1	V	Pollen prayer
NMa #6	269-75	5	1) -3) No text 4) A B E C H M U V	Preparation for dance last night
NMb #7	302-4	5	1) B_1C H M U V 2) B_2C H M U V	Prayerstick rite—Ninth Day
NMc #8	34-35	1	B V	Pollen prayer, on pollen figure
NMc #9	29-30	1	1) A_1B G V 2) A_2B G V	Prayer on sacred buckskin, myth
NS #1	244		Inadequate text	Prayerstick rite
NS #2	272	1	V	Pollen prayer [?]
PCL #1	573	1	F V	To medicine plant
PCM #1	149-70	6	Q R S T V	Prayer ceremony, protection for Emergence Myth narration

226

PP #1	72-77	7	1) $A_1B_1L_1N_1$ 2) $A_2B_2L_2N_2$	Prayer addressed to Monster Slayer and Born for Water given as an example of a Protection-way prayer
PW #1	18-23	6	1) $Q_1R_1S_1T_1V$ .... 4) $Q_4R_4S_4T_4V$	Prayer to rid one of the condition of prostituting
PW #2	40-41		1) A_1B C? .... 4) A_4B C?	Prayer of a hunter
PW #3	59-60	1	1) $A_1B_1G L V$ .... 4) $A_4B_4G L V$	Blessing part of Prostitution-way ceremony
RCH #1	75	1	V	Pollen prayer while sprinkling pollen on floor
RCH #2	78-79	1	1) $A_1G V$ 2) $A_2G V$	Prayerstick and jewel offering rite
RCH #3	79-80	1	V	Said while eating pollen
RCH #4	80	1	$(G V)^{14}V$	Early morning—Second Day
RCH #5	82-84	1	$G V(F_V{}^{HP})^{45}G V$	Said on sacred buckskin
RCH #6	84	1	V	Pollen prayer

TABLE 7–Continued

Alphanumeric Designation	Page No.	C*	Structure Diagram	Context
RCH #7	88-89	1	1) B_1C_1 V .... 4) B_4C_4 V 5) B_5C_5 V/B A?	At place of prayerstick and jewel deposit—Last Day
RSC #1	277	1	B G	None given
RMGW #1	134-35		1) A B_1 S T .... 4) A B_4 S T	Hoop ceremony
RMGW #2a	137-45	7	1) $A_1B_1C_1$ E N L_1N .... 4) $A_4B_4C_4$ E N L_4N	Offering at tree where pokers were collected
RMGW #2b	137-45	7	1) A_1B_1E L_1N .... 4) A_4B_4E L_4N	Offering at tree where pokers were collected
RMGW #2c	137-45	7	1) B_1E L_1N .... 4) B_4E L_4N	Offering at tree where pokers were collected

RMGW # 2d	137-45	7	same as RMGW # 2c	Offering at tree where pokers were collected
RMGW # 2e	137-45	7	same as RMGW # 2b	Offering at tree where pokers were collected
RMGW # 2f	137-45	7/4	1) A_1B_1G N .... 4) A_4B_4G N	
RMGW # 3	147-48	7	1) A_1L_1N .... 4) A_4L_4N	Hoop ceremony, said before going through hoops—First Day
RMGW # 4	154-55	7	1) $A_1B_1E L_1N$ .... 4) $A_4B_4E L_4N$ M	Hoop ceremony, said before going through hoops—Second Day
RMGW # 5	157	7	same as #4	Hoop ceremony—Third Day
RMGW # 6	158		No text	Hoop ceremony—Fourth Day
RMHW # 1	165		No text	Upright setout
RMHW # 2	170		No text	Conclusion of five night ceremony
RP # 1	100-2	1	1) B_1G V .... 7) B_7G V with additions	Rainbow Prayer said with offering made at Rainbow Bridge and elsewhere
RRP # 1	135-37		B C P U C V	Prayer to request rain
SFH # 1	13-17	8	B I J T U V	Figurine rite

TABLE 7–Continued

Alphanumeric Designation	Page No.	C*	Structure Diagram	Context
SFH # 2	17-18	5	B C H M U V	Figurine prayerstick rite
SFH # 3 and all odd numbers to SFH # 47				
	21-46	8	A B I J T U V	Figurine rite
SFH # 4 and all even numbers to SFH # 48				
	21-46	5	A B C H M U V	Figurine prayerstick rite
SGH # 1	11	1	V	Pollen prayer
SGH # 2	11	1	B V	Application of water
SGH # 3	11		B F C	At salt gathering place
SGH # 4	14	1	V	Leaving salt gathering place
SH # 1	346-47	7	B L N	Ash blowing
SH # 2	354-55	7	B L N	Ash blowing
SMGH # 1	89-127	6	1) Q₁ R S T S T V /T G V G V .... 4) Q₄ R S T S T V /T G V G V	Hoop ceremony, said on figure on buckskin surrounded by hoops
SMGH # 2	245-63	7	1) B A B E L N .... 4) B A B E L G M N K N	After line drawing around slain ghost, myth

230

SMGH # 3	265-71	4	B C M N	Offering of beads to tree
SMGH # 4	271-76	7	1) B_1 E L N . . . . 4) B_4 E L N	Bath under thunderstruck tree
SMGH # 5	278-82	7	1) B_1 E L_1 N . . . . 9) B_9 E L_9 N	Short ceremony or addition to other uglyway ceremonials
SMGH # 6	283-88	7	1) B_1 C E L N . . . . 4) B_4 C E L N	Jewel offering in coyote track
SMGRa # 1		6	Q R S T V	None given
SMGRb # 2	58-93		1) -4)?	None given
SMHH # 1	78-80	7	1) B_1 C F L V . . . . 4) B_4 C F L V	Offering to tree at poker collection
SMHH # 2	153-54	7	1) B_1 C F L V . . . . 8) B_8 C F L V/V	Prayerstick rite—First Day
SMHH # 3	159	7	same as SMHH # 2	Prayerstick rite—Second Day
SMHH # 4	170	7	same as SMHH # 2	Prayerstick rite—Third Day
SMHH # 5	174-77	7	1) B_1 F L V . . . . 12) B_{12} F L V/V	Prayer at the uprights

231

TABLE 7—Continued

Alphanumeric Designation	Page No.	C*	Structure Diagram	Context
SMHH #6	182-83	7	1) A B C F L V 2) A B C F L V/V	Prayerstick rite—Fourth Day
SMHH #7	225-27	7	1) B_1 C F L V . . . . 4) B_4 C F L V/F G U V	Prayer to pinyon at end of ceremonial
SMHM #1	224-25		1) A_1B_1 C F C F V . . . . 4) A_4B_4 C F C F V	Prayerstick offering to Snake, first day (text for parts 2 through 4 not fully available)
SMHR #1	1		No text	Prayer of instruction at beginning of myth recitation
SMHR #2	118-22	6	B Q R S T U V	For injury by water
SMHR #3	127	1	V	Prayer for rain
SMHR #4	161	7	1) A B C F L F L V . . . . 4) A B C F L F L V/U V	Prayerstick rite—First Day
SMHR #5	166		Questionable text	Prayerstick rite—First Day
SMHR #6	168		Questionable text	Prayerstick rite—Second Day

232

SMHR #7	174-75		Questionable text	Prayerstick rite—Third Day
SMHR #8	178-80		Questionable text	Prayerstick rite—Fourth Day
SMHR #9	185-87		V	House blessing
SMHR #10	187-89		1) -4)?	House blessing, setup application of uprights to one sung over
SMHR #11	191-200	7	1) A B_1 F L F V 2) B_2 F L F V . . . . 25) B_{25} F L F V	Altar setup
SMHR #12	209-10		Inadequate text	Prayer to pinyon at end of ceremonial, jewel offering
SWH #1	125-26		1) -4) P	Jewel and pollen offering at base of tree
SWH #2	128-29	8	F J V	Jewel offering on bone at cliff rose at end of hunt
UR #1	59-60	7	1) B_1 L G L N . . . . 8) B_8 L G L N	None given
UR #2	72-79	7	1) B_1 F L G L N . . . . 4) B_4 F L G L N	None given
WCW #1	241		No text	Special request

233

TABLE 7–Continued

Alphanumeric Designation	Page No.	C*	Structure Diagram	Context
WCW # 2	245		No text	Special request
WCW # 3	246		No text	None given
WH # 1	102	1	V	Hunter's meal blessing
WH # 2	102	1	V	Blessing of hunting structure
WH # 3	104	1	V	Pollen prayer, fire ceremony, first night of hunt
WNW # 1	173-79	6	Q R S T V	After unraveling—First Night
WNW # 2	182-83	5	1) B_1 C H M U V .... 6) B_6 C H M U V$_e$	Prayerstick rite—First Day
WNW # 3	187	5	1) A B_1 C H M U V .... 4) A B_4 C H M U V 5) B_5 C H M U V 6) B_6 C H M U V	Prayerstick rite—Second Day

234

WNW #4	189-90	5	1) B_1 C H M U V . . . . 8) B_8 C H M U V	Prayerstick rite—Third Day
WNW #5	192-93	5	1) AB_1 C H M U V . . . . 4) AB_4 C H M U V	Prayerstick rite—Fourth Day
WNW #6	203-5	7	1) B_1 L F G V . . . . 4) B_4 L F G V_e	Prayer at upright setout

BIBLIOGRAPHY

Aberle, David F. *The Peyote Religion Among the Navaho*. Chicago: Aldine, 1966.

———. "The Navaho Singer's 'Fee': Payment or Presentment." In *Studies in Southwestern Ethnolinguistics*, pp. 15-32. Edited by Dell Hymes. The Hague: Mouton, 1967.

Bauman, Richard, "Verbal Art as Performance." *American Anthropologist* 77 (1975): 290-311.

Ben-Amos, Dan and Goldstein, Kenneth S., eds. *Folklore: Performance & Communication*. The Hague: Mouton, 1975.

Brugge, David M. *Navajo Pottery and Ethnohistory*. Window Rock, Arizona: Navajoland Publications, 1963.

Evans-Pritchard, E. E. *Theories of Primitive Religion*. Oxford: Oxford University Press, 1965.

Finnegan, Ruth. *Oral Poetry: Its Nature, Significance and Social Context*. New York: Cambridge University Press, 1977.

Foster, Michael K. "Speaking in the Longhouse at Six Nations Reserve." In *Linguistic Diversity in Canadian Society,* edited by R. Darnell. Edmonton: Linguistic Research, 1971, pp. 129-54.

———. *From the Earth to Beyond the Sky: An Ethnographic Approach to Four Longhouse Iroquois Speech Events*. Ottawa: National Museums of Canada, 1974.

The Franciscan Fathers. *An Ethnologic Dictionary of the Navaho Language*. St. Michaels, Arizona: St. Michaels Press, 1910.

Frisbie, Charlotte J. *Kinaaldá: A Study of the Navaho Girl's Puberty Ceremony*. Middletown, Connecticut: Wesleyan University Press, 1967.

——. "A House Blessing Ceremonial." *El Palacio* 75 (1968): 26-35.

——. *Music and Dance Research of Southwestern United States Indians*. Detroit Studies in Music Bibliography, no. 36. Detroit: Information Coordinators, 1977.

——, ed. *Southwestern Indian Ritual Drama*. Albuquerque: University of New Mexico Press, 1980.

——. "Ritual Drama in the Navajo House Blessing Ceremony." In *Southwestern Indian Ritual Drama*, edited by Charlotte J. Frisbie. Albuquerque: University of New Mexico Press, 1980, pp. 161-98.

Geertz, Clifford. "Thick Description: Toward an Interpretive Theory of Culture." *The Interpretation of Culture*. New York: Basic Books, 1973, pp. 3-30.

Gill, Sam D. *A Theory of Navajo Prayer Acts: A Study in Ritual Symbolism*. Ph.D. Dissertation. University of Chicago, 1974.

——. "The Prayer of the Navajo Carved Figurine." *Plateau* 47 (1974): 59-69.

——. "The Color of Navajo Ritual Symbolism: An Evaluation of Methods." *Journal of Anthropological Research* 4 (1975): 350-63.

——. "The Shadow of a Vision Yonder." In *Seeing with a Native Eye*, edited by Walter H. Capps. New York: Harper Row, 1976, pp. 44-57.

——. "Prayer as Person: The Performative Force in Navajo Prayer Acts." *History of Religions* 17 (1977): 143-57.

——. "The Trees Stood Deep Rooted." *Parabola* 2:2 (1977): 6-12.

——. "Native American Religions." *The Council on the Study of Religion Bulletin* 9:2 (1978): 125-28.

——. "Native American Religions: A Review Essay." *Religious Studies Review* 5:4 (1979): 251-58.

——. *Songs of Life: An Introduction to Navajo Religious Culture*. Leiden: E. J. Brill, 1979.

Goddard, Pliney E., *Navaho Texts*, Anthropology Papers of the American Museum of Natural History, vol. 34. New York, 1933.

Goosen, Gary H. "Language as Ritual Substance." In *Language in Religious Practice*, edited by William J. Samarin, pp. 40-62. Rowley, Massachusetts: Newbury House Publishers, 1976.

Haile, Father Berard. *Creation and Emergence Myth of the Navajo According to the Hanelnehe, Moving-Up Rite,* Manuscript 171-2, Museum of Northern Arizona. Flagstaff, 1908.

——. *Female Mountainway Myth,* Manuscript 112-21, Museum of Northern Arizona. Flagstaff, 1935.

——. "Navaho Chantways and Ceremonials." *American Anthropologist* 40 (1938): 639-52.

——. *Origin Legend of the Navaho Enemy Way,* Yale University Publications in Anthropology, no. 17. New Haven, 1938.

——. "Navaho Upward-Reaching Way and Emergence Place." *American Anthropologist* 44 (1942): 407-20.

——. *Origin Legend of the Navaho Flintway.* Chicago: University of Chicago Press, 1943.

——. "Soul Concepts of the Navaho." *Annali Lateranensi* 7 (1943): 59-94.

——. *Head and Face Masks in Navaho Ceremonialism.* St. Michaels, Arizona: St. Michaels Press, 1947.

——. *Prayer Stick Cutting in a Five Night Navaho Ceremonial of the Male Branch of Shootingway.* Chicago: University of Chicago Press, 1947.

——. *Navaho Sacrificial Figurines.* Chicago: The University of Chicago Press, 1947.

——. *Legend of the Ghostway Ritual in the Male Branch of Shooting Way.* St. Michaels, Arizona: St. Michaels Press, 1950.

——. *Love-Magic and Butterfly People: The Slim Curly Version of the Ajiłee and Mothway Myths.* Flagstaff: Museum of Northern Arizona Press, 1978.

——. *Big Starway Liberation Prayer,* Manuscript 112-0, Museum of Northern Arizona. Flagstaff, n.d.

Heiler, Frederick. *Prayer: A Study in the History and Psychology of Religion.* New York: Oxford University Press, 1932. (Originally published as *Das Gebet,* 1928).

Hill, Willard W. *The Agricultural and Hunting Methods of the Navaho Indians,* Yale University Publications in Anthropology, no. 18. New Haven, 1938.

——. *Navajo Salt Gathering,* University of New Mexico Anthropology Series, Bulletin 3. Albuquerque, 1940.

Hymes, Dell. "Breakthrough into Performance." In *Folklore: Performance and Communication*, edited by Dan Ben-Amos and Kenneth S. Goldstein. The Hague: Mouton, 1975, pp. 11-74.

Kelly, Roger E. "Navaho Ritual Human Figurines: Form and Function." In *Navaho Figurines Called Dolls*, pp. 1-45. Santa Fe: Museum of Navaho Ceremonial Art, 1972.

Kitagawa, Joseph M. and Long, Charles H. eds. *Myths and Symbols: Studies in Honor of Mircea Eliade.* Chicago: University of Chicago Press, 1969.

Kluckhohn, Clyde. "Navajo Categories." In *Culture in History: Essays in Honor of Paul Radin*, edited by Stanley Diamond, pp. 65-98. New York: Columbia University Press, 1960.

—— and Leighton, Dorothea. *The Navaho.* Cambridge: Harvard University Press, 1946.

—— and Wyman, Leland C. *An Introduction to Navaho Chant Practice*, Memoirs, American Anthropology Association, no. 53. Menasha, Wisconsin, 1940.

Lang, R. W. and Walters, Harry. "The Remaking Rites of the Navaho: Causal Factors of Illness and Its Nature." In *Navaho Figurines Called Dolls*, pp. 46-75. Santa Fe: Museum of Navaho Ceremonial Art, 1972.

Lamphere, Louise and Vogt, Evon Z. "Clyde Kluckhohn as Ethnographer and Student of Navaho Ceremonialism." In *Culture and Life, Essays in Memory of Clyde Kluckhohn*, edited by Walter W. Taylor, *et al.*, pp. 94-135. Carbondale: Southern Illinois University Press, 1973.

Lowie, Robert H. *Primitive Religion.* New York: Liveright Publishing Corp., 1972.

Luckert, Karl W. "Traditional Navaho Theories of Disease and Healing." *Arizona Medicine: Journal of the Arizona Medical Association* 29 (1972): 570-73.

——. *The Navajo Hunter Tradition.* Tucson: University of Arizona Press, 1975.

——. *Navajo Mountain and Rainbow Bridge Religion.* Flagstaff: Museum of Northern Arizona Press, 1977.

——. *A Navajo Bringing-Home Ceremony: The Claus Chee Sonny Version of Deerway Ajiłee.* Flagstaff: Museum of Northern Arizona Press, 1978.

——. *Coyoteway: A Navajo Holyway Healing Ceremonial.* Tucson: The University of Arizona Press and Flagstaff: Museum of Northern Arizona Press, 1979.

Matthews, Washington. *The Mountain Chant*, Bureau of Ethnology, Fifth Annual Report, pp. 385-467. Washington, D.C., 1887.

——. "The Prayer of a Navaho Shaman." *American Anthropologist* 2 (1889): 1-19.

——. *Navaho Legends*, Memoirs, American Folklore Society, vol. 5. Boston, 1897.

——. "Some Sacred Objects of the Navajo Rites," Archives of the International Folklore Congress of the World's Columbian Exposition, pp. 227-47. Chicago, 1898.

——. *The Night Chant, A Navaho Ceremony*, American Museum of Natural History, Memoirs, vol. 6. New York, 1902.

——. *Navaho Myths, Prayers, and Songs,* University of California Publications in American Archaeology and Ethnology, vol. 5. Berkeley, 1907.

McAllester, David P. "Shootingway, an Epic Drama of the Navajos." In *Southwestern Indian Ritual Drama*, edited by Charlotte J. Frisbie, pp. 199-238. Albuquerque: University of New Mexico Press, 1980.

—— and McAllester, Susan W. *Hogans: Navajo Houses & House Songs.* Middletown, Connecticut: Wesleyan University Press, 1980.

Mitchell, Frank. *Navajo Blessingway Singer: The Autobiography of Frank Mitchell, 1881-1967,* edited by Charlotte J. Frisbie and David P. McAllester. Tucson: University of Arizona Press, 1978.

New Literary History, vol. VIII, no. 3 (1977). Issue on Oral Cultures and Oral Performances.

O'Bryan, Aileen. *The Dine: Origin Myths of the Navaho Indians*, Bureau of American Ethnology, Bulletin 163. Washington, D.C., 1956.

Reichard, Gladys A. "The Complexity of Rhythm in Decorative Art." *American Anthropologist* 24 (1922): 183-208.

——. *Social Life of the Navaho Indians with Some Attention to Minor Ceremonies.* New York: Columbia University Press, 1928.

——. *Prayer: The Compulsive Word.* New York: J. J. Augustin, 1944.

——. *The Story of the Navaho Hail Chant.* New York: Barnard College, Columbia University, 1944.

——. *Navaho Religion: A Study of Symbolism.* Princeton: Princeton University Press, 1950.

——. *Chant of Waning Endurance*, Manuscript 29-48, Museum of Northern Arizona. Flagstaff, n.d.

——. *Male Shooting Chant Evil Chasing*, Manuscript 29-48, Museum of Northern Arizona. Flagstaff, n.d.

——. *Navaho Male Shooting Chant [Holy]*, Manuscript 29-45, 46, Museum of Northern Arizona. Flagstaff, n.d.

Sapir, Edward and Hoijer, Harry. *Navaho Texts.* Iowa City: Linguistics Society of America, 1942.

Smith, Jonathan Z. "I Am A Parrot (Red)." *History of Religions* 10 (1972): 391-413.

Smith, Marian W. "Gladys Armanda Reichard." *American Anthropologist* 58 (1956): 914.

Smith, Wilfred C. "Comparative Religion: Whither—and Why?" In *The History of Religions: Essays in Methodology,* edited by Mircea Eliade and Joseph Kitagawa, pp. 31-58. Chicago: University of Chicago Press, 1959.

Spencer, Katherine. *Reflection of Social Life in the Navaho Origin Myth,* University of New Mexico Publications in Anthropology, no. 3. Albuquerque, 1947.

——. *Mythology and Values: An Analysis of Navaho Chantway Myths,* American Folklore Society, Memoirs, vol. 48. Boston, 1957.

Stevenson, James. *Ceremonial of Hasjelti Dailjis and Mythical Sand Painting of the Navajo Indians,* Bureau of American Ethnology, 8th Annual Report. Washington, D.C., 1891.

Tedlock, Dennis. "From Prayer to Reprimand." In *Language in Religious Practice,* edited by William J. Samarin, pp. 72-83. Rowley, Massachusetts: Newbury House Publishers, 1976.

——. "Verbal Art." *Handbook of North American Indians,* vol. 9, chapter 50. Washington: The Smithsonian, 1980.

Toelken, Barre. "The 'Pretty Language' of Yellowman: Genre, Mode, & Texture in Navaho Coyote Narratives." *Genre* 2 (1969): 211-35.

——. "Ma'i Joldloshi: Legendary Styles and Navaho Myth." In *American Folk Legend,* edited by Wayland Hand, pp. 203-12. Berkeley: University of California Press, 1971.

Tylor, Edward B. *Primitive Culture.* London: John Murray, 1873.

Wagner, Roland M. "Some Pragmatic Aspects of Navaho Peyotism." *Plains Anthropologist* 20 (1975): 197-205.

Wheelwright, Mary C. *Emergency Myth According to the Hanelthnaybe or Upward-Reaching Rite.* Santa Fe: Museum of Navaho Ceremonial Art, 1949.

——. *The Myth and Prayers of the Great Star Chant and the Myth of the Coyote Chant.* Santa Fe: Museum of Navaho Ceremonial Art, 1956.

Witherspoon, Gary. "The Central Concepts of Navajo World View (I)." *Linguistics* 119 (1974): 46-58.

——. *Language and Art in the Navajo Universe.* Ann Arbor: The University of Michigan Press, 1977.

Wyman, Leland C. "The Female Shooting Life Chant." *American Anthropologist* 38 (1936): 634-53.

——. *Beautyway, A Navaho Ceremonial.* Princeton: Princeton University Press, 1957.

——. *The Windways of the Navaho.* Colorado Springs: The Taylor Museum of Colorado Springs Fine Arts Center, 1962.

——. "Snakeskins and Hoops." *Plateau* 39 (1966): 4-25.

——. *Blessingway: With Three Versions of the Myth Recorded and Translated from the Navaho by Father Berard Haile, O.F.M.* Tucson, University of Arizona Press, 1970.

——. *The Red Antway of the Navaho.* Santa Fe: Museum of Navaho Ceremonial Art, 1973.

—— and Bailey, Flora L. *Navaho Upward-Reaching Way: Objective Behavior, Rationale and Sanction,* University of New Mexico Bulletin, Anthropology Series, vol. 4. Albuquerque, 1943.

——. "Idea and Action Patterns in Navajo Flintway." *Southwestern Journal of Anthropology* 1 (1945): 356-77.

——, Hill, Willard W. and Osanai, Iva. *Navajo Eschatology,* University of New Mexico Bulletin, Anthropology Series, vol. 4. Albuquerque, 1942.

—— and Kluckhohn, Clyde. *Navaho Classification of Their Song Ceremonials,* Memoirs, American Anthropological Association, no. 50. Menasha, Wisconsin, 1938.

Young, Robert W. and Morgan, William. *The Navaho Language.* Salt Lake City: Deseret Book Company, 1972.

INDEX

About the Author

Sam D. Gill is Associate Professor of Religious Studies at Arizona State University in Tempe. He is the author of *Songs of Life: An Introduction to Navajo Religious Culture.*